I Am Legend
as American Myth

ALSO BY AMY J. RANSOM
AND FROM MCFARLAND

*Science Fiction from Québec:
A Postcolonial Study* (2009)

I Am Legend as American Myth

Race and Masculinity in the Novel and Its Film Adaptations

AMY J. RANSOM

McFarland & Company, Inc., Publishers
Jefferson, North Carolina

Excerpts from the following works by Richard Matheson are reprinted by permission of Don Congdon Associates, Inc.: *I Am Legend* © 1954, renewed 1982 by Richard Matheson. *Beardless Warriors* © 1960, renewed 1988 by Richard Matheson. *The Shrinking Man* © 1956, renewed 1984 by Richard Matheson.

Library of Congress Cataloguing-in-Publication Data

Names: Ransom, Amy J., 1964– author.
Title: I am legend as American myth : race and masculinity in the novel and its film adaptations / Amy J. Ransom.
Description: Jefferson, North Carolina : McFarland & Company, Inc., Publishers, 2018. | Includes bibliographical references and index.
Identifiers: LCCN 2018022767 | ISBN 9781476668338 (softcover : acid free paper) ∞
Subjects: LCSH: Matheson, Richard. I am legend. | Matheson, Richard.—Film adaptations. | I am legend (Motion picture) | Race in literature. | Masculinity in literature. | Race in motion pictures. | Masculinity in motion pictures.
Classification: LCC PS3563.A8355 I1835 2018 | DDC 813/.54—dc23
LC record available at https://lccn.loc.gov/2018022767

British Library cataloguing data are available

ISBN (print) ISBN 978-1-4766-6833-8
ISBN (ebook) ISBN 978-1-4766-3267-4

© 2018 Amy J. Ransom. All rights reserved

No part of this book may be reproduced or transmitted in any form or by any means, electronic or mechanical, including photocopying or recording, or by any information storage and retrieval system, without permission in writing from the publisher.

Front cover: Will Smith in the 2007 film *I Am Legend* (Warner Bros. Pictures/Photofest)

Printed in the United States of America

McFarland & Company, Inc., Publishers
 Box 611, Jefferson, North Carolina 28640
 www.mcfarlandpub.com

In memory of my brother-in-law
Rickey Gene Martin (1957–2018)
You are loved

Table of Contents

Introduction: Adapting Richard Matheson's I Am Legend *Novel to the Screen*   1

One. Richard Matheson's *I Am Legend*: The Trauma of World War II and the Decline of Western "Right"   15

Two. Visualizing Apocalypse Through Compromised Masculinity: Vincent Price as *The Last Man on Earth*   58

Three. The Last White Man on Earth: Charlton Heston in *The Omega Man*   96

Four. The Color of the New Hero: Will Smith in *I Am Legend*   146

Conclusion: I Am Legend *as American Myth*   185

Chapter Notes   191

Filmography and Bibliography   198

Index   214

Introduction: Adapting Richard Matheson's *I Am Legend* Novel to the Screen

World War II marks a significant turning point in American history and society. The shocking attack on Pearl Harbor on December 7, 1941, irrevocably changed how the United States viewed its place in the world; its subsequent leading roles in the decisive invasion of the Normandy beaches on D–Day, the Liberation of Europe, and the use of atomic weapons to end the war in the Pacific positioned the U.S. as one of two superpowers. In this last "good war" (Chafe 4), young American men and their leaders appeared to have ensured the reign of democracy at home and abroad, fighting fascism in Europe and imperialism in Japan. Although they had not stopped the Holocaust, which took the lives of six million Jews and five million more political prisoners, prisoners of war, homosexual people, gypsies, and the disabled, they had prevented Hitler's program from becoming a fully Final Solution.

In spite of an exuberant material prosperity, the post-war years were far from peaceful as ideological demagogues like Senator Joe McCarthy spread the fear of communism at home. Our former ally, the Soviet Union, consolidated a bloc of power in Eastern Europe and Mao Tse Tung introduced his own form of communism to China. The Cold War had begun, fueled by the nuclear arms and the space races, with the first U.S. hydrogen bomb tested in November 1952 and the Soviet launch of Sputnik in October 1957. Such a climate of paranoia linked to developing technologies and foreign social systems fostered the rise of science fiction (SF). This multi-media genre both indulged contemporary fears by exploring the ultimate outcomes of the horrors unleashed since World War II and offered potential—although often fantastic—solutions to them. During the 1950s and the 1960s, then, well-fed, well-dressed, and well-housed Americans were entertained and titillated by a host of science-fiction monster movies like *It Came from Outer Space* (1953), *Them!* (1954), and *The Day the World Ended* (1955). Similarly books by writers like Arthur C. Clarke, Robert A. Heinlein, and Ray Bradbury filled the racks, and a cohort of talented young writers in Hollywood collaborated with producers bringing *The Twilight Zone* (1959–1964) and its imitators to television screens across the nation.

Rod Serling, of course, was the genius behind the cult series that so effectively explored the anxieties of its day, from fear of alien invasion to the end of the world, from the dark powers of the individual human imagination to the social problems of prejudice and the pressure to conform (see Carroll and Hunt; Presnell and McGee; Stanyard). While Serling wrote many of the series' episodes, he could not do it alone; he relied on a core group of scenarists, which included Charles Beaumont and Richard Matheson. Although, like many screenwriters, his is not a name recognized today by the general population, Matheson's work punctuates the second half of the twentieth century. In addition to his episodes of *The Twilight Zone*, the iconic 1950s SF-horror film *The Incredible Shrinking Man* (1957) is based on his novel. In the 1960s, he wrote many of the screenplays for Roger Corman's cult adaptations of Edgar Allan Poe's work like *House of Usher* (1960) and *The Pit and the Pendulum* (1961). In the 1970s, he penned the scenario for Steven Spielberg's first major work, the telefilm *Duel* (1971), and his novel *Bid Time Return* (1975) became the iconic fan fic, *Somewhere in Time* (1980). But perhaps his most influential work remains Matheson's early novel, *I Am Legend* (1954), an attempt to offer a scientific explanation for vampirism, which blurs the generic lines between science fiction and horror.

Set in the (then) near future (the mid–1970s), it features a lone protagonist, the "Last Man" figure, Robert Neville. This everyman, a war veteran, believes himself to be the sole survivor of an epidemic that has turned the rest of humanity into vampires. Under Matheson's pen, this highly unlikely fantasy scenario, however, becomes an extremely human story of one man's struggle to survive not only the nightly physical assaults of the monsters that surround him but also the moral challenge of living completely and utterly alone in the world. Over the course of the last 60 years, this compelling tale has repeatedly inspired Hollywood insiders to undertake its adaptation to the screen.

At least four feature-length adaptations have been made to date[1]: *The Last Man on Earth* (1964, dir. Sidney Salkow, perf. Vincent Price), *The Omega Man* (1971, dir. Boris Sagal, perf. Charlton Heston), *I Am Legend* (2007, dir. Francis Lawrence, perf. Will Smith), and *I Am Omega* (2007, dir. Griff Furst, perf. Mark Dacascos). Like its protagonist, the legend has not died as evolving reboots continue to be announced on IMDb.com. What exactly is it about this short novel, considered a minor classic in the vampire sub-genre, that has inspired film executives and major movie stars to buy into the power of its story for well over half a century? How and why has Matheson's tale become a legend in its own right?

In *Living in the End Times* (2010), a study of Western civilization's recent apocalyptic turn, world-renowned cultural theorist Slavoj Žižek comments briefly on the 2007 film version of *I Am Legend*. He asserts that "one of the best ways to detect shifts in the ideological constellation is to compare consecutive remakes of the same story" (61). Since Matheson's death on June 23, 2013, a growing number of scholars have begun to explore the meaning of his landmark novel and the films it has inspired, sometimes offering a comparative approach. The handful of studies that address the body of *I Am Legend* adaptations (Brooks; Casali; Chenille; Hantke; Ingold; Moreman; Pulliam and Fonseca), however, remain limited in their scope, several of them simply published versions of conference papers. Thus, to date, no one has undertaken the significant task that Žižek called for in 2010—until now. This book offers a detailed, contextualized comparison of Matheson's novel and all four full-length film versions of it. By situating Matheson's original narrative in its post–World War II context, drawing out the various contemporary anxieties it invokes, and then re-examining the social and historical context for each of its subsequent film adaptations, this study reveals how various production teams have appropriated and often radically reworked Matheson's original story to reach audiences across the twentieth century and into the new millennium.

The sustained filmic interest in adapting a literary work that has until very recently been mostly ignored by both mainstream literary and by SF critics reflects the durability and the polyvalence of Matheson's original narrative framework. Although the success of the 2007 theatrical film adaptation and Matheson's passing in 2013 have spurred a sequence of homage volumes to the man and his oeuvre, these book-length treatments rarely offer a scholarly analysis grounded in social history and/or literary and cultural theory. Whereas the number of academic analyses of Matheson's work has begun to rise, particularly in relation to the growing number of zombie apocalypse texts and their analyses, only a handful of rigorous book-length treatments of his work exist. These include a volume of essays in French (Chenille *et al.*)—the acts of the first academic conference held on Matheson—and two recent books in English: the edited volume *Reading Richard Matheson: A Critical Survey* (Mathews and Haedicke) and a two-author study *Richard Matheson's Monsters* (Pulliam and Fonseca). This book, then, fills a gap in the scholarship on a highly significant but underappreciated figure in post–World War II SF/horror/fantasy literature and visual media, looking particularly at his most seminal and influential work and offering a serious academic examination of a popular and enduring cultural text, a contemporary American myth.

As such, this study invokes various iterations of film, gender, and race theories to support its hypotheses about the changing meanings of Matheson's iconic novel and the films it inspired. It also takes into account, and sometimes responds to, previous academic criticism of these works. Because popular culture texts are by their very nature polyvalent—open to various interpretations—not all readers of this book will agree with all of its positions, including possibly that of Matheson himself. Some of the interpretations proposed here may appear surprising, or even absurd, to some audiences, but all rest upon close readings of the texts coupled with current trends in critical theory about film, race, and gender. And while it does view Matheson's biography and his opinions expressed in interviews as relevant to his literary production, it also frequently scratches below the surface, finding meanings that remain in the author's unconscious. Similarly, it suggests interpretations that only some readers and viewers may identify with or find compelling. This is particularly the case for the applications of queer theory to the text, but may also be true for its discussions of race, which remains a compellingly controversial topic in American society. Above all, this study's goal is to reassess Matheson's significance as a major figure in SF, fantasy, and horror literature, film, and television.

Theoretical Frameworks: Star, Adaptation, Queer and Critical Race Theories

Of the many approaches to such a rich body of texts, this study focuses primarily on questions of race and gender, and to a lesser extent, class in the original Matheson novel and its film versions. It necessarily pays particular attention to the Everyman protagonist, Robert Neville, and his transformation over time, analyzing the novel's and films' representations of race and race relations, masculinity, femininity, and at times even a closeted queer sexuality as these vary from adaptation to adaptation. These examinations are deeply rooted in the changing historical context of the second half of the twentieth and first decade of the twenty-first centuries. Beginning with the post–World War II and Cold War context of Matheson's 1954 novel, this study examines how the literary work reflected anxieties specific to its time, following a similar trajectory for the film adaptations from the Civil Rights–Vietnam era and then the post–9/11 period. This analysis is grounded in a variety of theoretical approaches, drawing most heavily from the disciplines of literary and cultural studies, but also from adaptation theory and Richard Dyer's star theory from the realm of film studies. It ultimately reveals that *I Am Legend*'s film versions both transform and yet also reinscribe various aspects of the literary text's original vision of its hero and his confrontation with racial and gendered Otherness.

Adaptation Theory

As adaptations of an original literary work, with the later films also adapting aspects of earlier films, *The Last Man on Earth*, *The Omega Man*, *I Am Legend*, and *I Am Omega* can be read fruitfully through the lens of adaptation theory, an approach implicitly applied throughout this book. First and foremost, this approach eschews the notion that fidelity to the original is the most important criterion for judging the merits of an adaptation. Like any comparative study, the following chapters underscore the similarities and differences between each film and Matheson's literary model, as well as those between the films themselves, considering changes in the socio-political climate of their production and reception. That said, departures from the original text will not be labeled as "good" and "bad" in and of themselves; instead, this analysis seeks to explain why such changes were made. It follows Brian McFarlane, in that while

> many adaptations have chosen paths other than that of the literal-minded visualization of the original or even of "spiritual fidelity," making quite obvious departures from the original. Such departures may be seen in the light of offering a commentary on or, in more extreme cases, a deconstruction [...] of the original [22].

McFarlane borrows a definition of deconstruction from structuralist literary theory: "bring[ing] to light the internal contradictions in seemingly perfectly coherent systems of thought" (Sturrock 14; qtd. McFarlane 22). The close analyses of these films distinctly reveal the contradicting messages that they convey about race, masculinity, and their protagonists' status as heroes.

Adaptation theory thus sees film adaptations as working in dialogue with their original source text, other adaptations of it, as well as with other precursor films in the same genre or treating a similar theme. Margaret Montalbano points out in her reading of adaptations of Stoker's *Dracula* that

> this dialogic relationship that prevails in the adaptation process may be further explicated by Mikhail Bakhtin's concept of "heteroglossia," which asserts the "primacy of context over text" so that the meaning of every utterance—every text—is determined by the social, historical situation in which it is produced and received. From this perspective, even a word-for-word reproduction of a given text could not be considered identical to the original as a result of the differing temporalities in which each was produced and received; it would be considered, instead, a new text to be put into dialogue with its predecessors [386].

This dialogue thus extends out from the text to the society that produced it; thus, in the chapters that follow outlining the socio-historical setting for each of the texts considered will be essential to laying the groundwork for the analysis.

According to pioneer of adaptation theory Robert Stam, "[a]n adaptation consists in an interested *reading* of a novel and the *circumstantially shaped* 'writing' of a film" ("Introduction" 46; emphasis added). Thus, in addition to discussing the circumstances—that is the socio-historical and political context of the film in question—another central question to address will be: "What was the filmmakers' interest in revisiting Matheson's novel at this point in time?" Not only will I look at why they did so, but also how, asking as well, "What aspects of their literary model does each of its translations or interpretations on film retain, alter, eliminate, or underscore?" and "What do these changes signal about the evolving climate of American culture?" To further complicate this question, as we will see with *The Omega Man* and the 2007 film *I Am Legend*, adaptors may not always appear to have read—in a literal sense—the literary model that they are purportedly adapting.

In addition to a direct literary precursor, the adaptations considered here also have several filmic precursors upon which they draw inspiration for their visual imagination of the end times. For any film, adaptation or not, a team of visual artists—from the director of photography to the set designers, assisted by all sorts of technicians and led by the film's director—must work together to translate the written words of the screenplay into the visual imagery of the film. Just as the writer cannot work in a void and few ideas are completely original, always already informed by a body of texts that came before, so the filmmaking team draws inspiration from the visual arts and the film canon. *The Last Man on Earth*, for example, thus participates in an entire body of black and white apocalyptic film narratives. Among the significant corpus of postapocalyptic films produced before 1964, a handful of films stand out as precursor texts for the first film adaptation of *I Am Legend*, including the major studio production, *The World, The Flesh and The Devil* (1959) and the low-budget American International Pictures release, *The Last Woman on Earth* (1960). Featuring a mere three survivors, two men and one woman, these films resemble Matheson's Last Man scenario more closely than other apocalyptic visions from the 1950s and 1960s and so will also be considered in the pages that follow.

Richard Dyer's Star Theory

Instead of taking an *auteur* approach to the films, which focuses on directors as "authors" of the text, this book insists upon the significance of the actor cast in the lead role—the man who literally embodies the character of the Last Man. Richard Dyer's theorization of the star is merely an astute articulation of common sense, particularly given the mediatization of lead actors and actresses as commodities from the earliest days of the studio system to today's corporate media conglomerations and inter-media synergies. It is useful, however, to summarize the elements that comprise the star as a *constructed* image (Dyer, *Stars* 97)—a collage "made out of media texts that can be grouped together as *promotion, publicity, films* and *criticism* and *commentaries*" (Dyer, *Stars* 60). Because it is constructed in part through text, but also, of course, through the images made of the star, Dyer compares the star image to a character in a novel. Also, because of its composite construction, he views the star image as a polysemic *"complex totality"* (Dyer, *Stars* 63). Thus, as the various aspects that make up the composite image of the star may at times contradict each other or evolve over time, the star may serve as a vehicle for multiple meanings. At the same time, these various elements contribute to the illusion of a unified totality, focused as they are on a single individual, but comprised of his or her various roles, critical responses to these performances, media coverage of off-screen lives, and so on. Henceforth, when Vincent Price, Charlton Heston, and Will Smith are referenced here, the intent is not to signal the actual individual—the real life person (although his actions certainly inform his image)—but rather his "star image," this mediated social construct.

Just as we might analyze a character in a novel—obviously, in this case, Richard Matheson's Robert Neville—we may analyze the "star image" and what it brings to a character in a film. For the star image is a *sign*, an icon loaded with meaning. Thus, when Vincent Price's interpretation of the on-screen character Robert Morgan is invoked, not only will the ways in which the *film* characterizes him be involved, but also how the star image contributes to viewer interpretations of the character. Again, critics have long seized on this aspect of the star phenomenon in their judgments as to whether or not an actor has been miscast or the extent to which he or she "incorporates" a given film character. As Dyer explains:

> The film may, through its deployment of other signs of character and the rhetoric of film, bring out certain features of the star's image and ignore others. In other words, from the structured polysemy of the star's image certain meanings are selected in accord with the overriding conception of the character in the film [*Stars* 127].

Ideally, the studio's, the producer's, the director's, and the writer's goals all match, and casting process concludes with the choice of an actor whose star image does not conflict with the character he is chosen to play. However—as illustrated by criticism of Vincent Price as miscast in *The Last Man on Earth*—not only can there be conflict between the various individuals involved in a given film's decision-making process, this process cannot "guarantee that the particular aspects of a star's image it selects will be those that interest the audience" (127). In the end, this study follows Dyer's conclusion that

> although good cases can certainly be made for both a selective use of a star image and perfect fits between star images and film characters, it seems to me that the powerfully, inescapably present, always-already-signifying nature of star images more often than not creates problems in the construction of character [*Stars* 129].

Queer Theory

Queer theory is based on the notion that, rather than something innate to males and females, gender is a social construct, an aspect of human identity that is performative in nature. This field is particularly fruitful in the realm of film studies when it is cross-referenced with Dyer's star theory. Following Judith Butler's assertion, as outlined in *Gender Trouble: Feminism and the Subversion of Identity* (1990), that humans "perform" their masculinity and femininity, queer theorists look more specifically at how gay identities are performed and represented. Queer theorists, however, often generalize their ideas, applying them to all forms of gender and sexual expression that society might deem non-normative (Hall; Pearson; Wilchins). Clearly, actors perform roles; because of the continued heteronormative (i.e., straight equals normal) nature of American society, most film and television roles remain highly coded in terms of the "masculinity" and "femininity" of the characters they are meant to depict. For example, in Neill Blomkamp's *Elysium* (2013), Jodi Foster plays the role of Delacourt, the ruthless head of the elite off-world society's security forces, in an aggressive, decisive, inflexible manner that attributes the female character with traits traditionally seen as masculine and thus proper to such an authoritarian, militaristic role. Following the logic of queer theory, this non-normative gender characterization encourages a majority heterosexual audience to be unsympathetic to this villain character.

While on the one hand such gendered depictions are meant to reflect something about the character's role in the fictionalized image of society he or she evolves in (Delacourt is as ruthless and uncaring as the apartheid society that she protects), at the same time, consumers also internalize such images as normative and non-normative models for their own gendered identity (the masculinized Delacourt may be perceived as a "butch" lesbian fantasy figure *or* conversely as a frigid, castrating "bitch" whom "normal" males should avoid as a sexual partner). Thus, as Steven Cohan makes clear in his study of 1950s films that both mirrored and constructed a norm for the American male:

> While this norm was repeatedly invoked, as the movies readily illustrate, it was just as often subverted. Viewing masculinity as a masquerade helps to articulate more precisely why a hegemonic representation like the fifties' *Man in the Gray Flannel Suit* could dominate the culture and yet be subject to change [...]; why such a normative standard of masculinity is never stable or coherent or authentic [...]; and why *it has to exist alongside a range of alternative forms of representation* [xi; emphasis added].

Although the dominant model of on-screen masculinity in the fifties was that of the middle-class, white-collar breadwinner, competing models continued to appear, as witnessed through the decade's rise of more muscular, he-man types like Charlton Heston. Horror and science fiction films appear often to juxtapose a normatively masculine hero with male characters who are less so, and with a monster who is obviously Other. The actor cast in a lead male role, however, brings more than just his physical appearance; in addition, he brings the baggage of his prior roles, as well as his "real" life activities—rumored or actual—to audiences' reception of him in any new role, as well as their expectations or desires about his relationship to normative models.

Harry Benshoff's pathbreaking study *Monsters in the Closet: Homosexuality and the Horror Film* (1997) has been particularly fruitful in studying horror film and its potentially non-normative gender representations. Benshoff's scholarly articulation of something many horror fans have long intuited reveals that "the figure of the monster throughout the history of the English-language horror film can in some way be understood as a metaphoric construct standing in for the figure of the homosexual" (4). For example, with its sexual overtones, the female vampire film lends itself readily to such readings, as Benshoff observes of Lambert Hillyer's *Dracula's Daughter* (1936) and its blatantly lesbian coding of Countess Marya Zeleska's (Gloria Holden) lust for Janet's (Marguerite Churchill) blood. Less immediately evident is Benshoff's queering of the horror trope of the love triangle (monster, hero, female lead), as he shifts the trajectory of desire in Victor Halperin's *White Zombie* (1932) from plantation owner Murder Legendre (Bela Lugosi) to Neil Parker (John Harron), rather than to his new bride, Madeline (Madge Bellamy). Such analyses shed light on why sexuality is so often a latent or blatant element of horror films' thematics and marketing, as Benshoff demonstrates how we can interpret these films as both subversive expressions of oppositional desires, which at the same time reinforce the dominant ideology's concerns about "deviance."

Benshoff's work also signals the playful applications of queer theory, which on the one hand offers a useful tool for the reinterpretation of literary and popular culture texts with the serious political aim of questioning the hegemonic status of heteronormative sexuality in contemporary Western society. On the other hand, it allows for ludic appropriations of ostensibly "straight" texts by audiences, both gay and straight, who reinterpret such texts as "queer" via the slash reading. Particularly in the realm of fan fiction and fan video, slash texts take purportedly heterosexual characters, like Batman and Robin or Captain Kirk and Mr. Spock, and reinterpret them as gay.

Critical Race Theory

In the same way that theorists conceive gender as a cultural construct and a performed aspect of individual identity, race can be viewed in this light. Critical race theory (CRT) provides a theoretical framework for the sophisticated deconstruction of race representations in cultural texts. As Isiah

Lavender III, a pioneer in applying CRT to the study of SF in *Race in American Science Fiction* (2011), asserts, "Critical race theory challenges the assumption that whiteness is a neutral or unmarked identity in American culture" (Lavender, "Critical" 185). Richard Dyer, in "White" (a 1993 article) and *White* (a 1997 book), and Toni Morrison, in *Playing in the Dark: Whiteness and the Literary Imagination* (1992), offer models for teasing out how "whiteness" is constructed in American culture through film and literature. As Lavender also asserts, "While highlighting the socially constructed nature of race, [CRT] simultaneously acknowledges that race is a 'real' category in terms of its material effects and suggests that racism is more or less permanent" ("Critical" 186). Thus, although the science of genetics has radically changed how we understand race and ethnicity in the twenty-first century, the racial categories commonly used in everyday discourse and official U.S. data-gathering documents like "black" and "white," "African American" or "Caucasian" or "white non-Hispanic" are fictions. Their very nature as constructions is revealed in the way that race terminology changes over time, moving from "Negro" or "colored" to "Black" and "African American." Not only are these categories constructed by official institutions, popular culture images also contribute to our perception of them. At the same time, these categories have *real* impact on individual lives, as discussions of historical racially-motivated violence make eminently clear.

Critical race theory "exposes the hypocrisy at the heart of a government and society under the influence of racism, oppression, white patriarchal supremacy, economic equality and imperialism" (Lavender, "Critical" 186), but it does so in the hope that by exposing injustice and prejudice it can also foster understanding and create a society in which justice and opportunity can be had by all. Above all, it acknowledges that because of the complex history of race relations in the U.S., Americans' feelings about race are complex. By analyzing and untangling how the popular cultural texts we consume both play on deep-seated racist fears and offer utopian hopes for change, CRT fosters understanding that can form the basis for change.

Becoming Legend: Scholarship on I Am Legend *and Its Film Adaptations*

Already in the early 1980s, W. Warren Wagar attempted to get a fix on what he perceived as a then contemporary fascination, even obsession, with apocalyptic narratives. In his preface to *Terminal Visions: The Literature of Last Things* (1982), a study whose scope encompasses apocalyptic fictions well beyond the present examination of one particular cycle of Last Man narratives, Wagar argues that "we do indeed live in an endtime, an era in history marked by the collapse of the traditional civilizations of the non–Western world and by the senescence of the national-bourgeois social order in the West" (xiii). That impression has become all the more urgent since the September 11, 2001, attacks on the World Trade Towers by the Al-Qaeda terrorist group. But while we are obsessed by visions of Last Men, we also continue to hope for a savior, a hero. Over the decades, Matheson's novel has repeatedly supplied filmmakers with a basic narrative that addresses these concerns, but one supple enough to tailor to their own times.

In addition to the body of literature, referenced throughout this study, dealing with Matheson's novel and one or more of its film adaptations at a time, a handful of scholars have previously attempted to explain the staying power of Matheson's *I Am Legend* as a myth for the contemporary era. However, most of these comparative studies began as conference papers and thus— by force of the twenty-minute time limit of the genre—remain truncated, merely scratching the surface in the amount of time available to their authors (Brooks, Casali, Chenille, Ingold). Significantly, two of these (Brooks and Ingold), were presented a few years apart at the same conference, *The Image of the Hero in Literature, Media and Society*. Christopher Brooks' "When Is a Hero Not So? America, Robert Neville, and *I Am Legend*" (2004) identifies Neville's moral ambiguity and posits Matheson's novel and its followers as questioning the U.S.'s assumed role as arbiter of right—a notion developed in greater detail here. More recently, Charles Ingold reexamines Neville's ambiguous status as hero in "Hegemony and Patriarchy in Portrayals of the Protagonist and Antagonists in Film Versions of *I Am Legend*" (2010). He sees the films as increasingly effacing that ambiguity, concluding that recent films support "hegemonic and patriarchal structures in ways that the original novella did not" (217).

Steffen Hantke observes a similar trend in his excellent analysis of the most recent big screen production, "Historicizing the Bush Years: Politics, Horror Film, and Francis Lawrence's *I Am Legend*" (2011), which also addresses the earlier film adaptations. Hantke usefully cites Peter Biskind's study of Cold War film as presenting "not one but several warring ideologies" (Biskind 16). He admits, however, that the Will Smith vehicle retains a "lingering sense of an oppositional meaning [which] may originate from the source material" (177–78), a line of argument developed for each of the film adaptations in chapters to come. Finally, in two separate chapters of their expansive survey, *Richard Matheson's Monsters* (2016), June Pulliam and Anthony J. Fonseca focus on representations of masculinity in *I Am Legend* (67–78) and its film adaptations (120–26), but the brevity of their analysis leaves room for the more extended and nuanced discussion found here.

The deep analyses in the chapters that follow thus acknowledge previous scholarship on these literary and filmic texts, sometimes rebutting or nuancing earlier critics' assertions. In the end, the goal is to demonstrate the complex and sometimes contradictory nature of the ideological messages about race, gender, and class conveyed in this series of popular culture texts, ultimately revealing how and why *I Am Legend* has become an enduring American myth.

In the first chapter, "Richard Matheson's *I Am Legend*: The Trauma of World War II and the Decline of Western 'Right,'" a cultural studies approach informs the literary analysis of the original novel—the text behind what has become a contemporary myth. Whereas previous scholarship tends to link Matheson's original narrative to the context of the Cold War, reading it in tandem with other SF-horror narratives of the long 1950s, this study identifies a more compelling origin for the sense of trauma that pervades the text: World War II, with the Korean War functioning as a trigger event for its composition. Chapter One, then, examines the original 1954 novel within the context of post-war America, focusing on its author's biography as well, which included active duty in Europe. It invokes Matheson's realist combat novel *The Beardless Warriors* (1960) to demonstrate how the behaviors of Robert Neville resemble those of the trauma victim and how masculinity is compromised, rather than reinforced, by the battle experience. The chapter concludes with a discussion of how *I Am Legend*'s engagement of the questions of race, class, and gender undeniably expresses anxiety about living in the nuclear era, but at the same time critiques the binary logic of the Cold War and the West's self-conception as the culmination of "civilization" and the U.S.'s increasingly entrenched position as the arbiter of right.

Chapter Two, "Visualizing Apocalypse Through Compromised Masculinity: Vincent Price as *The Last Man on Earth*," examines how the novel's first screen adaptation appropriates its source text, producing a relatively faithful version of the core story. Still reflecting many Cold War anxieties, it maintains the vampire narrative and engagement with concerns about science's role in mid-twentieth-century America. It looks in particular at how casting Vincent Price suggests a closeted queer identity for the Last Man. Jamil Y. Khader has argued that Matheson's Neville can fruitfully be read through the lens of queer theory ("Will the Real"), and this notion is applied here to the novel's first film adaptation. With Vincent Price, an actor repeatedly viewed as a "high-toned sissy" (Tyler 330), cast as the protagonist, a queer reading of this filmic text seems almost inevitable. Reading another Matheson novel, *The Shrinking Man* (1956), in tandem reveals further evidence of a crisis of masculinity that finds expression in fears of apocalypse and human extinction.

For the second film version of Matheson's Last Man narrative, director Boris Sagal worked with the ultra-masculine Charlton Heston in the loosely adapted *The Omega Man*, countering any perceived queerness that may have lingered from the earlier Vincent Price vehicle. This film, the object of Chapter Three, "The Last White Man on Earth: Charlton Heston in *The Omega Man*," clearly foregrounds the question of race. During the film's scripting, screenwriters John William Corrington and Joyce Hooper Corrington drew on the contemporary context of the late 1960s race riots, the Black Power movement, and fear of a white apocalypse. Their scenario reverses the ethical lesson of Matheson's novel, reinscribing contemporary notions of heteronormative white masculinity while at the same time portraying these as under threat. Not only does he embody a hypermasculine hero, Heston's star persona, informed by his roles in 1950s and 1960s biblical epics, contributes to his iteration of "Dr. Robert Neville" as a Christ-like image of self-sacrifice by the end of the film. The film engages, however, with race in a sometimes radical fashion and, although it has been critiqued as an expression of white anxiety over urban racial violence (Nama; K. Patterson), this analysis reveals the text to be much more ambivalent in its descriptions of race roles and race relations.

Significantly, a hiatus in interest in adapting Matheson's text to the screen occurs in the 1980s. Given its emphasis on material prosperity fueled by neoliberal economics coupled with an increasingly conservative social agenda, the Reagan-Thatcher era in some ways resembles the 1950s; under Ronald Reagan's leadership, the nation appeared largely united, recovered from the humiliation of Vietnam through limited military victories, and the Cold War was soon to be over. Not only were the social tensions different, but perhaps Robert Neville represented too mundane a hero for the glamorous eighties. That decade did, however, see the rise of Stephen King as America's most popular author, a writer who mainstreamed precisely the horror of the mundane largely invented by Rod Serling, Charles Beaumont, Richard Matheson, and the writers of the *Twilight Zone*. It created its own heroes and monsters, radically blurring the lines between the two, with the mass murderer-serial killer topping the list of box-office draws, as seen in the success of horror and SF franchises like *Friday the 13th* (1980) and *Terminator* (1984), in which the title figure could be a villain in the first installment and a hero in the next, *Terminator 2: Judgement Day* (1991).[2]

Discussions about a new adaptation of the Matheson novel, however, began to occur in the 1990s, but the project was not realized until much later with a radically different approach to casting the last man on earth. Just as Pearl Harbor had been a shock in 1941, the September 11, 2001, terrorist attacks on the World Trade Towers in New York City rocked America, creating a new climate of fear and inspiring a new sub-genre of disaster films, including many remakes of 1950s SF-horror films (Briefel and Miller). The time was ripe for a resurrection of Matheson's narrative framework and his hero, but the casting of African American actor Will Smith—a figure already linked to a number of successful SF film projects—offered a completely new and updated spin to the story. Chapter Four, "The Color of the New Hero: Will Smith in *I Am Legend*," thus examines how this major race reversal of the central character functions in the 2007 blockbuster, partially answering earlier critiques that implicitly viewed both the novel and *The Omega Man* as potentially racist texts. The casting of an African American as Robert Neville is a highly significant move, both in its confirmation of trends involving the mainstreaming of minorities in American society and its reflection of a society working toward the necessity of envisioning the hero as a person of color. Almost immediately after this film was released, a direct-to-DVD adaptation of Matheson's novel was shot and premiered on the Syfy (then Sci-fi) network in 2009. *I Am Omega* also cast a multiracial actor, martial arts star Marc Dacascos, as its protagonist, thus further reinforcing the idea that the color of America's future is changing. The chapter concludes with a discussion of the SF hero's role as a tool in the construction of the post-white nation.

Finally, the book's conclusion, "*I Am Legend* as American Myth," summarizes how its analysis resituates Matheson's signal work along with its film versions within specific socio-historical contexts and partially rehabilitates these ambiguous and polyvalent texts. Countering charges of racism, it asserts instead that the 1954 novel already begins to grapple with the problem that the work's most recent film adaptations address through their choice of heroes of color: the death of the white male hero. If we recall the conclusion of Matheson's story, Robert Neville states with irony, "I am legend": he, the lone survivor of his race (for all surviving "humanity" has mutated into vampire-hybrids) has become a mythical figure. At the same time, though, the novel problematizes the white man's violence, standing as a statement of guilt, of failure, of the final self-destructiveness of white, Western, imperialist society—a social model shown as bankrupt by the horrors of the Holocaust, Hiroshima and Nagasaki, the Korean War, the Red Scare, and so on. Neville's realization at the end of the novel reveals that *he* is the monster[3]; while he had believed himself to be rightfully killing in self-defense, he realizes that he has perpetrated genocide upon the new race of humanity that has evolved after the plague. This condemnation of the white man implied in Matheson's post–World War II novel offers the archetypal core that has made this such a compelling story over the decades since, as American society comes to grips with the death of the last white man and embraces the future of a newly colored society—one that is not only postcolonial and postmodern, but also post-white.

ONE

Richard Matheson's *I Am Legend*
The Trauma of World War II and the Decline of Western "Right"

> *And, before science had caught up with the legend, the legend had swallowed science and everything* (Richard Matheson, *I Am Legend* 29).
>
> *Horror he had adjusted to. But monotony was the greater obstacle* (111).
>
> *And the dark men dragged his lifeless body from the house. Into the night. Into the world that was theirs and no longer his* (162).

Sometime in the near future, an epidemic has decimated the human population leaving a lone protagonist, Robert Neville, as the last man on earth. Or so we think. As he goes about the daily business of sole survivor—scavenging food, fuel and other supplies, maintaining his home, and painfully reminiscing about the events that have brought him here—we learn that he is not, after all, alone. For the plague has transformed the rest of humanity into apparently mindless, undead creatures; like the vampires of legend, garlic repels them and they can be dispatched by a stake through the heart. Using the scientific method along with a methodical procedure for their slaughter, Neville comes to understand the relationship between the plague and these vampires; but then he discovers another survivor whose story completely overturns his current understanding of the world. Rather than one type of vampire, there are two; the second of which has remained sentient, dependent on blood, but intelligent enough to supply its nutritional needs without slaughter. Because of Neville's indiscriminate campaign of terror against all vampires, however, the new society condemns him to death as a relic of the past; ultimately, Neville understands his fate, realizing at the narrative's conclusion: "I am legend" (170).[1]

In his handbook, *Richard Matheson on Screen: A History of the Filmed Works* (2010), Matthew R. Bradley proposes that "[f]ew works published in the twentieth century affected literary and cinematic horror as profoundly as Richard Matheson's third novel, *I Am Legend*" (118). In 2012, the World Horror Writers Association named it the vampire novel of the century (Pulliam and Fonseca 67), and writers of the caliber of Ray Bradbury and Stephen King (293) have long acknowledged Matheson's influence on the development of horror as a popular media genre after World War II. But as Cheyenne Mathews attests, academics have been somewhat slow to recognize the significance of his contributions ("Introduction" xii-xiii); June Pulliam and Anthony J. Fonseca even title the introduction to their recent study of his work "The Most Famous Horror Writer You've Never Heard Of" (ix). Nonetheless, in the introduction to a 2003 interview of Matheson, Jack O'Connell and James Sallis assert that "when the dust finally settles and something like perspective begins to descend, we suspect, like many of our boomer cohorts, that the writer who will have influenced us most and defined our era best will be Richard Matheson" (195).

With the blockbuster success of Francis Lawrence's 2007 eponymous film adaptation of *I Am Legend*, a new generation of fans and academics has discovered this seminal text. Thus, Matheson's work now figures in a number of master's and doctoral theses defended in the U.S. (Ethridge; Hudson), France (Hautecloque), Austria (Wenk), Denmark (Svensson), and even in Serbia (Sarovic). Among these, Christian Wenk could still nonetheless assert in 2008 that "Matheson has had such an enormous—*although often forgotten*—influence on modern Gothic fiction and film" (187; emphasis added). Unfortunately, it appears to have taken the writer's passing in 2013 for a significant number of scholars to remember him. Since then the academic literature on Matheson has begun to snowball, as a mere handful of scholarly articles has grown over the last five years into a respectable body of secondary literature, including edited volumes in French (Chenille *et al.*) and English (Mathews and Haedicke; Pulliam and Fonseca), as well as a special issue of an online Spanish journal (Roas).

In his recent "biocultural critique," Matias Clasen, like scholars before him, correctly situates *I Am Legend* in its obvious and immediate sociopolitical context of the Cold War, discussing how it addresses contemporary anxieties about nuclear energy and fears of an apocalyptic attack from the Soviet Union. But when he asks, "What is it about this novel that has invested it with canonical status?" (313), Clasen raises an as yet largely unexplored avenue for a fruitful exegesis of the text, attributing the power of its expression of Robert Neville's particular anxiety by linking it to Matheson's own biographical stresses as a young writer struggling to support a family (315; see also Pulliam and Fonseca 1–2, 7). Matheson admitted to interviewer Pat

McGilligan that "[w]hether it's built in or whether that came from my environment [an immigrant family during the Depression], I don't know, but I have this dread of financial insecurity" (253). Indeed, Raymond Carney asserts that "Matheson, far from dissociating himself with his heroes, goes to some lengths to emphasize their biographical similarity to himself" (13). And Matheson told interviewer Robert Arnett that "[m]ost of the characters are me, in one form or another, since it's one man against insuperable odds" (60). As we shall see, the fears of Robert Neville—an avatar of Matheson himself and an entire generation of men—reflect very personal fears, including those of the GI returning to a changed America and changing expectations of masculinity.

Clasen also identifies an argument made here in depth, in this and the following chapters, regarding both the text's timeliness in its own day, but also its continued significance more than half a century after its initial publication: "*I Am Legend* is the story of a troubled man in troubled times, at once intensely personal and highly dependent on local, sociohistorical anxieties. *Yet, the story retains its power to engage and to disturb in contexts far removed from that of its production*" (313; emphasis added). Following Clasen, this study links the power of Matheson's writing not to its literary accomplishment, but rather to its ability to touch a deeply affective register as it communicates the fears and anxieties of an Everyman protagonist, a protagonist whose biographical trajectory often resembles that of his creator. Then, the chapters that follow address how a text so deeply rooted in the personal and cultural anxieties of its own time has proven so adaptable across the decades, developing Christopher Brooks' assertion that "*I Am Legend* continues to be re-issued because it responds to the political status of the United States and, especially today, gestures directly to our tenuous status as an arbiter of right" (477).

Richard Matheson: A Legend in SF-Horror Writing

Until very recently, scholars have largely neglected Richard Matheson's major contributions to the development of the SF, fantasy, and horror genres in the second half of the twentieth century (Wenk 187). Along with the other writers of the Southern California school of writers (Pulliam and Fonseca 9), many of whom also wrote for film and television, Matheson's work must be recognized as establishing the framework for modern horror, which became with Stephen King and the slasher films of the 1970s a major genre for the end of the millennium. Christian Wenk argues for his significance, positing that "[h]aving inherited the legacy of the American Gothic from Lovecraft and Poe, Richard Matheson was, along with Jack Finney, Shirley Jackson and Ray Bradbury responsible for providing new impetus to the Gothic of the twentieth century" (186). Indeed, interviewer Douglas E. Winter describes Matheson as "perhaps the most influential writer of horror fiction of his generation" (24).

Richard Burton Matheson was born in 1926 in Allendale, New Jersey, to a Norwegian immigrant couple who were practicing Christian Scientists.[2] They moved to Brooklyn when young Richard was three and he eventually studied structural engineering at Brooklyn Technical High School. In 1943 he enlisted in the Army engineering program, and in 1944 he was placed in the infantry and saw combat. After the war, he pursued a BA in journalism at the University of Missouri, later publishing his first story "Born of Man and Woman" (1950) in the *Magazine of Fantasy and Science Fiction*. Soon after, he moved to California and continued to pursue a career in writing fiction and for the screen, working for a time at the Douglas Aircraft factory to pay the bills. In the Los Angeles area he met Ray Bradbury, Charles Beaumont, William F. Nolan, and mystery writer William Campbell Gault, all of whom helped along his career by reading drafts and creating a network for publication. In 1952, he married Ruth Ann Woodson; they had four children, three of whom also became writers: Chris Matheson, Richard Christian Matheson, and Ali Matheson.

Among the nearly one hundred short stories Matheson has published in magazines like *Galaxy Science Fiction* and *Playboy* during the 1950s and 1960s figure the minor classics "Third from the Sun" (1950) and "Duel" (1971). His short fiction has been collected in 21 various volumes, most notably in the *Shock* trilogy (1961–1964) followed by *Shock Waves!* (1970), and Gauntlet Press has recently reissued his complete short fiction in a three-volume set edited by Stanley Wiater (Matheson, *Collected*). His first novel, *Someone is Bleeding*, appeared in 1953, which he quickly followed with *I Am Legend* and *The Shrinking Man* (1956); other recognized titles include *Hell House* (1971), adapted to film as *The Legend of Hill House* (1973), as well as *Bid Time Return*, the latter also published as *Somewhere in Time* upon its 1980 film adaptation directed by Jeannot Szwarc, starring Christopher Reeve and Jane Seymour. In all, Matheson has published nearly 30 novels, including a number of Westerns during the 1990s.

Early in his career, Matheson's fiction fed his screenwriting; his short stories formed the basis for seven of his 14 *Twilight Zone* teleplays, such as "Death Ship" (1953/1963) and "Little Girl Lost" (1953/1962),[3] and Rod Serling adapted two more Matheson stories himself. They also appeared later on Serling's *Night Gallery* (1969–1973) and the *Outer Limits* (1995–2002) series reprise. His first television gigs were episodes for the Western series *Buckskin*

(1959), *Wanted: Dead or Alive* (1959), and *Have Gun—Will Travel* (1960). His skills as a teller of science-fictional, supernatural, or uncanny tales appeared in episodes of *The Alfred Hitchcock Hour* ("Ride the Nightmare," 1962), *Star Trek* ("The Enemy Within," 1966), as well as television movies like *The Night Stalker* (1972) which popularized the character of Carl Kolchak (Darren McGavin), *Dracula* (1974) starring Jack Palance, and *Scream of the Wolf* (1974). Matheson's best-known works for the big screen include his free adaptations of Edgar Allan Poe works for Roger Corman's now classic cycle of films for American International Pictures. Others have also adapted his short fiction to the big screen as recently as *What Dreams May Come* (1998), *The Box* (2009), based on "Button, Button" (1970), and *Real Steel* (2011), based on "Steel" (1956), both of which had been *Twilight Zone* episodes although on separate iterations of the series, airing in 1986 and 1964 respectively. Regrettably, *Jaws 3-D* (1983) represents his last major studio contract as a screenwriter, although he later helped his son Richard Christian Matheson with the Gene Hackman, Dan Aykroyd crime comedy *Loose Cannons* (1990).

Matheson continued publishing new fiction through the 1990s, virtually right up to his death at the age of 87 in 2013. He returned to the Western with titles like *Journal of the Gun Years* (1991), *The Gun Fight* (1993), and *The Memoirs of Wild Bill Hickok* (1996). *Abu and the 7 Marvels* (2002), illustrated by William Stout, offers *Arabian Nights*–like fare to younger readers. Tor Books began re-issuing Matheson's earlier work in both paper and e-book formats, also publishing new suspense and fantasy novels like *Now You See It* (1995) and *Other Kingdoms* (2011), as well as "inspirational fiction" such as *The Path: A New Look at Reality* (1999). In addition, Gauntlet Press/Edge Books has published a number of limited editions of his works, including his *Twilight Zone* scripts (2001–2002), as well as his fictionalized memoir, *Generations* (2012). This long and productive career, with contributions to a number of popular genres of film and literature, had earned him The World Fantasy Award for Lifetime Achievement as early as 1984 and the Horror Writers Association Bram Stoker Award for Lifetime Achievement in 1991; he was inducted into the Science Fiction Hall of Fame in 2010. But he remains best remembered for one of his earliest works of fiction.

Matheson's SF-Horror Classic: I Am Legend

First issued as a Gold Medal paperback in 1954 (Bradley 118), Matheson's short novel of the last man on earth blends horror and science fiction as it occurs in its contemporary readers' future, taking place from January 1976 to January 1979, as the titles of its four sections indicate. Set in the Los Angeles suburbs, with references to Compton Boulevard (25) in Gardena—where

Matheson lived in the 1950s (Bradley 119)—Inglewood and Santa Monica (49), *I Am Legend* (henceforth *IAL*) brings its apocalyptic scenario of humanity's decimation into the very backyard of his contemporaries. It tracks the struggles of a sole survivor, helping establish the tropes of a literary and filmic sub-genre which would burgeon in the years after the United States dropped atomic bombs on Hiroshima and Nagasaki and the ensuing Cold War with the Soviet Union. It cannot claim full primacy as a novel of nuclear apocalypse, given that George R. Stewart's *Earth Abides* (1949) and Judith Merril's *Shadow on the Hearth* (1950) antedate it. However, *IAL*'s implementation of disease as a rational explanation for the Gothic horror trope of the vampire offers a radical variation on both the nuclear holocaust and traditional vampire narratives.

In part one, chapters one through five of this relatively short novel, an omniscient third-person narrator introduces us to its sole protagonist Robert Neville and his daily routine, an almost ritualized inspection of his house and yard, and the endless search for evidence of damage caused by unnamed assailants, "*them*" (14).[4] The reader's first clue to the identity of Neville's antagonists appears in his concern with mirrors and garlic as part of his protective apparatus. This detailed outlining of his domestic routine—what Adryan Glasgow refers to as "vampire maintenance" (37)—and the insistence on a ritualized structuring of the daylight hours recurs as a consistent leitmotif in all of the novel's subsequent film adaptations. Although "he was a man and he was alone" (15), or rather, precisely because he was a man alone, Neville's survival, as well as his sanity, hinge upon the rigid observance of precautionary measures taken to maintain his living space, as well as constant foraging for food and supplies because of the absolute breakdown of pre-catastrophe social and economic structures. Such routines also help keep at bay the deep sense of loneliness, both spiritual and physical, that he experiences.

Much of the novel's appeal lies in the intimate relationship it establishes, even though it is narrated in the third person, between its protagonist and its readers. Of those who have commented on *IAL* in print, only Nina Auerbach finds Robert Neville completely unsympathetic, characterizing him as a "singular, nasty hero" (138). Most critics find him empathetic even while understanding his ambiguous heroism, but Ted Krulik goes so far as to find that "with his stoic, self-reliant way of life and his dynamic physical struggle against the vampires, he is a hero we can admire" (4). Although none of us have had to face the trauma of being the last human on earth, many readers have faced periods of depression when we have felt as if we are completely and utterly alone. Indeed, Matheson admits having drawn on his own sense of isolation when "young and single" (Dawidziak 13). The text thus allows us to identify with Neville and the survival mechanisms that he develops; Matheson accomplishes this through tiny details that many of the filmmakers reproduce or adapt. These iconic tropes include Neville's vehicle, a "Willys station wagon" (23), the SUV of the 1950s; his obsession with time and clocks; his search for solace in alcohol; and his musical connoisseurship. Neville listens—perhaps idiosyncratically since he otherwise appears to be an average working-class American male—to Beethoven's (16), Mozart's (89), and Schubert's (134) symphonies, Schoenberg's *Verklärte Nacht* (19), and Brahms (28). His record collection also includes Leonard Bernstein's Symphony No 2, *The Age of Anxiety* (30), a work expressive precisely of the Cold War angst Matheson's novel has been seen as symptomatic of (Ruiz 44). In addition, Matheson self-consciously signals the tropes of his own fiction as his protagonist listens to Flemish composer Roger Leie's *The Year of the Plague* (20). Neville often defuses a stressful situation with wry, dark humor; however, he also snaps periodically, expressing rage and sadness in a manner over and above what might have been deemed socially acceptable for a male of his era in more normal circumstances.

After establishing the routines of the peaceful daylight hours, the novel disrupts the order Neville has so carefully reestablished by staging an assault on his dwelling. With nightfall, his peaceful suburban home on Cimarron Street (17) becomes the object of an all-out attack; at first, former neighbor Ben Cortman shouts, "Come out, Neville!" (18). The protagonist tries to block out the assault which first manifests itself through sound; he cannot see his assailants because he has boarded up all of his windows. He turns up the volume on his record player, but cannot block out the racket of the creatures outside. The fear and horror elicited by this nightly assault represents the second element that all film versions of the story maintain, expressive of a primal human fear of the creatures that go bump in the night.

The next day's activities reveal Neville's more active measures to protect himself. Not only does he load stranded bodies into his car, taking them to a burning pit of corpses; he also finds and dispatches, driving a wooden stake into their hearts, a number of what readers soon learn to call vampires (27). Here, Matheson introduces the tension between scientific truth and superstitious belief; the text has made clear that the original Neville is not, at first, an "analytical" (13) man. Even as he acts, the narrator asserts that "[i]t was insane, there was no rational argument for" (26) the fact that only wooden stakes worked; "[i]t seemed fantastic" (27). Matheson then draws upon his readers' knowledge of the supernatural vampire—"their staying inside by day, their avoidance of garlic, their death by stake, their reputed fear of crosses, their supposed dread of mirrors" (27)—to describe Neville's assailants. At the same time, Neville realizes that "[t]hings should be done the right way, the scientific way" (27). Although without scientific training of any formal kind, a trait with which subsequent adaptations will break, Neville determines to learn all he can, to apply that knowledge to devise experiments, and ultimately to develop a "scientific" explanation for the vampire. Critics acknowledge Matheson's contribution here, referring to his work as the first "contemporary" or "modern" vampire narrative (Weinstock, E-mail; O'Connell and Sallis 197; Wenk 187).

Neville's thoughts, relayed by the narrator, often turn to Kathy and Virginia, his dead daughter and wife, as his backstory is gradually revealed through memory flashback passages, a formal technique maintained in all of the film adaptations of the novel. One day, having gone to visit Virginia's tomb, Neville falls asleep, waking late—too late to make it home before nightfall. This dramatic episode of a race against the sun and an encounter with the horde outside the protagonist's door also recurs in the films. As Mary Pharr points out, in spite of the novel's greater emphasis on the vampire hordes than on what Gregory A. Waller calls the "King-Vampire," the novel nonetheless provides the slayer Neville—an updated version of Stoker's Abraham Van Helsing—with an individual nemesis, former neighbor Ben Cortman, a figure greatly transformed in most of the films. Here again we see the novel's contribution to the genre, as Charles Hoge asserts: "Matheson essentially invented the notion of the undead apocalypse, in which living humans were converted into monsters dedicated to destroying and consuming those living who remained" (11).

Part two of the novel, dated March 1976 and spanning chapters six through fourteen, continues to develop Neville's struggle to survive, giving him greater agency as he follows up on his resolution to study and understand the phenomenon that threatens him nightly. It also fills in his backstory through the first in a series of flashbacks, which present the novel's secondary characters, his wife, daughter, and neighbor. It introduces the catastrophe to come through the device of ominous dust storms (51), depicting the early stages of Virginia's illness, soon revealed to be a widespread epidemic, "the plague of 1975" (88). Another flashback within a flashback depicts his dead daughter, Kathy, in Neville's arms (70). During these sequences, Neville and Virginia informally speculate as to the source of the illness, quickly linked not only to blood-borne pathogens carried by mosquitoes and fleas (54–55), but also to the dust storms, themselves linked to bombings (56) and germ warfare (57). But Neville's post-apocalypse research brings him—all too late— to a more complete understanding of the disease and its legendary origin, as he ultimately realizes that "[t]he vampire was real. It was only that his true story had never been told" (88). The self-taught researcher uses a microscope to link the disease to a bacterium, mutated by the bombings and spread by the dust storms. Finally, he identifies two separate types of vampire, the mindless brutes that assail him nightly and a second, more intelligent and "civilized" sort. As Pulliam and Fonseca observe, in addition to the relentless monsters that assail Neville each night, unbeknownst to him, another "group of functional infected who were transformed before death" (69) have been gathering. Although Anne Morey cites Patrick Whalen's *Night Thirst* (1991) as an early example of this trope popularized by Stephenie Meyer in her *Twilight* saga (2005–2008), with the Cullens' ability to control their thirst as opposed to the animal-like "newborns" (Morey 4), Matheson's *IAL* predates it by nearly half a century.

This last discovery proves fatal when he meets Ruth, whom he believes to be another human survivor in Part III, chapters 15 through 19. But first, a seemingly minor encounter occupies a good bit of a chapter and is found in most of the film's adaptations, as well as in its most important literary precursor text, Mary Shelley's *The Last Man* (1826). Neville, touchingly, discovers a dog, a potential companion, a sign of hope, indeed, "a miracle" (94); the dog's death (110) only serves as a warning sign pointing toward the futility of hope and Neville's eventual fate. When this tragic sequence is followed by Neville's encounter with Ruth, it simply reveals the depths to which he has sunk. Afraid of his hermit-like appearance, Ruth has fallen unconscious, and while he brings her into his home at nightfall, his thoughts are not hopeful, but wary: "He had doubted too long. His concept of the society had become ironbound" (127). While he wants to question her, learn about her, he also considers that she may be infected and so does not want to know more. He realizes that the idea that she might stay, that they might be together and have children, "was more terrifying" than any alternative (139). And, of course, as he suspects, he learns that she is after all infected. Ruth reveals to Neville the existence of a parallel, surviving society, which—through science—has been able to dominate the blood lust that consumes the mindless vampires that roam the night. They have developed a pill, as Ruth explains in a letter to Neville when she leaves him, "It was the discovery of this pill that saved us from dying, that is helping to set up society again slowly" (155). Subsequent film adaptations refocus the intelligent vampires' adaptation to their newly evolved condition onto the hero's search for a cure that will restore the plague victims to their full humanity.

Part Four, chapters 20 and 21, offers a rapid climax to the existence of Robert Neville, the last man on earth, and further develops its image of the posthuman society to which Ruth belongs. Another dramatic sequence maintained in most of the films, opens with the January 1979 arrival of a contingent from the new society not only to capture Neville, but also to dispatch with brutality the other, rival, strain of their race. These "dark-suited men [...] were more like gangsters than men forced into a situation. There were looks of vicious triumph on their faces, white and stark in the spotlights. Their faces were cruel and emotionless" (158). Puzzled by the fact that they should choose to slay violently at night, rather than the relatively peaceful executions he has been administering by day, Neville sympathizes more with the mindless vampires than with these purportedly rational ones. Neville is captured as, "tears running down his face" (159–60), he attempts to save Ben Cortman, his nemesis but also his only remaining friend. As "the dark men dragged his lifeless body from the house. Into the night. Into the world that was theirs and no longer his" (162), Neville realizes that humanity's reign over the earth has come to an end.

Neville is confronted by his captors, his status as "the last of the old race" revealed (167). Ruth gives him an envelope full of pills and his fate becomes clear, but Neville even comes to accept this fate, willingly swallowing them. Thus, the last man on earth passes into legend himself, with one of the most effective and moving conclusions in science-fiction and horror literatures.

Given the power of its telling, the polyvalence of its allegories, the intimate identification between its protagonist and reader, it is no wonder that Matheson's novel continues to move us today and that filmmakers have, over the decades, wanted to appropriate the story and make it their own, altering its details—and also its conclusion—to suit their own needs and to reflect the interests and preoccupations of their contemporary audiences. However, as already suggested above, there are key threads maintained by all of the story's adaptors, and there are key reasons as to why this particular text holds such enduring appeal for the post-war American audience. First and foremost, *IAL* offers a truly *urban* legend. Unlike, for example, many vampire films set in remote mountain castles or werewolf films set in the backwoods, Matheson's novel and its film adaptations all clearly address the anxieties of city dwellers. Next, it invokes all of the Cold War anxieties about science and the environment, from nuclear fallout to biological warfare, imbricating these with fears of pandemic, a fear already sparked by the tuberculosis and polio epidemics, greatly heightened since the advent of AIDS. Finally, it explores the boundaries of life and death, linking these to questions about the survival of the human race and its possible evolution into something beyond. While the later film adaptations largely drop the vampire trope, they opportunistically adopt other identities for the threatening "them."

I Am Legend *as Cold War Allegory:*
SF's Ambivalence to Science

The variety of positions critics have taken as to the "meaning" of *IAL* reveals the work's complexity as a literary text, but whatever their particular focus—race, class, or gender roles—most agree with David Oakes' assertion that "Matheson's work concentrates on humanity's ability to destroy itself, reflecting cultural aspects of the Cold War years such as the threat of nuclear holocaust" (63). Another reason for the novel's polysemic adaptability appears in its generic fluidity. While I have referred to Matheson's contribution to the "horror" genre—a term that the author himself eschewed in favor of "terror" (O'Connell and Sallis 200)—in fact, much of his work blurs the lines between SF and the fantastic broadly conceived. Indeed, reveling in this generic indeterminacy, Matheson relates to interviewers that "I once had a clipping that described my writing perfectly: offbeat" (O'Connell and Sallis 199). This "offbeat" style, which we can associate with other writers of the California group, the overall tone of which *The Twilight Zone* brought to the small screen, precisely destabilizes readers' and viewers' expectations through its seemingly random appropriation of the tools and tropes of one genre in order to complicate a narrative that initially appears to belong to another.

The ambivalent climate of fear and complacency that dominated America in the fifties worked as a perfect incubator for this style, which developed most obviously in the SF-horror films that dominated the decade. Already in the path-breaking essay, "The Imagination of Disaster" (1966), Susan Sontag links 1950s horror film to the "sensuous elaboration" (41) of the decade's fears of apocalyptic nuclear holocaust or alien invasion, synthesizing the "independent sub-genre" into a handful of formulaic plot elements (38–40). Distinguishing them from SF novels—a move I am not ready to make—Sontag argues: "Science fiction films are not about science. They are about disaster" (41), "the aesthetics of destruction" (41). Naming such works as *Rocketship X-M* (1950), *The War of the Worlds* (1953), and *The World, the Flesh and the Devil*, Sontag argues that they reflect "the deepest anxieties about contemporary existence" (48). She continues that not only do they reveal "these new anxieties about physical disaster, the prospect of universal mutilation and even annihilation, the science fiction films reflect powerful anxieties about the individual psyche" (48).

Subsequent examinations like Vivian Sobchack's seminal study, *The Limits of Infinity: The American Science-Fiction Film, 1950–1975* (1980), build on Sontag's early work, but also establish the groundwork for later critics like Steven Cohan to assert that "[a]long with their generic cousins (the equally popular alien-invasion films), the atomic-monster films of this period have long been read as transparent parables of cold war containment" (130). One of the problems, however, that these early critics felt they must address is where these monster and disaster films fit on the generic spectrum and where to situate them in the timeline of cinematic history. Again, following Sontag, film studies scholars tend to divorce films like *The Thing from Another World* (1951) and *Them!* from the fiction that spawned them, reading them instead as a new iteration of the 1930s classic horror film.[5] In his literary history, *Monsters, Mushroom Clouds, and the Cold War: American Science Fiction and the Roots of Postmodernism, 1946–1964* (2001), M. Keith Booker makes similar arguments, however, about popular literature, placing Matheson at the core of such trends since his "books of the 1950s contain some of the most representative science fiction expressions of the concerns of the decade" (84).

Matheson avers that, for him, *I Am Legend* was a work of science fiction as he conceived it (Dawidziak 12). But the novel fits into this cross-generic trend as it begins with a monster taken from the pages of "supernatural horror" (Lovecraft), the vampire, and then transforms it into an apocalyptic pandemic, all the while invoking science as both its cause and its explanation. It is precisely in its engagement with science that Matheson's novel, then, most clearly reflects Cold War ambivalence about the potentially destructive power of science, as well as the scientific method's potentially comforting role as an epistemological tool for man's understanding of the universe.

Science and the Apocalypse

Through flashback sequences, in which the Last Man figure Robert Neville converses with his late wife, Virginia, *IAL* speculates as to how the apocalypse came about. Reflective of the often vague, half-informed discourses that tended to heighten, rather than calm, contemporary fears about the effect of a nuclear event, the text establishes relatively loose connections between the etiology of the vampire plague and a recent war. Ultimately, it remains coy as to whether the pandemic resulted from a genetic mutation caused by nuclear fallout or if it was the direct result of biological warfare.[6] At the very beginning of the epidemic, the couple speculates about the origin of the vaguely defined illness that has affected "[h]alf the people on the block" (54). Neville first accuses "some kind of virus," pointing a finger at a range of causes from "the storms and the mosquitoes" (54) to "[e]verything from germ warfare on down" (57). Virginia seconds his concerns about "[m]osquitoes [...], flies, sand fleas" which "carry diseases" (55), while Neville questions the efficacy—now also attributing potential blame to a chemical agent—of the "spray" being used to fight "the age of the insect" (55).

This discourse invokes the mutant insects of the "so-called big bug films" of the era typified by *Them!* released the same year as Matheson's novel (Leskosky 319).[7] Furthermore, unspecified "bombings" are blamed for causing genetic mutation in insects, including a "strain of giant grasshoppers" in Colorado (56). These comments refer to the ongoing testing of nuclear weapons during the Cold War, including the first Soviet nuclear test drop on August 29, 1949, and the November 1, 1952, drop of the first hydrogen bomb in the Pacific by the U.S. As Jerome F. Shapiro describes in *Atomic Bomb Cinema* (2002), throughout the 1950s SF-horror films would explore both a nuclear holocaust resulting from war, as in Arch Oboler's *Five* (1951) or Roger Corman's *The Day the World Ended*, as well as mutations caused by ongoing nuclear testing, like in Corman's *Attack of the Crab Monsters* (1957), and even the possible use of atomic power in the space race, thematized in *Attack of the Giant Leeches* (1959). In response, Virginia ironizes, "And they say we won the war" (56), giving victory to the insects. Her attitude about the bombings and their vicissitudes begins to problematize their moral rightness, casting a shadow upon what has obviously proven to be a hollow victory.

The vectors of blood-borne bacteria transmitted to humans by mosquitoes and fleas allow Matheson to draw upon the tropes of the plague narrative, aspects of *IAL* which are both borrowed from its precursor texts and found in its descendants, today's zombie apocalypse narratives. While evidence for a connection to Mary W. Shelley's *The Last Man*—itself inspired by the cholera epidemic, which had begun in India in 1817 to 1821 (Arnold 30) and then moved to Europe only after that novel's publication—remains tenuous, there are numerous textual similarities between the two novels.[8] More direct influences may be found in M. P. Shiel's last man narrative *The Purple Cloud* (1901), which features a plague and, of course, Albert Camus' *The Plague* (1947). Published in English translation (1948) only a few years earlier, that novel achieved international acclaim for its French author, contributing to his receipt of the Nobel Prize for Literature in 1957. *The Plague* has also been read as an allegory for the Nazi Occupation and the French Resistance during World War II (Henry; Lunde). Significantly, James R. Giles observes a similar phenomenon of Othering plague victims, recalling "Camus's division in *The Plague* of human beings into the categories of plague carriers and plague fighters" (25), which we see in *IAL*.

After this speculative flashback, the narrative returns to Neville's post-catastrophe present, both reinforcing Virginia's statement questioning the war, its methods, and results but also gainsaying the couple's speculated causes for the plague: "only talk of insect carriers and virus, and they weren't the causes. He was sure of it" (59). Unsatisfied with idle speculation about bombings and chemical agents, Neville realizes that he must identify the origin of his (and humanity's) predicament in order to combat it. Finally understanding that there is something else that he can do besides methodically manufacturing the instruments of death (the wooden stakes he prepares on his lathe by day), securing his fortress through constant maintenance to his home's assaulted facade, and effecting sorties by day to kill the dormant creatures, Neville decides that he can also use reason to comprehend what appears as irrational, as completely Other. Unlike his film avatars, all of whom have scientific training and two of whom are military officers, however, Matheson's Neville is an average Joe who must train himself in the scientific method of observation and reflection.

Science as Tool for Survival?

Matheson thus directly engages the scientific discourse also prevalent in the SF-horror fiction and films of the period. The novel's second paragraph begins, "[i]f he had been more analytical" (13), initially coding Neville as ignorant and unreflective, admitting that he "had no anatomical knowledge" (27). However, he soon realizes: "You have a mind, don't you? .... Well, *use* it!" (19). First, "[h]e had to do a lot of reading, a lot of research" (38); next, "an experimental fervor had seized him and he could think of nothing else" (39). He acts on that fervor by kidnapping a vampire and observing the effects of the sun on her. Perhaps precisely because he is self-taught, however, Neville's trial and error approach seems repeatedly to bring him back to square one, as we read again and again: "The first step, and already you've fallen flat on your face" (60); "Step number one, then, was reading about blood" (77); and, then, "[t]he first step was to get a microscope" (83). The novel's ambivalence as to the efficacy of the scientific method as a means to arrive at the truth appears in these mixed messages. On the surface, Neville's assertions about the right way to do things is validated; at the same time, however, the text reveals their inefficacy. Eventually, he does make progress, moving from reading, to experimentation, to observations, finally reaching a point at which, "I won't believe anything unless I see it in a microscope" (135). Ultimately, Neville realizes that bacteria are the true cause, and that "[t]he flies and mosquitoes had been a part of it. Spreading the disease causing it to race through the world" (82).

Neville's research eventually links not only the source of the pandemic, but also his own immunity, to the war and his personal role in it as a soldier. He later explains his suppositions to Ruth:

> [W]hile I was stationed in Panama during the war I was bitten by a vampire bat. And, though I can't prove it, my theory is that the bat had previously encountered a true vampire and acquired the *vampiris* germ. [...] But, by the time the germ had passed into my system, it had been weakened in some way by the bat's system. It made me terribly ill, of course, but it didn't kill me, and as a result, my body built up an immunity to it. That's my theory, anyway. I can't find any better reason [144].

Thus Neville explicitly links his current existence as the sole surviving human, his Last Man status, to his experiences as a soldier, which led to his inoculation against the pandemic that has transformed the rest of humanity into vampires. But the mention of the vampire bat bite as an immunizing factor also links Matheson's plague to traditional lore and literary interpretations of the supernatural vampire via the trope of the bat.[9] Furthermore, Neville's research includes not only physiology, blood, and bacteriology (79), but he also consults historical and literary accounts of vampirism as authoritative sources to help him grapple with the problem.

The novel's logic nonetheless rests upon an epistemological conundrum. The scientific cause and explanation for the pandemic is identified as a revenant from forgotten superstitions, vampirism: "And, before science had caught up with the legend, the legend had swallowed science and everything" (29). Just as he cannot trust science to provide the truth, neither can he trust religious superstition; as Christopher M. Moreman points out, Neville "strikes an ambivalent relationship with Christianity throughout the novel" (132). Both explanatory models for the universe, the secular/scientific and the religious/superstitious fail the novel's ambiguous hero; not only is he alone, bereft of all human society and companionship, Neville is also spiritually and intellectually lost, without an adequate model to understand the world he lives in. This blurring of the boundaries between science and religion—evocative of Arthur C. Clarke's third law that "any sufficiently advanced technology is indistinguishable from magic"—in which both models lead simply to fear and wonder, typifies the Cold War context in which Matheson wrote. But the seeds of the Cold War, of course, were planted at the conclusion of World War II.

Robert Neville, Vampire Slayer

For Matheson *IAL* was ultimately a vampire story; in his own recollection, the novel originated directly as such, as he told *Twilight Zone Magazine*: "I got the idea for it when I was seventeen years old in Brooklyn and saw *Dracula*. I figured if one vampire was scary then a whole world full of vampires should be really scary" (qtd. Neilson 1075; see also McGilligan 252). Explicitly acknowledging his novel's literary heritage, Matheson begins chapter three with a citation from Bram Stoker's *Dracula*: "'The strength of the vampire is that no one will believe in him.' / Thank *you*, Dr. Van Helsing, he thought" (28). Of course, reading a work of fiction as part of his "scientific" research reveals the problematic nature of his self-taught methodology, exposing the paradoxical logic of the text's Gothic aspects, which have been adequately laid out by David A. Oakes. Nonetheless, Neville becomes, of course, a vampire slayer, drawing on the wisdom of Van Helsing for his epic but doomed battle for human survival, spending much of the day sharpening stakes and stocking up on garlic, although he offers scientific explanations for their efficacy.

Neville, the Righteous Slayer?

In *Slayers and Their Vampires: A Cultural History of Killing the Dead* (2006), Bruce McClelland identifies the steps taken by and special characteristics of the vampire hunter. He does not engage *IAL* at all in his analysis, perhaps because Neville ultimately cannot conform to his heroic vision of the slayer. And yet, McClelland reveals how vampire literature positions the slayer as arbiter of right precisely by demonizing the vampire:

> To label something evil is to magically circumscribe it and to effectively push the obligation to proof of goodness onto the thing so designated. To define what constitutes anathema, to excommunicate *ex officio*, is of course to assert or reassert, with full authority, *one's own unquestionable status as good* [xiii; emphasis added].

At first glance, with the victims of the vampire plague depicted as mindless, subhuman monsters, Neville's war against them appears completely justified. Under nightly siege in his bungalow bunker, "he still heard them outside, their murmuring and their walkings about and their cries, their snarling and fighting among themselves" (18). He refers to them impersonally as "they" (13, 17, 65); "*them*" (14, 19, 26), even as "*that*" (29), or as "bastards" (17, 20, 30); his former neighbor has become "completely alien to him now" (65). Compared to dogs and wolves, they are subhuman animals: "crouching on their haunches like dogs, eyes glittering at the house, teeth slowly grating together; back and forth, back and forth" (22); "[o]utside they howled and pummeled the door, shouting his name in a paroxysm of demented fury" (46). Furthermore, there appears to be no human social interaction between them, as

> he saw another man and a woman on the lawn. None of the three was speaking to either of the others. They never did. They walked and walked about on restless feet, circling each other like wolves, never looking at each other once, having hungry eyes only for the house and their prey inside the house [65].

As prey, besieged by these walking dead, these ambulatory "corpses" (65), certainly Neville is justified in killing as many of them as possible? As he later explains to Ruth, "If I didn't kill them, sooner or later they'd die and come after me. I have no choice; no choice at all" (146).

The Moral Ambiguities of Slaying

Through the first two thirds of the novel, then, both Neville and the reader largely assume the righteousness of his slaying. That is, until he meets Ruth, the woman from the newly evolving society of vampire hybrids. Only when he makes contact with an Other and begins to engage in dialogue with her is his righteousness fully questioned, as Ruth's evident humanity and her description of the new social order reveal that the victims of a different strain of the epidemic actually remain sentient. Although even then, he at first asserts, "it was better not to know anything about the people you killed" (127), he now at least refers to them as "people."

That said, cracks in the façade of Neville's justifications for his ruthless slaying actually appear quite early in the novel. Albeit rationally convinced that he is the last human being and that these rival monsters will prey on him if given the slightest chance to do so, Neville struggles with his actions: "Robert Neville's hands fumbled on the stake and mallet. It was always hard when they were alive; especially with women [....] Well, what *else* can I do? he asked himself, for he still had to convince himself he was doing the right thing" (26). Long before his encounter with the new society, then, the narrative questions whether or not its hero is acting in justifiable, although preventative rather than reactive, self-defense.

In this respect, Matheson's reworking of the vampire novel was then radically new, as Gregory Waller observes. In *The Living and the Undead: Slaying Vampires, Exterminating Zombies* (1986/2010), Waller interprets *IAL* as "consciously demythologiz[ing] certain assumptions about violence, heroism, faith, and ritual that inform Stoker's novel and other vampire stories" (257). Describing Neville's vampire slaying as "a methodical, futile exercise in genocide" (18), Waller underscores the moral ambiguities faced even by such traditional vampire hunters as the figure's ur-model, Van Helsing.[10] Furthermore, Waller compares Neville's experimentation to find a cause for the plague as "disturbingly similar to the notorious experimentation conducted in Nazi concentration camps on Jews and other 'subhuman' species" (261). With these references to genocide and concentration camps, Waller thus doubly signals the World War II context of the Holocaust, to which we will turn in a moment. There lies here an implicit accusation about the violence underlying the scientific model of experimentation. The novel depicts Neville's use of the vampires to further his knowledge, his "dominating medical gaze" (Stephanou 25), as similar to Nazi scientists' use of camp inmates for their experiments on human survival in extreme cold and high altitude, in addition to testing human reaction to poisons and various illnesses (Spitz 44–45). That gaze becomes increasingly justified in the films' association of Neville with institutionally authorized scientific credentials.

The Mark of the Slayer

For Waller, "*I Am Legend* suggests that in a world that does not contain Good or Evil, violence, even when it is directed against the undead and when it is undertaken in the name of survival, necessarily dehumanizes and creates monsters" (262). McClelland is more conservative, refusing to question the slayers' moral imperatives; he nonetheless realizes that even in the conventional vampire novels he treats, the slayer becomes just as marked, as much of a pariah as the vampires themselves:

> The heroic nature of the vampire slayer is predicated on his ability to identify the force that saps the energy from the life of the community. Something unnatural, unholy, invades and disturbs the natural order of things [....] Yet because this intruder is invisible or, at the very least, unnoticeable—he is one of us, after all—

only those with a special understanding of his nature are able to intervene and stop the hemorrhage. Like the vampire, the slayer must be marked—externally, by some sign of birth or accident; internally, by his symbolic connection to the world of the dead [7].

Matheson's novel exploits these aspects of the slayer in a number of ways. First, he describes his slayer in terms of being dead himself or being much like the supposed monsters he kills. In fact, by boarding up his own home, he "had made the house a gloomy sepulcher" (15); having survived yet another onslaught, Neville sprawls exhausted on the floor, "his legs and arms like dead limbs" (46). After meeting Ruth and bringing her to his tomb-like home, "Robert Neville sat there wondering why he didn't feel more compassion for her. Emotion was a difficult thing to summon from the dead, though" (131).

Then, a note from the now-escaped Ruth shifts him from his throne of the righteous with a direct accusation: "I *had* a husband, Robert. You killed him" (154). Later, when Neville is now the sentient vampires' captive, Ruth explains the existence of two types of vampires to justify her own society's Neville-like massacre of beings whose "brains are impaired" (166). She makes clear, though, that he was also murdering her kind, accusing him as "one who killed the dead *and* the living" (166). And, finally, of course, in Matheson's dramatic reversal at the novel's conclusion, Neville realizes that he himself is the "legend," the monster that must be exterminated in the eyes of the so-called "new society" (170; 158).

Of particular interest here is the specific "mark" of the slayer alluded to by McClelland, which Neville bears, a mark specifically linked to his identity as a combat veteran, also a somewhat sexualized passage: "As he washed, he looked into the mirror at his broad chest, at the dark hair swirling around the nipples and down the center line of his chest. He looked at the ornate *cross he'd had tattooed* on his chest one night in Panama when he'd been drunk" (21; emphasis added). We have just learned that he "never wore pajama tops; it was a habit he'd acquired in Panama during the war" (21); the novel thus establishes Neville's backstory as a returning vet in its first chapter. Regarding the nature of his tattoo, a cross, he reflects that while on the one hand he had been a "fool [...] in those days," on the other that the cross may have "saved his life" (21). Not only does the text indulge in an instance of the paradoxical survival of an irrational aspect of the vampire's Gothic apparatus (religious symbols are still anathema to this creature of hell), it also suggests that Neville—like Matheson himself, and other protagonists like Scott Carey in *The Shrinking Man* and Lionel Barrett in *Hell House*—had been a soldier. And much later, the novel reveals the fateful connection between his tour of duty in Panama and the apocalyptic virus that has transformed most of humanity into vampires, leaving Neville behind as ostensibly the last human man.

Neville's *Bildungsroman*, then, from the human being that he was before the apocalyptic event, takes him through various stages of development. From the loving husband and father who tearfully brought his daughter's body to be destroyed, then rebelled and buried his wife against the state of emergency orders, he becomes a besieged, reactionary survivor, living at the bare minimum, half dead himself. He draws on religious lore partially to protect himself from the creatures that haunt him and takes on the role of the vampire slayer. He then turns hopefully to science perhaps to find a way out of the impasse that has become his existence, but that, too, fails, simply leading him back to violence. Both of the dominant paradigms of his civilization, the Judeo-Christian tradition and the secular worldview of science, have failed him; both are implicated in the violence that rules his daily life. Both also paradoxically fed the fires of the real-life war that Matheson's generation had lived through; American participation in World War II was linked of course to the defense of secular, Enlightenment ideals of freedom and democracy, but it was also frequently linked to Christian notions of moral right. At the same time, our enemy, Nazi Germany, invoked Christianity (Abrams xxxiv). And, of course, what brought it to an end were the ultimate fruits of Western techno-science: weapons of mass destruction.

I Am Legend elides any explicit reference to World War II itself, but that war undeniably subtends and permeates the text and its imagery. Perhaps significantly—although it may simply be a coincidence—its protagonist's name eerily recalls that of another questionable war "hero," French commander-in-chief on the Western Front in World War I, Robert Nivelle (Clayton; Rolland).[11] Not only can we see Neville's slaying as a vampire genocide, the human plague victims thrown into open pits invoke the mass graves of the Holocaust. Through Neville's characterization as an ex-soldier, vampire slaying becomes an allegory for the soldier's role as Nazi or "Jap" killer in World War II. Through its mise-en-scène of Neville's violent vampire-hunting activities *IAL* raises the question of the just war, a question brought to the fore once again just before its publication as American soldiers were again sent overseas, this time to Korea. Another work in Matheson's oeuvre, one that explicitly deals with the experience of World War II combat, a fictionalization of his own tour of duty, the mainstream novel *The Beardless Warriors* supports this interpretation.

World War II and the Crisis of White Right: Matheson's Beardless Warriors

Vincent Chenille and Marie Dollé, editors of the proceedings of the most comprehensive scholarly event to date dedicated to Matheson's work, a

2008 conference held in France, observe that "Richard Matheson knew war because he was wounded during the campaign in Alsace in 1944–1945 and this experience undoubtedly constitutes one of the keys of his oeuvre" (8). During World War II, Americans fought in Europe and in the Pacific to protect the purported values of freedom and equality, values which were perceived as under assault by the racial Other of Japanese imperial oppression, particularly after Pearl Harbor. Incidences of Japanese brutality, such as the Death March of Bataan and the fanaticism of the kamikaze pilots ready to die for the emperor, were incomprehensible to Americans. The war in the Pacific seemed therefore a fully justified and just war. That is, until August 6 and 9, 1945, when the immediate apocalyptic destruction and long-term devastation of radioactive fallout wreaked upon innocent civilians, women and children became a reality. Thereafter, the use of atomic weapons cast a dark cloud over the U.S.' sense of rightness. In Europe, again, putting an end to Nazi racial fanaticism and the insanity of Hitler's Final Solution—even to an America not free of its own racial tensions and violence—appeared fully to justify the U.S. presence. And yet, did not the racial inequality at home find a merely amplified echo in the notion of Aryan supremacy used to initiate the Shoah? Furthermore, when the war concluded, the U.S. became retroactively implicated in war crimes as it recruited former Nazis among the many scientists and intelligence operatives deemed a necessary evil to fight the Cold War against Soviet Russia and to win the nuclear arms race.

World War II, as much as it has been portrayed as a heroic war, in which we were unquestionably the "good guys," nonetheless left a mark on the American collective psyche, a mark which obviously informed the entire Cold War and anti–Communist hysteria of the House Committee on Un-American Activities and McCarthyism. Would we have feared the Soviets so much if we had not used nuclear weapons first? The American use of the annihilating force of the atomic bomb to end the war had made nuclear war a reality, and thus was responsible for creating the very Cold War climate of paranoia of which *IAL* has consistently been read as symptomatic. As historian James T. Patterson reminds us, "16.4 million Americans, the vast majority of them young men, joined the armed services during World War II" (*Grand* 13). These masses of young men were indoctrinated into a system that asserted, in the words of General Leslie McNair in 1942, director of training for American ground forces: "We must lust for battle; our object in life must be to kill; we must scheme and plan night and day to kill" (qtd. Patterson, *Grand* 7). Even President Harry S. Truman told church leaders: "When you have to deal with a beast, you have to treat him as a beast" (qtd. Patterson, *Grand* 7). Thus, in addition to a repressed sense of guilt at the national level, at the individual level, as well, millions of American young men—including Richard Matheson—had, albeit under orders, killed other Japanese and German young men. They had lived in extremely difficult conditions of physical discomfort, including cold, hunger, mud, and illness, as well as of extreme physical danger and mental stress. Those men who had seen combat in World War II suffered great difficulties in reinsertion into civilian life after the war, including post-traumatic stress disorder, some returning to find that their wives had fared perfectly well without them, or had even left them. Furthermore, because the war was overwhelmingly seen as a just war, there seemed to be no support even to consider the question of guilt that might be felt by combat veterans who had killed.

About his own experience, Matheson tells an interviewer: "I ended up being tossed into the infantry and being sent overseas as an eighteen-year-old soldier" (Winter 26).[12] Although he began to unpack his World War II combat experiences in an allegorical fashion through his earlier fictions, *I Am Legend* and *The Shrinking Man*, he did not address them directly until 1960 with the publication of a realist war novel, *The Beardless Warriors*.[13] This text, which "may well be Matheson's most underrated novel" (Pulliam and Fonseca 207), offers an explicit discourse on the moral dilemma of killing and the dehumanizing effect that war has on its protagonist, Everett Hackermeyer. "Hack," as his father-figure sergeant calls him affectionately after he has proven his worth on the battlefield, realizes that although he was never good at anything before, he now learns that he is good at killing.

The most obvious trait shared by both the horror novel and the war novel is the graphic depiction of the violent sundering and dismembering of the human body. Indeed, *IAL* describes Neville's vampire-hunting scenes not much differently than the combat scenes in *The Beardless Warriors*. Like Neville, Hack has conflicted feelings about what he is doing. On the one hand, he is fascinated with death: "Hackermeyer stared at the dead German soldiers. He couldn't take his eyes away, he was so fascinated by the bloody mangle of them" (118). In another incident, his difference in this respect from his fellow soldiers is revealed, along with a reason for him to feel guilty about killing the enemy. Stuck in a foxhole with a dead German soldier, whereas his fellow American Linstrom gags and vomits, Hackermeyer is riveted with fascination at the sight of the maggot-ridden corpse. While he does experience some nausea, he reflects, "Still, there had been a certain satisfaction in it and in the sight of the other dead Germans that day. They reminded him that the Germans were, after all, only human, and could be killed just as easily as anyone else" (127). Hackermeyer learns, then, that not only can he coldly contemplate death, he can also mete it out.

During combat the mediocre young man with no advantages from his life at home discovers a hidden talent for killing. The similarity between the descriptive passages of Hackermeyer's spree on the killing fields and Robert Neville's Van Helsing–like rage is fascinating, and merits citation at length:

The Beardless Warriors	*I Am Legend*
"Hackermeyer's heart rocked and hammered. His breath spilled out in bolting gasps. His lips began to shake. His features grew distorted as aggression, raw and murderous, flooded out of him. He couldn't miss! Every shot resulted in a fallen enemy. The earth was littered with his prey. There were no comrades on the slope; just him and all his enemies, offering themselves as targets. He sank and sank into a blood-filmed haze. The slope became the landscape of a dream, amorphous, misted over. The bloated figures drifted toward him in an endless horde, falling, executed at his hands, to be replaced by more who, in their turn, fell to silent and submissive death" (192).	"He jerked open the door and shot the first one in the face. The man went spinning back off the porch and two women came at him in muddy, torn dresses, their white arms spread to enfold him. He watched their bodies jerk as the bullets struck them, then he shoved them both aside and began firing his guns into their midst, a wild yell ripping back his bloodless lips. He kept firing the pistols until they were both empty. Then he stood on the porch clubbing them with insane blows, losing his mind almost completely when the same ones he'd shot came rushing at him again. And when they tore the guns out of his hands he used his fists and elbows and he butted with his head and kicked them with his big shoes" (47).

Indeed, so effective a killing machine does Hackermeyer become that he imagines his M1 submachine gun had become part of his arm and that he is picking off Germans "like targets in a shooting gallery" (227). This prescient imagery invokes to today's reader the possibilities of such transformations in SF films like *The Terminator* or *Transformers* (2007), but also our own children playing first-person-shooter video games. Hack is not, however, a remorseless killer, and like Neville, he questions the ethics of his actions:

> He closed his eyes and shivered. What the hell was wrong with him? Why was he becoming so bloodthirsty? No matter what the problem was, the only solution he could think of was violence. He tried to reason away the disturbance. He was in a war; it was his job. Except he knew that, somehow, it had become more than a job to him [239].

On the one hand, the grunt has been told that Germans are inhuman, as a conversation with a fellow private, Linstrom, reveals: "'What I mean,' continued Linstrom,' is that, you know, they're trained so—so strictly that they're like machines. They can't think for themselves. They have no—imagination [....] That's what makes them so inhuman'" (79). Just as the vampire slayer, in McClelland's account, must dehumanize the vampires in order to exterminate them, so, the American soldier must dehumanize his enemy. On the other hand, Hack knows that these young men are still fellow humans; indeed, Hack at first has trouble referring to the enemy as "Krauts"—the dehumanizing, derogatory term—and repeatedly refers to them as "Germans." Ultimately, stuck in a fox hole and unable to leave, Hack almost finds solace, for at least there in the dark, womb-like cave, everything is simple, with one imperative only, to survive, while "[o]utside lay only the relentless terrors of complexity" (182).

Sergeant Cooley, who has seen the young soldier's value in combat and taken him under his wing, also assumes a mentoring role, explicitly discussing the soldier's dilemma. After Hack, in his berserker battle rage, has killed a surrendering German, Cooley confronts the youth, admitting that "when we kill, we ain't men, we're animals—and that ain't giving much to the animals. Uncle Sam says, Okay boys, kill all the Krauts you like. Enjoy yourself" (245). Cooley's discourse implicitly acknowledges that war is governmentally sanctioned mass murder, even allowing for a certain pleasure in such deadly violence. He goes further admitting, "We all know killing can be fun. Hell, it's exciting" (245). However, he also admonishes the young soldier: "But the excitement goes fast, Hack—real fast. And if you get wrapped up in it, it'll wind up making you sick. It can turn you into so much an animal you'll never get back from it" (245). This animal-like state isolates the individual, essentially turning the professional killer into an antisocial being; paradoxically, murder undertaken for the collective good can easily turn into a loner's perverse pleasure. Like Hack, in his role of vampire slayer, Robert Neville finds himself slipping further and further into this state of inhuman isolation, a state ironically self-justified as the will to survival for the human race, of which he believes himself to be the last remaining individual. Indeed, Cooley completes his homily with a negative example, a young man he knew who, "after a while, Hack, he got to looking like a zombie" (246). Through his character's speech, then, Matheson directly connects the slayer to the monsters he kills.

This passage tellingly invokes the major thesis of *IAL*, which ultimately questions the right of its hero. Neville is revealed to have been a murderous villain, not only by reputation—his legend among Ruth's new society—but in reality, as well, since he has been indiscriminately murdering both mindless predatory vampires, as well as the sentient, human-like form. Just as the machine-like Germans who "can't think for themselves," according to Linstrom, resemble zombies, so does the American soldier on a killing spree resemble, in Cooley's words, a "zombie." Hunter and hunted, friend and foe, victim and prey are all alike in this world of moral ambiguity. Thus, Christopher Brooks asks in the title of his insightful reflections on the enduring qualities of Matheson's novel, "When Is a Hero Not So?" He answers his query,

> When "we" are killing "them" to our advantage, we see our cause as just—as does Robert Neville. [But as the balance of power and demographics shift] *I Am Legend* establishes new ground for the vampire story *and* for political introspection. Neville comes to view himself as anything but a hero while seeing his own violent past being played out before him, watching as the skillful killers of the "new society" execute the remaining old vampires [480].

Hackermeyer thus resembles in many ways Matheson's Robert Neville—not the scientist officer of the novel's film adaptations—but an average, even uneducated grunt, placed into an insane situation that ultimately changes him forever. Just as Hack must rethink the paradigm of the Germans being inhuman, robot-like fighting machines, so, too, Neville is forced to reconsider the humanity of the vampires he has been ruthlessly killing. In *IAL*, Neville's role as vampire hunter extraordinaire is thoroughly undermined as he learns that, in addition to the mindless zombie-vampires, another form of humanity has learned to survive with the virus and retain its capacity for reason, and that to them, he is the ruthless murderer. As the last *homo sapiens* as we know it, Neville is the legend. In this reversal, in which the hero becomes the monster, Matheson's literary text questions the values of white, Western civilization. Through references to Jews and Germans, it invokes the Nazi genocide in the name of white supremacy, and through its scientific explanation for vampirism, while at the same time repeatedly invoking "the superstition," "the legend," of the vampire, it equates Western techno-science with an unquestioned religion, condemning both in the long term.

If Matheson was able to express his concerns about the moral ambiguity of combat even in a war touted as "good" in a realist novel, why does he wait until 1960 to do so? Why, as he wrote in the 1950s, does his horror fiction deal in this veiled manner with such real life issues? As the next section argues, Robert Neville's situation—and the reason Matheson is able to tell it in such a compelling fashion—resembles that of a victim of post-traumatic stress disorder (PTSD). Certainly, the survivor of an apocalyptic pandemic, forced to fight for his survival every night and scavenge for food and supplies every day, constantly under stress, would suffer from traumatic stress. But none of us has ever experienced such a situation; Matheson succeeds in relating it with such realism by drawing on the extreme situation of his own combat experience. It should be clarified that drawing on the author's biographical experience to shed new light on the meaning of his writing is not the same as diagnosing Richard Matheson himself as having suffered from PTSD. His protagonist Robert Neville, however, appears very clearly as displaying such symptoms.

Robert Neville, Trauma Victim and the Korean War as Trigger

Not insignificantly, trauma theory began as an effort to understand the "shell shock" of returning World War I veterans, and the field came into its own in relation to the sufferings not only of World War II veterans (Vickroy 16; Tal 117–119), but also those of Holocaust survivors (Langer; LaCapra). His experiences as a soldier, followed by the loss of his wife and daughter have left Robert Neville with a textbook case of post-traumatic stress disorder. With "trauma, defined as a response to events so overwhelmingly intense that they impair normal emotional or cognitive responses and bring lasting psychological disruption" (Vickroy xi), we understand Neville's extreme reaction to the events which led to the utter collapse of the world as he knows it: compulsively to repeat the acts of killing he had been forced to commit during the war by a socio-political system of which he, too, is a victim. According to Laurie Vickroy, the trauma victim displays "situational-contingent behavior" such as "helplessness and other discomforting adaptive or defensive psychic responses" (23). On the surface, many of the behaviors that Neville engages in can be seen merely as adaptive survival strategies for life in the vampire apocalypse; the behaviors of the trauma victim, however, are also developed to "deal with" the psychological impact of an extraordinary event. Thus, Neville's obsessive-compulsive checking of the safety of his home (13–14); his "relaxing hobby, hunting for Cortman" (119); his excursions to hunt and kill other vampires, and so on, represent such coping mechanisms.

In one of the novel's key passages, already partially cited above as part of Neville's transformative process from a man of action into a man of science, he has an epiphany about memory:

> The past revealed nothing to help him [....] The past had brought something else, though; pain at remembering. Every recalled word had been like a knife blade twisting in him. Old wounds had been reopened with every thought of [his wife] [59].

Neville suffers because of a past that he cannot fully recall, but which at the same time obsesses him, intrudes upon the present so that he cannot move forward. When he discovers Ruth, attempting to comprehend her presence, for example, an uncontrollable memory of his wife emerges: "he thought the past was dead. How long did it take for the past to die?" (149). He manages to describe for Ruth one of his many traumatic experiences, Virginia's return from the grave and his act of slaying her, putting a stake through her heart. Shaking uncontrollably, he explains memory's tenacious hold:

> "Almost three years ago I did that. And I still remember it, it's still with me. What can you do? What can you *do*?" He drove a fist down on the bar top as the anguish of memory swept over him again. "No matter how you try, you can't forget or—or adjust or—*ever* get away from it!" [150].

In terms of the narrative's overt logic, his nostalgia for the past represents Neville's sense of loss over his wife's death and his current desire "to love and be loved" (79). Significantly, although these memories of Virginia refuse to leave him, he *can* remember. Trauma victims' relationship to memory is paradoxical, as the American Psychiatric Association's *Diagnostic and Statistical Manual* (fifth edition, 2013) reveals.[14] On the one hand, the diagnostic criteria include the inability to control memory: "Recurrent, involuntary, and intrusive distressing memories of the traumatic event(s)" (APA 271). On the other, the inability to remember at all figures on the same list: "Inability to remember an important aspect of the traumatic event(s)" (APA 271). Neville clearly suffers from this paradoxical relationship with memory; plagued by uncontrollable recollections of Virginia, he nonetheless cannot remember the event that holds the key to his current situation. Once again, like the trauma victim suffering from PTSD he nonetheless re-enacts the battle situation again and again through his violent vampire-hunting activities.[15] The act that begins in part to free him from the past is his final recovery of the key memory that solves the problem of the entire vampire plague and his own immunity, a memory explicitly connected to his military service in Panama.

The trauma victim, then, suffers from a disrupted relationship with memory and time, as the traumatic memory comes to repeat itself, or its very blockage results in other symptoms:

> Traumatic experience can produce a sometimes indelible effect on the human psyche that can change the nature of an individual's memory, self-recognition, and relational life. Despite the human capacity to survive and adapt, traumatic experiences can alter people's psychological, biological, and social equilibrium to such a degree that the memory of one particular event comes to taint all other experiences, spoiling appreciation of the present. This tyranny of the past interferes with the ability to pay attention to both new and familiar situations. When people come to concentrate selectively on reminders of their past, life tends to become colorless, and contemporary experience ceases to be a teacher [Vickroy 11–12].

The novel's narrative structure involves frequent flashbacks to provide the backstory for the vampire plague and Neville's survival; memories intrude, unwanted:

> He was getting disgusted at this increasing nostalgic preoccupation with the past. It was a weakness, he knew, a weakness he could scarcely afford if he intended to go on. And yet he kept discovering himself drifting into extensive meditation on aspects of the past. It was almost more than he could control [...] [79].

But above all, Neville cannot get a grip on time itself: "Time was caught on hooks and could not progress" (69). Indeed, his constant knowledge of time is crucial as he must always return to his bunkered home before sunset; a near fatal incident occurs precisely because he forgot to wind his watch and therefore returns home late (40–42). As critics have observed, time is an overarching theme in Matheson's oeuvre (see, for example, Bacon; Comer; Tunc). To cite only two examples, in *Bid Time Return*, the protagonist wills himself back in time to find the woman of his dreams; in the *Twilight Zone* episode, "The Last Flight," a World War I pilot is projected forty two years into the future.

Seeking to understand the phenomenon of the vampire plague cognitively, through science, does represent a first step for Neville to move forward, but part of this cognitive process, however, involves remembering, to seize some piece of lost knowledge that he believes may solve the current problem. Neville is thus locked in a struggle to recover a repressed memory of some type:

> Now he sat in the living room, listening to Mozart's Jupiter Symphony and wondering how he was to begin, *where* he was to begin his investigation.
> He knew a few details, but these were only landmarks above the basic earth of cause. The answer lay in something else. Probably in some fact he was aware of but did not adequately appreciate, in some apparent knowledge he had not yet connected with the over-all picture[....]
> Maybe if he went back. Maybe the answer lay in the past, in some obscure crevice of memory. Go back then, he told his mind, go back.
> It tore his heart out to go back [51].

Matheson offers, then, a flashback, Neville's memory of his wife's transformation through the illness; her increasing pallor and her appearance, in her own words, "like a ghost" (53). Fictional engagements of trauma frequently involve ghosts, these revenants from the past, signs of the return of the repressed, as Vickroy interprets the ghost in Toni Morrison's *Beloved* (1987), for example, as a sign of the violent past of slavery in the U.S. (x).

The Last Man in Matheson's novel is first haunted by his wife, who, even before death resembles a revenant, but then who literally returns from the dead. Having lost his daughter to the pandemic and having seen the mass graves into which its victims are unceremoniously dumped like so much trash and burned to prevent their rising, he cannot bear to see his wife's body undergo the same abject treatment. Neville secretly buries her, and she, of course, returns. Similarly, Ben Cortman represents another literal revenant, Neville's former neighbor and co-worker, another figure from his past who returns nightly to haunt him. Neither of these reminders, however, helps him recover from his traumatized state.

It is another memory that returns which represents the key to unlocking the riddle of the past, the passage cited above in which Neville finally remembers the very origin of his predicament, the bat bite during his tour of duty in Panama (144). Uncovering the secret of the original trauma, one that explicitly connects his past as a soldier to his present, monstrous existence provides a new level of understanding that allows Neville to act in a way that might bring about a change in the current stalemate. Unfortunately, science still only brings Neville to a partial understanding of the Others in his environment. The text ultimately questions his vampire slaying activities by revealing the indiscriminate slaughter of Others to be misguided, since many of Neville's victims had actually been the sentient version of the plague's victims, members of the "new society," a problem that brings us to the related issues of race, class, and gender as they are engaged in Matheson's novel.

Before turning to the question of race in *IAL*, however, I would like to pose one more question about the novel's genesis and its links to Matheson's biography, looking more precisely at the context leading up to the novel's publication in 1954. What was it in the early 1950s that inspired Matheson unconsciously to write such a vivid portrait of a man suffering from trauma traceable back to a combat-related experience? Certainly the novel's paranoid, claustrophobic climate, as nearly every scholar writing on the novel has observed, reflects the general climate of the Cold War. Cold War strategy and the "domino effect" theory led, however, to a hot war in the early 1950s. Since for Americans, Korea truly seems to be, in historian Bruce Cumings' words, "Forgotten, never-known, abandoned" (xv), it took a French critic to remember its significance. Thus, without elaborating, Vincent Chenille asserts that "Richard Matheson conceived *I Am Legend* during the Korean War" (99), in his brief, but enlightening overview of the various versions of *IAL* in print and film.[16]

The Korean War thus appears as a trigger—an environmental element that might inspire the unconscious work of memory and recovery—allowing these repressed events to appear in the subtext of Matheson's writing. In their descriptions, which seek to recover this lost tragedy, recent histories of the Korean War allow the construction of parallels with the themes of Matheson's fiction, *I Am Legend*, in particular. For example, in his 2010 history Cumings stresses elements that I emphasize in this analysis of Matheson's novel:

> [T]his book is about a forgotten or never-known war and therefore, ipso facto, is also about *history and memory*. Its major themes are the Korean origins of the war, *the cultural contradictions of the early 1950s in America*, which buried this conflict almost before it could be known, the harrowing brutality [...] of a supposedly limited war, the recovery of this history in South Korea, and the way in which this unknown war transformed the American position in the world—and history and memory [xvii; emphasis added].

Cumings further argues that "the Korean War, more than any other war in modern times, is surrounded by residues and slippages of memory" (62). The reason for this, he argues, is that during the first few months of the conflict that began in June 1950, coverage of our South Korean allies' atrocities appeared widely "in popular magazines of the time such as *Life, The Saturday Evening Post,* and *Collier's*" (Cumings xviii). This widespread early coverage was then abruptly shut off like a water tap in January 1951, when news correspondents were placed under military command and General Douglas MacArthur's policy of censorship was strictly enforced (Cumings 84). The extent of the early coverage and the graphic nature of the images must certainly have entered the American unconscious, providing yet another element to fuel the flow of anxieties in the 1950s. But its abrupt halt denied the population the ability to process it; like the repressed traumatic memory, it festered below the surface, returning indirectly, in unexpected situations.

Historians have only recently begun *Rethinking the Korean War* (2002) as William Stueck titled his account, spurred in part, perhaps because of the formation of the 2005 formation of the Truth and Reconciliation Commission of the Republic of Korea (TRCK). New studies shed light on the atrocities committed, such as *The Massacres at Mt. Halla: Sixty Years of Truth Seeking in South Korea* (2014) revealed by Hun Joon Kim, and underscore its nature precisely as a Cold War conflict, as Richard C. Thornton's *Odd Man Out: Truman, Stalin, Mao, and the Origins of the Korean War* (2000) argues. Not only did President Truman ultimately threaten using the bomb (Cumings 34), because it occurred during the McCarthy period of anti–Communist witch hunts, accurate news coverage became that much easier to suppress.

Cumings underscores the extent of racism as a factor in the Korean War, a conflict which took on the colors of a sort of Yellow Peril narrative,[17] identifying the "gooks" a decade and a half before U.S. Marines stepped onto the soil of Vietnam. This racism perhaps mitigated the consciences of some soldiers as the effectiveness of napalm was test-run in Korea, but reports reveal the impact that launching chemical attacks on civilians left its own scars. Not only our own atrocities, but those of our allies, certainly place a cloud of moral questionability over the action, as Kim declares that "[m]ass arrests and civilian killings during the early phase of the Korean War [...] were a nationwide practice. Within a three-month period, at least 300,000 people were detained and subsequently disappeared nationwide" (19). As Cumings argues:

> For Americans Korea is just one among several wars best forgotten, since we are batting only one for four in big wars since 1945, just another transient episode among a myriad of interventions in Third World countries that do not bear close examination if one cares about amour propre, but have unsettling ways of coming back to haunt us [63].

This haunting is visible not only in *I Am Legend*, but in the Cold War SF-horror genre. Having seen a glimpse of what was happening in Korea in 1950, Americans happily accepted MacArthur's order to suppress the unpleasant details of atrocities. The problem with the repressed is that it tends to return in unexpected and uncontrollable ways.

Shrinking Men: The Impaired Masculinity of the Returning Vet

In *Masked Men: Masculinity and the Movies in the Fifties* (1997), Steven Cohan links Hollywood's portrayal of male protagonists in the post–World

War II era as reflective of a "crisis in national confidence" and "the culture's self-examination, directed at the imperiled state of American manhood" (x). Cohan links this crisis, which particularly affected working-class men, to post-war economic prosperity and what became essentially a re-positioning of men as domestic consumers, a role previously held by women:

> The initial postwar economic boom gave apparent evidence of America's transformation into a seamless middle-class society, with the ability of *working men* to buy a refrigerator, car, even a house apparently signaling their rise in social status. *But the dominance of an emerging upper middle class, identified through a man's corporate or professional employment,* was confirmed by the culture's equation of normative masculinity with white-collar labor. This corporate setting ended up relocating masculinity in what had previously been considered a "feminine" sphere, primarily by valuing a man's domesticity (and consumption) over his work (and production) as the means through which he fulfilled societal expectations of what it took to be "manly" [xii; emphasis added].

This shift, which sought to attach masculinity to bread-winning and consumerism thus valorizing the new white collar middle class, left working-class men struggling to conform to the new model of post-war life in the suburban tract-home developments which burgeoned after the war. *IAL* offers a clear reflection of these specific anxieties in its depiction of Robert Neville as a working-class man under siege.

Neville's Compromised Manhood

The novel emphasizes not simply Neville's status as the final human, but underscores his gendered identity as "the last *man* in the world" (78; 83; emphasis added); "he was a *man* and he was alone" (15; emphasis added). His loneliness becomes not only a mental and emotional void, but also a physical longing. In this postapocalyptic setting, however, any chance of a "normal" sexuality has expired with the last human woman.[18] Now, the undead females have come to obsess him, and his violent slaying activities become sexualized in the narrative[19]:

> It was the women who made it so difficult, he thought, the women posing like lewd puppets in the night on the possibility that he'd see them and decide to come out.
> A shudder ran through him. Every night it was the same. He'd be reading and listening to music. Then he'd start to think about sound-proofing the house, then he'd think about the women [...].
> All the knowledge in those books couldn't put out the fires in him; all the words of centuries couldn't end the wordless, mindless craving of his flesh.
> The realization made him sick. It was an insult to *a man*. All right, it was a natural drive, but there was no outlet for it any more [19; emphasis added].

Again, the text underscores that this is not just a general insult, but one specifically targeting his manhood. A number of other Matheson protagonists struggle with this notion of self-discipline, of the mind's role in controlling the body, most explicitly the wayward husband in *Earthbound* (1982) realizes that an enduring marriage occurs at a higher level than the mere physical. Similarly, the afterlife imagined in *What Dreams May Come* is not just about the mind's control over the body's shape, image and desires, but also about ridding the human person of the body's constraints. In this and other passages, Neville feels betrayed by his body and its ostensibly uncontrollable sexual desire; this lack of self-control represents a certain form of un-manning.

Sexuality in the Apocalypse

On a different occasion, a series of *double entendres* allows Neville to act symbolically on his desires as he thinks about "the lustful, bloodthirsty, naked women flaunting their bodies at him [....] He actually found himself *jerking off* the crossbar from the door. Coming girls, *I'm coming. Wet your lips now*" (33; emphasis added). Later, Neville admits that he had contemplated "the most terrible of solutions to his need," ostensibly considering necrophilia with an undead woman (136), but while zombie erotica has become a minor sub-genre today (see, for example, Gates and Holt), such perversion was clearly out of the question in the conservative 1950s. Thus forced into celibacy by his condition as "the only one left in the world" (101), Neville sublimates his sexual drives into the intellectual activity of his research. So successfully does he repress his physical desire that when Ruth arrives, "he felt no physical desire for her [....] His sex drive had diminished, had virtually disappeared" (136). Indeed, he fears the very possibility of sexual contact, emotional involvement, or especially, reproduction (139); "he had become an ill-tempered and inveterate bachelor again" (139).

In the postapocalyptic situation, normative gender roles for the heterosexual couple have completely disappeared. Although Neville does not consciously make this mental connection, the narrator downplays Ruth's secondary sexual characteristics as the protagonist notices that "[h]er figure was very slim, almost curveless. Not at all like the women he'd used to envision" (130). Later, he repeats the observation, mentally noting "the slight eminence of her breasts [...] [s]he had a body like a young girl" (136). Just as Ruth does not display the characteristics of his image of womanhood, from her perspective Neville already appears like a monster, since he has stopped caring about either his appearance or the niceties of social life. When he first spots her, he chases her, lunging at her; "[h]e didn't realize how frightening he looked; six foot three in his boots, a gigantic bearded man with an intent look" (123). Not only does he look like a monster, "[h]e didn't realize that his voice was devoid of warmth, that it was the harsh, sterile voice of a man who had lost all touch with humanity" (125).

Domesticating Neville

While Neville's secondary sexual characteristics as a male are indicated (his height, his beard, his hairy chest), the novel begins slowly to feminize him. At first he is depicted maintaining his suburban home, performing the masculine chores of nailing loose boards and the pseudo-carpenter's task of making wooden stakes, phallic symbols *par excellence*, on a lathe. Once again, the postapocalyptic situation, however, has disrupted the proper division of labor in a patriarchal society. Although he initially refuses to perform the woman's work of laundry, cleaning up, doing the dishes (14–15; 21), with no public sphere to circulate within, Neville is forced to remain in the private. His situation reflects what Cohan refers to as the new domestication of the male image in post-war era. From his earlier sloppiness, he appears to have begun taking care of his home (although not his person), if we can accept Ruth's compliments at face value; perhaps her comments are simply flattery to obtain his confidence, but she remarks, "You've certainly done a wonderful job" (135) and "[i]t must have taken a lot of work to get your house like this," admiring a mural of the woods that he has painted on his living room wall (136). Thus, although Neville has converted his suburban tract home into a tomb-like bunker for safety, he has also made it "homey."

Furthermore, after a symbolic castration occurs he becomes excessively emotional, reflecting at times the hysteria associated with the feminine in a Freud-obsessed 1950s America. Frustrated by his inability to leave his bunkered bungalow at night, he turns to alcohol as a release. Angered by the thought of "them," he squeezes his drinking glass, which shatters and cuts his hand; not only does the blood spilled represent an enticement for the vampires outside, "the sliced-open flesh" (30) of the wound invokes the imaginary castration that Freudian psychology attributes to all women in the infantile imagination. Thus feminized physically, Neville also loses control emotionally, expressing alternately "[c]old fear" (41; see also 22), "terror" (42), "pain" (33; 43), "sorrow" (36); breaking down in grief over the loss of his wife and daughter, "he sobbed like a lost, frightened child" (47). He becomes hysterical, filling the room "with his gasping, nerve-shattered laughter" (67), then later breaks down into tears again. Although he often feels "rage" (21; 37) and "fury" (91), grief appears to be his predominant emotion[20]; perhaps because of the apocalyptic situation he is allowed to express feelings that "real men" in the 1950s should not. In a flashback to his daughter's death, he "felt the tears running slowly down his cheeks as he carried her" (73). He reaches a point where he fears for his sanity, so scary has the emotional rollercoaster become: "You're not going to go flying off in twenty different directions. You can't take that any more; you're an emotional misfit" (83).

Just as he seeks control over the vampires via his research and experimentation, drawing upon his rational mind becomes a means through which he attempts to control his emotions and the "craving for violence" (92). In a brief interlude, Neville rediscovers his humanity, expressing an almost maternal instinct when he discovers that he is not completely alone in the world: a dog has managed to survive the epidemic and the vampire's onslaughts. The thought of companionship raises Neville's hopes; he nurtures the animal, patiently luring it into his home by leaving food and milk outside. He even goes "shopping," taking pet supplies from the local grocery store: "Lord, you'd think I was having a baby or something, he thought" (98). He thus explicitly characterizes his behavior as motherly, feminine. This episode, which fills nearly twenty pages of the short novel, extends hope, only to dash it: "In a week the dog was dead" (110). After this, Neville so thoroughly succeeds at repressing all of his emotions that he becomes numb, thus losing the very humanity he fought so hard to maintain:

> In a world of monotonous horror there could be no salvation in wild dreaming. Horror he had adjusted to. But monotony was the greater obstacle [...]. From that day on he learned to accept the dungeon he existed in, neither seeking to escape with sudden derring-do nor beating his pate bloody on its walls [111].

This reading departs from earlier critics who have observed the domestic bent in Matheson's fiction in order to draw other conclusions. For example, Ted Krulik, reading Neville as a latter-day Robinson Crusoe (a comparison drawn from Neville's own reflections; 83), argues that despite his daily routine of making coffee and sharpening stakes, Neville enjoys a "freedom from the responsibilities we all face in tending to a job, a home, automobile, family [...]. All the fruits of modern technology lie before him" (2–3). Although this characteristic of the last man—his ability to pillage the entire world— occurs in the film versions of the narrative, pace Krulik, Neville's routine is hardly carefree and his home turns out to be a prison, "Great! he thought. Another day stuck in this boarded up rat-hole!" (34). Trapped—indeed, Keith Neilson identifies "the man in a trap" as a recurring trope in Matheson's oeuvre (1074)—he experiences "the feeling as if he were expanding and the house were contracting" (35), "as if he had mislaid the exit from this house of horror" (70). Significantly, in Matheson's script for *Duel*, David Mann (Dennis Weaver)—his family name says it all about his status as another Mathesonian Everyman—is as much a prisoner of his family life, appearing as a hen-pecked husband when he calls home to his wife and kids, as he is of the tanker truck that persists in running him down, an external projection of the inner angst of the white American male.[21]

Krulik connects Neville to a frontier mythology of masculine self-reliance, somewhat blithely asserting that

Matheson reveals a belief that living in an unknown frontier can be beneficial to man. Natural self-reliance in facing a wilderness is missing from our machine-age existence [....] Carey [of *The Shrinking Man*] and Neville are representative of the frontier spirit, seeking survival in the face of cruel hardships [....] The lengthy, mundane descriptions of Neville's daily life [...] vividly illustrate what we would have to go through if we had to rebuild civilization around our needs [....] In a violent world, Neville has the strength to meet violence with violence. With his stoic, self-reliant way of life and his dynamic physical struggle against the vampires, he is a hero we can admire [3–4].

Stefan Dziemianowicz comes closer to the mark in his survey of Matheson's work, "Horror Begins at Home: Richard Matheson's Fear of the Familiar" (1994), correctly fingering his very domesticity as something that threatens Neville. As works of horror and suspense fiction, Matheson's novels hinge upon "the idea of the individual trying to survive in a world which unexpectedly turns hostile to his existence" (Dziemianowicz 29). Not only does this describe Neville's protagonists, but it also fits the returning real-life GI. Significantly, a good number of *Twilight Zone* episodes, including scripts written by Matheson or adapted from his stories by Rod Serling, also feature men in uniform in distress, as seen in "And When the Sky Was Opened" and "The Last Flight." Indeed, Cheyenne Mathews explores this crisis of masculinity in relation to the aesthetics of film noir in several of Matheson's *Twilight Zone* episodes ("Private") and Pulliam and Fonseca's study views this as a leitmotif of his entire screen and fiction writing career.

As Dziemianowicz observes: "A fragile dynamic exists between the personalities of Matheson's characters and the security of their surroundings [which leads] to feelings of insecurity about themselves that threatens their very identities" (29). *I Am Legend* signals its protagonist's identity crisis from its very first paragraphs, as Neville "looked at the distorted reflection of himself in the cracked mirror" nailed to a door (13). Although its purpose is to repel the vampires, we soon learn that these preventive measures are not fully reliable in the same way that this mirror cannot be relied on to provide Neville with a true image of himself. Or perhaps the passage signals that, indeed, the cracked mirror reflects this flawed specimen of humanity.

As Matheson asserts of his fiction in general, "I'm strictly rooted in tract developments and suburban activities" (O'Connell and Sallis 206), just such a development is the setting of *I Am Legend*. The original Neville figures clearly the situation of the returning war veteran struggling to survive in the new reality of suburban consumerism; his difficulty in doing so relates precisely to his working-class origins, which have not fully equipped him for life in this new society of conformity and domesticity. To return to the biographical reading of the novel, although he eventually made a living in the white-collar profession of Hollywood writer, when he was writing his first novels,

Matheson worked on the production line in the aerospace industry (Bloom 171).[22] He makes his own working-class, immigrant background clear in interviews: "I came from a background where you didn't consider being a creative writer as a logical means of making a living" (McGilligan 234).

This point is significant because one of the seemingly minor alterations that the film adaptations operate on their characterizations of Neville is his transformation from an uneducated working-class man who probably served as a regular GI into a middle-class, trained scientist and a military officer. Furthermore, recent misreadings of Matheson's Neville as a "bourgeois" subject directs attention away from his working-class origins. In an otherwise perceptive Marxian analysis of *IAL*, Cheyenne Mathews argues that

> *I Am Legend* again depicts the vampire as a reconfigured social entity, this time in the wake of such a capitalist war, and presents another stage of Marxist historical class struggle as a *bourgeois* character, Robert Neville, combats a rising class of vampire proletariat [92; emphasis added].

This argument rests, however, upon a factual error, for Neville is clearly depicted as working class throughout the novel; Pulliam and Fonseca also refer to Neville as "white middle-class man" (71). It must be noted that before the apocalypse, he and Cortman worked "at the plant" together and his tattooed, hairy chest also reflects his wartime experiences as a common soldier, rather than an officer. Furthermore, Neville's immigrant origins tend to situate him in the working, rather than the middle classes. Whereas other critics, like Cristina Castellana, understand that Neville's "role has shifted from factory worker to vampire slayer" (29), Mathews elides what is more than just a detail. First, as a member of the proletariat himself, Neville cannot fully be implicated in the Western establishment elite that is implicitly condemned as having led humanity to the brink of destruction. He is as much a victim, perhaps, as the vampires he slays. In addition, understanding Neville as a working class man is essential to a full understanding of the relationship between his crisis in masculinity and why he is the last *man*, and not just the last *person*. But above all, he is also the last *white man*, although the meaning of his whiteness in Matheson's novel, is not quite what previous critics—wishing to see in *IAL* and allegory of the contemporary crisis in U.S. race relations—have argued it to be.

Black Bastards: Neville as the Last White Man

In her analysis of "films that work in an oppositional manner toward whiteness," Gwendolyn Audrey Foster includes *The Incredible Shrinking Man*, the film adaptation of Matheson's 1956 novel ("Monstrosity" 67). Looking more deeply into Matheson's oeuvre supports the argument that *IAL*, published only two years before *The Shrinking Man*, also reveals "the cracks and fissures," to use Foster's expression, "of performative whiteness" (*Performing* 2). Foster, following Richard Dyer in *White* (1997), argues that

> whiteness is a master narrative that is increasingly being questioned and marked. Postmodernists reconfigure identity as a performance that is itself fractured, unstable, and mutable. White performances are simulacra, falsely stabilized by master narratives that themselves are suspect, and whiteness itself is a construct that needs constant upkeep. It is in the cracks and fissures of performative whiteness that we can begin the dismantling of whiteness as a norm [*Performing* 2].

Neville's whiteness is both constructed and deconstructed in Matheson's text,[23] thus undermining the entire righteousness of the white man's burden, particularly within the context of World War II when Hitler used Nazism to pervert the civilizing mission into genocide. Although World War II served as a catalyst for the Civil Rights movement at home, rather than African Americans, the novel's real other "race" is the Jew.

Constructing Neville as "White"

There is no doubt that Robert Neville is constructed as white from the beginning of the novel: "He was a tall man, thirty-six, born of English-German stock, his features undistinguished except for the long, determined mouth and the bright blue of his eyes" (14). Thus, he is linked not only to a WASP (white Anglo-Saxon protestant) identity, but also to Hitler's master race through his father's ethnic origins (27). As he gets a grip on his emotions through rational thought and scientific experimentation: "He found, to his surprise, that he actually gleaned pleasure from practicing orderliness. I guess I got old Fritz's blood in me, after all" (85). Returning to the biographical reading of Matheson's fiction, the mention of "Fritz" displaces the author's Norwegian heritage onto the related German ethnicity for his protagonist Neville. This assimilation of the American Neville to the German harks back to *The Beardless Warriors*' blurring of the lines between ally and enemy, thus undermining binary discourses of Self and Other, us and them. It also establishes a connection between Neville's experimentation and Nazi laboratories, further reinforcing his monstrosity and its origin in Western techno-science.

Neville himself directly engages—albeit with biting sarcasm—discourses of race prejudice and minority status early in the novel, facetiously rambling while on a drinking binge that "vampires are prejudiced against. The keynote of minority prejudice is this: They are loathed because they are feared" (31). He then mentally invokes the vampire's power and status in the "Dark and Middle Ages" (31), but then introduces a relativistic interrogation of the hatred the vampire instilled in past times, asking "are his needs any more shocking than the needs of other animals and men?" (32). Neville then cites various flawed humans, from arms manufacturers to distillers of grain alcohol to the parents of neurotic children, nonetheless concluding with another rhetorical question: "would you let your sister marry one?" (32). The white male protagonist's ambivalence about racial difference appears in these passages, which both recognize the wrongness of racial prejudice but at the same time question his willingness to embrace the racial Other. Such contradictions appear more clearly when they are examined in tandem with passages that work to other the vampires, who appear at times to be constructed as "black."

Black and White or Fifty Shades of Gray?

Kathy Davis Patterson picks up on Matheson's characterization of the vampires as "black bastards" (35) and the new society's representatives as "dark men" (160). Invoking the May 17, 1954, decision in *Brown v. Board of Education* case, in which the Supreme Court ruled against school segregation, Patterson argues that *IAL* is a parable about white anxiety over integration (19). She, of course, invokes many of the passages I recruit here, to make her case that "the tableau of a white man being dragged from his house by 'dark men' into a world that is 'no longer his' is a stark concretization of white racial anxieties in 1950s America and serves as a powerful metaphor for the inevitable failure of segregation" (25). In their more recent, conventional discussion of race and masculinity in *IAL*, Pulliam and Fonseca concur with Patterson, citing her work to assert that

> *I Am Legend* spends much time considering the import of a changing view of masculinity in an evolving world. It presents a society where homogeneous Caucasian (read "white") manhood is no longer defined by the male ability to wield physical and political power over women, children, and nonwhites [67].

While this claim is not inaccurate, the present analysis resists the implication that Neville is as fully sexist and racist as suggested by earlier studies, insisting that he expresses an often contradictory range of emotion and opinion typical in individuals in relation to such controversial subjects.

Patterson's (and later Pulliam's and Fonseca's) otherwise perceptive reading thus describes Matheson's ambivalent text in terms that, to put it frankly, are simply too black and white. Certainly Neville is constructed as white, but the story ultimately questions his position of dominance as such. As Patterson so perspicuously concludes, with the narrative's stunning reversal "readers are left with a story in which the white Western male has become a monster, the 'legend' to be feared" (25). Patterson completely elides for the sake of her argument passages that repeatedly qualify the vampires as white ("white-faced men," 22; "Their screaming white faces," 42; "their grayish-white faces," 43). Furthermore, although he frequently dehumanizes the vampires, referring to them with the impersonal "they" as discussed above, Neville at times rehumanizes his victims, again calling into question his own moral imperatives. In a striking scene, during which he is slaying a female vampire, "he felt a twinge when he realized that, but for some affliction he did not understand, these people were the same as he" (39). As his survival instinct ostensibly kicks in, and he eventually slaughters her, he must mentally justify his actions: "she's one of them and she'd kill me gladly if she got the chance" (39). However, as he watches her die, "she stopped moving, stopped muttering, and her hands uncurled slowly like white blossoms on the cement" (39). Once again, the vampire's whiteness appears in this poetic moment.[24]

Matheson's narrative thus blurs the racial lines too thoroughly to be read as a neat allegory of white anxiety about the changing place of blacks in an American society originally constructed by whites for whites upon the backs of black labor. Instead, this story's blackness itself is more metaphorical than literal, taking on a theological connotation: the blackness of sin and evil. Religion and the Judeo-Christian underpinnings of a Western civilization that has revealed its underlying barbarity in World War II and its aftermath is a recurring theme in Matheson's novel and its filmic followers. As Cohan observes, a "religion boom" occurred in post-war America (126); Matheson draws on this trend, a move certainly fitting in an apocalyptic novel,[25] featuring an evangelist in a flashback sequence. The prophet's words inevitably can be read as playing on racist fears during this end-time, as he preaches over a loudspeaker: "Do you want to be changed into a black unholy animal?" (113)—but they can equally be read as the metaphorical blackness of sin. The preacher rants: "God has set loose the second deluge upon us [...]! He has opened the grave, He has unsealed the crypt, He has turned the dead from their black tombs—*and set them upon us!*" (113). Such passages undeniably label the vampires as black, but just as many passages associate them with whiteness.

Kathy Patterson's linkage of school segregation to *IAL* certainly anticipates concerns about race that Matheson's novel will be recruited to express in its adaptation to film, particularly in *The Omega Man*. It is productive, then, to clarify how World War II contributed to the types of racial tensions that she invokes and to examine the *real* race issue that subtends *IAL*: that of anti–Semitism and the Holocaust. In their Oxford University Press histories of post-war America, both William H. Chafe (*The Unfinished Journey: America Since World War II*, 1995) and James T. Patterson (*Grand Expectations: The United States, 1945-1974*, 1996) emphasize the significance of gender, class, and race as "fundamental reference points for understanding how power and resources are divided in our society" (Chafe vii). Both insist that World War II represents a major turning point in American society, in particular regarding gender roles, class associations, and race relations. With African Americans "enlisting at rates far higher than their proportion of the population" (Chafe 4) and justifiably questioning the fact that they were willing to risk their lives for democracy in Europe when Jim Crow still limited their own freedom at home, World War II served as a catalyst for the Civil Rights movement. As early as 1941, A. Philip Randolph led the first March on Washington Movement (Chafe 18), but the 1950s and 1960s represented the height of the movement with the Montgomery Bus Boycott in 1955 and 1956, the Greensboro sit-ins beginning in 1960, and the March on Washington of August 1963. These activities culminated, of course, in the passage of the Civil Rights Act in 1964.

Simply moving out of the Jim Crow south changed the lives of many African Americans, as the war economy undeniably allowed for a mass migration: "As late as 1940, 75 percent of all blacks lived in the rural South. During the next decade, more than a million moved to northern and western industrial areas" (Chafe 18–19). Much has been made about white fears of integration, including Kathy Patterson's reading of *IAL* as just such an expression; the chronology, however, simply doesn't bear out this reading. As historian James T. Patterson clarifies the situation:

> While blacks crowded into ghettos, whites found ample space in the mushrooming suburbs. In Chicago, 77 percent of home-building between 1954 and 1960 took place in suburban areas. *As of 1960 only 2.9 percent of people in these suburbs were black, roughly the same percentage as had lived in Chicago suburbs in 1940.* "White flight," indeed, was rendering restrictive covenants unnecessary even before the Supreme Court decision in 1948. Many white urban residents, anxious to escape the influx of blacks, sold their houses to blacks and—racial covenant or no—took off for the suburbs. This process led to the creation of a few "salt-and-pepper" areas of racial mixing, but *neighborhood desegregation rarely lasted for long* [Grand 28; emphasis added].

Whereas these concerns will prove to be valid for the 1971 film adaptation, *The Omega Man*, they are a less compelling argument for Matheson's 1954 novel, published too early in this period. Although the class action lawsuit, which eventually resulted in the May 1954 *Brown v. Board of Education* decision, had been filed in 1951, neighborhood desegregation was still in its infancy at the time Matheson's novel was published.

Anti-Semitism and *I Am Legend*

As if the weight of killing European and Japanese soldiers in combat, dropping atomic weapons on Hiroshima and Nagasaki, then engaging in a new war in Korea were not a heavy enough burden for Americans' guilty consciences, a lingering sense that the liberation of the Nazi death camps in summer 1944 was too little, too late must have also weighed upon some minds. Although we were fighting Nazi Germany, according to William H. Chafe,

> anti–Semitism also remained a corrosive presence in America. The FEPC found a significant pattern of employment discrimination against Jews in New York; *Fortune*

magazine insisted on talking about Jewish "clannishness"; and numerous right-wing politicians defended violence against Jews in America and insisted that the war itself was a Jewish plot [24].

As early as 1942, American knowledge of the concentration camps was widespread, but while "Congress denounced the Nazi policy of genocide, American Jewish organizations held rallies demanding action, and individual leaders pleaded with people like Eleanor Roosevelt to intervene" (Chafe 25), nothing was actually done. The U.S. maintained a strict entrance visa policy preventing large numbers of Jewish refugees from entering the country; Roosevelt's war refugee board was not created until January 1944, only a few months before the liberation (Chafe 25).

The racial conflict that *IAL* engages directly, then, is the problem of anti–Semitism. For the Anglo-Germanic Neville in this post–World War II context, like the vampires he slays, the minority that is constructed as both different and yet not always visibly so is, of course, the Jew. As Christian Wenk observes, "the only other round characters in *I Am Legend* both carry Jewish names" (205). He refers here to Ruth, creating a somewhat tenuous link between the messenger from the new society and the biblical Ruth,[26] and to Ben Cortman, a fascinating character who deserves greater attention than he has generally been given in the secondary literature. As Wenk also notes, his first name, Benjamin, refers to the youngest of Jacob's sons, all founders of the twelve Hebrew clans (214). Many Jewish family names end in "-man," like Adelman, Bauman, and more stereotypically, Goldman; more than such compelling clues, however, Matheson gives us an explicit sign of Cortman's identity. Through his experimentation, Neville realizes that while Cortman fails to react to a crucifix like a "normal" vampire, instead when he holds up a Torah, this particular vampire shrinks tellingly (140). Neville later explains to Ruth that individual vampire's reactions to the cross vary depending upon what religious tradition they were raised in; he attributes the repellent power of these religious symbols to a deep-seated, unconscious psychological reaction to a meaningful object from the vampire's former life. The fact that Virginia retained enough of her former intelligence to return home, coupled with Ben's ability to remember Neville's name, suggest that *all* of the vampires, at one level or another, may be more than mindless bloodthirsty organisms, thus again calling into question the slayer's indiscriminate killing. In turn, the novel implicitly condemns race-based violence through its treatment of the relationship between Neville and Cortman.

Cortman represents, in essence, the only surviving and still recognizable aspect of Neville's pre-holocaust life. From the beginning of the novel, he appears as a particular nemesis, the only individualized member of the zombie-like vampires, leading the nightly assault on Neville's home. But Matheson develops their former, ostensibly friendly relationship through narrative flashbacks of Neville's fragmented memories, revealing that the two men used to car pool "to the plant," talking "about cars and baseball and politics" (65). As their families are both stricken by "the disease," they discuss more serious matters, as well (65). Indeed, Neville borrows Cortman's car when he illicitly buries his wife, Virginia. Their current antagonism—and one of the few, vividly described incidences of hand-to-hand combat occurs as Neville and vampire-Cortman fight (43–45)—has roots in a happier past. After the epidemic, having a nemesis almost helps Neville remain sane: "[i]t had become a relaxing hobby, hunting for Cortman; one of the few diversions left to him" (119). Neville attributes Cortman with an intelligence absent in the others: "[h]e felt, further, that Cortman relished the peril of it. If the phrase were not such an obvious anachronism, Neville would have said that Ben Cortman had a zest for life" (119).

Cortman's ability to speak and to remember something of his past life clearly sets him apart from the rest of the undistinguished horde, a phenomenon that generally differentiates *IAL* from earlier vampire narratives, which focus on a "master vampire" figure, as Mary Pharr observes (94). Here, Cortman remains the closest thing to a leader, the first to arrive at sunset with his persistent taunts of "Come out, Neville!" (18; 20).[27] When he is attacked by the members of Ruth's "new society," Neville realizes that "he didn't want them to destroy Cortman like that [...] that he felt more deeply toward the vampires than he did toward their executioners" (158). Thus, given Cortman's significance, then, Wenk's argument that "the threatening Other in *IAL* rather expresses anti–Semitic tendencies than issues concerning African Americans" (214) appears valid. To clarify, Matheson's novel allegorically condemns the Holocaust and ultimately expresses sympathy for the persecuted Jews.

Before concluding this chapter, a final word on the question of race in *IAL*, also present in *The Shrinking Man*, is in order. In addition to their indirect depiction of the vicissitudes of combat on the individual soldier and the collective burden of allowing the Holocaust to occur, through their exploration of the apocalyptic destruction of human life linked to "bombings" and "winds from the east," these works also make an implied, yet clear reference to the dropping of the atomic bomb on Hiroshima and Nagasaki. Mick Broderick includes articles on American SF-monster films from the 1950s in his volume on *Hibakusha Cinema: Hiroshima, Nagasaki and the Nuclear Image in Japanese Film* (1996). Read through this lens, the vampires of *IAL* also resemble *hibakusha*, "pronounced *he-back-sha*, meaning 'atom-bomb affected person/ s'" (Broderick 17n1). Just as Neville experimented on the vampires and the Nazis experimented on concentration camp victims, as Broderick explains in his introduction, "the principal medical establishment in Hiroshima after the war [was] the Atomic Bomb Casualty Commission, with its policy of research without treatment" (3). Thus, "US scientists were collecting and collating evidence of just such effects at radiological institutes which refused to treat *hibakusha* but nevertheless studied them by the tens of thousands" (3). It is not, then, a huge leap to liken the vampire hordes to the ambulatory survivors of the nuclear holocaust; linking the *hibakusha* to the victims of the Shoah, the vampire hordes can be read together as the vengeful return of the repressed victims of the white, Anglo-Saxon, protestant male, embodied by Neville, until he embraces his own extinction as the most logical solution to his predicament.

Conclusion

Published as it was in 1954 and openly thematizing the reinsertion of an ex-GI into the rapidly growing suburban American culture, at a very basic level Matheson's novel expresses unresolved anxiety about sixteen million American men's personal experiences in World War II, in particular the moral dilemma of the soldier as professional killer, something Matheson knew firsthand as he served in Europe. Support for this chapter's thesis appears not only in veiled World War II references in *I Am Legend* and *The Shrinking Man*, but most clearly in Matheson's "mainstream" novel, *The Beardless Warriors*.

Not only was Richard Matheson a combat veteran, so are his most recognized protagonists, Robert Neville and Scott Carey. *IAL*'s characterization of Neville first establishes him as a specimen of rugged masculinity and appears to support his crusade-like struggle against the vampires, as he methodically exterminates them in order to reduce their threat upon his own life. It gradually, however, undermines both his masculine self-determination and the ethical position of his war-like acts of violence. Neville turns to science for answers, finding only partial ones. It is solely through his direct communication with the Other that he begins to understand the changing world he now lives in, contact which eventually brings about his tragic realization of the ethical tenuousness of his own position. As Cristina Castellana observes, Neville "remained passionate about [his] values and true to [his] cause, but instead of achieving hero-status, [he] ruptured and became [a] symbol of ignorance and defeat" (30).

Thus drawing on the literary and filmic tradition of Gothic horror, but also in response to specific individual and collective experience, namely the killing fields of World War II, memories of which may have been resurrected by coverage of the U.S.'s decision to put another generation of young men fighting in Korea, *IAL* problematizes the white male's role as arbiter of right. As we have seen, then, the racial dynamics of Matheson's *IAL* are much more about white guilt and expiation of crimes of commission and of omission during World War II and the Korean conflict than an expression of white anxiety about being overrun by blacks in the suburbs.

As we shall see, Matheson's original text will prove to be more "progressive" (Hantke 182) in its oppositional ideology than its film adaptations. Gwendolyn Audrey Foster links an entire spate of "bad-white body" ("Monstrosity" 39) films to the difficulties of integrating World War II and Korean War veterans into a changing American society. She argues that *The Incredible Shrinking Man*, the film adaptation of Matheson's 1956 novel, "questions the historical validity of the dominance of white maleness in the 1950s" (Foster, "Monstrosity" 50). We can say the same for Matheson's other mid–1950s novel, *I Am Legend*. Unlike his subsequent film avatars, the original Robert Neville fully embraces his status as "legend" and his civilization's replacement by a new society; Matheson's dark conclusion holds out no hope for its Last Man or the human civilization he represented:

> Robert Neville looked out over the new people of the earth. He knew he did not belong to them; he knew that, like the vampires, he was anathema and black terror to be destroyed. And, abruptly, the concept came, amusing to him even in his pain.
> A coughing chuckle filled his throat. He turned and leaned against the wall while he swallowed the pills. Full circle, he thought while the final lethargy crept into his limbs. Full circle. A new terror born in death, a new superstition entering the unassailable fortress of forever.
> I am legend [170].

None of his future iterations, interpreted on the big screen by Vincent Price, Charlton Heston, and Will Smith, can match the absolute finality of Neville's ultimate awareness. Like him, though, they will be reflections of their times: the ongoing Cold War, the Vietnam era, or post–9/11.

Two

Visualizing Apocalypse Through Compromised Masculinity
Vincent Price as *The Last Man on Earth*

"Another day. Another day to start all over again" (Robert Morgan, *The Last Man on Earth*).
"I can't live a heartbeat away from hell and forget it."
"You're freaks. All of you. All of you, freaks! Mutations."

The first film adaptation of *I Am Legend*, *The Last Man on Earth* has been all but forgotten, even characterized as "a reprehensible adaptation" (197) by Ryan Baker. Jonathan Malcolm Lampley notes "[t]he film's failure to generate much interest among either critics or audiences in 1964" (95). Not only have many fans and critics dismissed the film as a low-budget affair, miscast and unconvincingly shot in Italy, Matheson himself pans the film as an unfaithful adaptation of his work (Weaver 307). Yet, Lampley nonetheless argues that "in some ways it has become the most consistently influential project of Price's 60s output [...] anticipating the rise of a new cinematic sub-genre: the apocalyptic zombie horror movie" (95). Both Matheson's novel and its first adaptation's influence on the reinterpretation of a monster pulled from Haitian folklore in George A. Romero's now iconic *Night of the Living Dead* (1968) is well documented (Berger 56–57; Bradley 118; Christie 67; Glasgow 31; Lampley 97; Mitchell 96; Moreland 79–80). This minor work has thus made a major contribution to the horror film genre through its inspiration of today's most-exploited monster.

On closer examination, when judged on its own for what it is, *The Last Man on Earth* (henceforth *LMoE*) is a coherent, yet complex, popular culture text, a satisfying and unique contribution to the vampire/zombie canon. Filmed only a decade after the publication of its literary model, the Vincent Price vehicle shares many of the same social, political, and psychological con-

Two. Visualizing Apocalypse Through Compromised Masculinity   59

cerns of its literary model. The recent crisis in the Bay of Pigs (1961) may have made the Cold War feel a bit more urgent, but M. Keith Booker's notion of the "long 1950s," stretching from 1946 through 1964 (25), places it in the same decade as Matheson's novel. What, then, sets this film adaptation apart from its literary precursor? This chapter explores that question, focusing on the continued relevance of the film's Cold War context, but also on the visual and aural translation of a written narrative to the big screen. Most importantly, it looks at how the incarnation of a fictional character—alive only in the minds of author and readers—is transformed via the performance of a flesh and blood actor, himself a "real" person, but also a star persona surrounded by a mythology of his own. It also looks at how Matheson himself imagined bringing *I Am Legend* to the screen with a brief examination of his now published, but still unfilmed script, "The Night Creatures."

In *Rational Fears: American Horror in the 1950s* (1996), Mark Jancovich asserts that, in general, "Matheson's fiction seems to be preoccupied with the male anxieties of the 1950s" (130; see also Hagood; Pagnoni Berns; Pulliam and Fonseca). At the core of those anxieties lay concerns about the notion of masculinity: what it means to be a man itself. Jancovich draws on the work of Steven Cohan whose *Masked Men: Masculinity and the Movies in the Fifties* (1997) analyzes the competing images of masculinity battling for prominence on the big screen in the decade prior to the first film adaptation of Matheson's Last Man novel. As Anne Morey suggests in another context, "[m]ale stardom was a referendum on preferred modes of masculinity" (8). The suave, sophisticated model of bourgeois manhood embodied by Cary Grant and Gregory Peck that dominated the Fifties, however, was becoming increasingly identified with the phenomenon of the "Man in the Gray Flannel Suit"[1] whose alienation became fodder for the short stories of California writers like Matheson, his friends Charles Beaumont and Robert Bloch, as well as Anthony Boucher on the east coast. We can also see the anguish suffered by this type in *Twilight Zone* episodes, like Matheson's "Nick of Time" and "Nightmare at 20,000 Feet."

By the end of the 1950s, Cohan argues, the crisis in masculinity had become full blown. The result: the refined image of bourgeois, consumerist masculinity was gradually nudged off the screen by more rugged models for the ideal male, including Kirk Douglas, Robert Mitchum, and Charlton Heston. Given the context in 1964, what, then, does it mean to cast Vincent Price, an actor characterized as one of Hollywood's "professional sissies" (Tyler 330), as Robert Neville's analogue, Robert Morgan? The obvious, practical explanation is that American International Pictures and other low-budget producers frequently capitalized on Price's star presence to help market their brand of low-budget SF-horror film. But the reasons why this Last Man text reflects a contemporary crisis in evolving images of masculinity and a growing awareness of homosexuality's latent presence throughout American/Western society also bear reflection. When read through the lenses of star theory and queer theory, *The Last Man on Earth* can be read as an expression of contemporary anxiety about homosexuality spreading like a contagion. This reading of a queer subtext in *LMoE* is further supported by an examination of Matheson's *The Shrinking Man* (1956), making an explicit link between the returning GIs' anxieties about reinsertion into an increasingly mainstream and homogeneous American post-war society and the crisis in masculinity. The threatening queer found in that novel reflects a deepening of that crisis; at the same time, however, Vincent Price was cementing his reputation as Hollywood's greatest "scream queen" of them all.

Vincent Price as Scream Queen

Vincent Leonard Price, Jr. (1911–1993)[2] was born in St. Louis, Missouri, to a well-off merchant's family; he attended Yale University, studying art history and the fine arts. He developed his acting skills on the London stage during the 1930s. Through the late 1930s and into the 1940s, he played a number of secondary and leading roles in noir and historical films, like *Laura* (1944) and *Dragonwyck* (1947), but Price never quite found his niche. Kevin Heffernan argues that the tides turned in Price's career as a second-tier leading man with *House of Wax* (1953), after which he became a first-tier horror star (97). During the 1950s he took the lead in horror classics like *The Fly* (1958), *The House on Haunted Hill* (1959), and the richly gimmicky *The Tingler* (1959). Roger Corman turned to Price through the 1960s, using his established reputation in the genre to market the artsy Poe adaptation cycle, a collaboration that also made Richard Matheson a name familiar to Price and to horror audiences. Within the context of the long and productive career of Vincent Price, however, *LMoE* represents a very minor episode. In her biography of her father, Victoria Price mentions it only once:

> In January 1963, AIP sent Vincent to Rome to shoot *The Last Man on Earth*, a science-fiction thriller in which he played, with commendable restraint, the only man on earth, immune to a plague which was transforming the human race into vampires [258].

In spite of his repeated over-the-top characterizations of what today seem transparent as campy queers, Price's private sexual life remains a mystery. Kevin Heffernan cites a 1960 *Time* magazine article referring to Price as a "sort of a sissified Bela Lugosi" (97); Harry Benshoff quotes film historian Ed Sikov as stating that "in 1939 the Hollywood gossip mill knew of and subtly acknowledged Vincent Price's homosexuality" (216). Price was married three times, with a son and a daughter; the latter born when he was fifty years old (Price 235). Denis Meikle refers to rumors of affairs with both male and female co-stars (136; 198), and Price's "innately effeminate and over-theatrical manner" (16) as possibly resulting in his difficulties and ultimate type-casting in horror roles in Hollywood. In addition to his acting career, Price pursued his interest in art and antiques, activities often coded as queer,[3] but which also lent him an air of respectability to counteract his presence in the minor genre of horror, according to his daughter (Price 190). Price was a dedicated Democrat (Price 221), and, partly due to his presence in the art community, Eisenhower appointed him to the Indian Arts and Crafts Board (Price 222).

Price worked regularly almost up until his death in 1993. In the 1970s, he incarnated *The Abominable Dr. Phibes* (1971), bringing a psychedelic sensibility to his work, but his stage work in the role of Oscar Wilde in *Diversions and Delights* (1977–1979) certainly clinched his association with things queer.[4] Already in the 1960s, he had played the role of the villain Egghead on the *Batman* (1966–1967) television series, starring Adam West. His now iconic status brought him voice roles in Hanna-Barbera's *The 13 Ghosts of Scooby Doo* (1985), Disney's *The Great Mouse Detective* (1986), but most famously on Michael Jackson's *Thriller* music video (1982). He also hosted PBS's *Mystery* from 1981–1989. As a living legend, he appeared in *The Monster Club* (1981), and his last major role was as the Inventor in Tim Burton's *Edward Scissorhands* (1990). His distinctive voice and elegant stature, but also his talent as an actor allowed him to create a persona that could be desperately hovering on the brink of madness, perversely sinister, or—increasingly so in his later life—cannily avuncular. More than any other single actor, particularly given the length of his career—over forty years in the genre—Price came to represent horror itself.

In *Monsters in the Closet*, Harry Benshoff argues that many actors who have become typecast as horror leads may be read as "queer" star personae: Bela Lugosi's pronounced accent gives him a non-normative foreignness, as does Peter Lorre's accent and short stature. Boris Karloff's (William Henry Pratt), Russian sounding stage name and lisped delivery (when allowed lines, for example, in *The Mask of Fu Manchu* [1932] or *The Raven* [1935]) suggest something fey. Like these horror stars of an earlier generation but even more so, Vincent Price emerges in the 1950s with a distinctly "queer" star persona, an image that will build across the 1960s to be blatantly exploited in the 1970s in what Benshoff refers to as "homo-horror" (14).[5] In his extended discussion of the *Phibes* franchise Benshoff asserts that "a deliberate and overarching camp aesthetic is used to nominate the protagonist as queer [....] Price's bigger-than-life performances and somewhat effeminate persona have made him a favorite among queer spectators for years" (208).[6]

From his earliest roles in Gothic romance films like *Dragonwyck*, Price's characters' sexuality had repeatedly been suggested as non-normative (Benshoff and Griffin 35); already in the 1940s Benshoff asserts that "Laird Cregar, Vincent Price, *et al.*, played queer homicidal maniacs" (231). But his performances in Roger Corman's Poe cycle offer the most clear-cut examples of the male scream queen at work. The association of Edgar Allan Poe and his literary works to non-normative sexuality has been well documented, from his real-life marriage to thirteen-year-old cousin Virginia Clemm to the incest of "The Fall of the House of Usher" (1839) and the necrophilia of "Morella" (1835). Roger Corman and his production team, including Richard Matheson who scripted a number of these films, generally exploited the lurid aspects of Poe as they translated his works to film. The Corman-Matheson-Price collaborations in *House of Usher*, *The Pit and the Pendulum*, *Tales of Terror* (1962), *The Raven*, as well as *The Comedy of Terrors*, scripted by Matheson but directed by Jacques Tourneur, and *The Tomb of Ligeia* (1964), scripted by Robert Towne, underscore the queer aspects of Poe's oeuvre specifically drawing upon Vincent Price's star image to do so.[7]

As might be expected, then, over the years critics' reception of his performance in *LMoE* has proven to be highly ambivalent. As already mentioned, Matheson himself felt that Price was horribly miscast (Foreword 9), an opinion shared by others since (Dawidziak 15; McGee 208). Price was arguably a poor choice if the film sought to interpret Neville as Matheson had actually written him; Price hardly embodies the working-class, ex-military, hairy chested Everyman that Neville first appears to be in *Legend*. Denis Meikle, usually a sympathetic critic to Price, opines, "Given that he represents the focus of the film for the whole of its 86-minute running-time, his limp-wristed approach to the role is nothing short of a dereliction of duty" (106). Others, however, have been kinder. Charles Mitchell describes his performance as "both convincing and remarkable" (96), in contrast to the actor's usual style. Some critics note Price's effort to tone down his performance, an over-the-top emotionalism appropriate to the "queer homicidal maniacs" and "campy madm[e]n" (Benshoff 231; 205) he was typically cast to play, appreciating his understated portrayal of Robert Morgan. Indeed, much of this negative criticism derives precisely from critics' insistence on comparing Price's Morgan to Matheson's Neville (two quite different characters, really), and their watching Price play Morgan as they have watched Price play Roderick Usher and Nicholas Medina. Nonetheless, drawing on the queer coding of his star persona sheds insight on the various meanings we can gather from this filmic text.

And yet, the film is frequently described as a "relatively faithful" adaptation of Matheson's novel (Pulliam and Fonseca 120). *LMoE* certainly reproduces its claustrophobic feel and its intimate portrayal of Neville and his everyday life, particularly as Price carries the film in an effective toned down desperation. While Price may not be Neville the way Matheson wrote him, he makes an effective Last Man in this film. Charles Mitchell pays tribute to his performance, described as:

> both convincing and remarkable. Price takes some chances along the way. Few actors would dare to tackle the scene where Morgan watches the home movies and mixes laughter and tears in an extended take. Price is marvelous in conveying the world weariness of his character, and his voice-over narration is a perfect film noir touch. The picture is essentially a one-man show [96].

Just as Neville's consciousness focalizes the novel, Price rarely shares the screen, with the exception of the flashback scenes, Ruth's arrival, and the final conflict with the black-shirted members of the new society. In addition to a near identical mirroring of the narrative structure, *LMoE* retains Neville's relationship with Ben Cortman, but its stunning reversal of the novel's conclusion in which the hero maintains his position of righteousness sets a precedent for later films.

The Last Man on Earth *as "Relatively Faithful" Adaptation*

The very title of Robert Stam's seminal essay, "Beyond Fidelity: The Dialogics of Adaptation" (2000), disavows a long tradition of criticism that judged film adaptations based on their purported fidelity to a literary original. That tradition can be seen in the frequently negative reactions to the various film adaptations of Matheson's novel, beginning with *The Last Man on Earth*. The present study agrees with Stam's assertion that "[t]he notion of fidelity is highly problematic for a number of reasons" (55), but at the same time it admits with Linda Hutcheon that a comparative approach is largely inevitable (6). Even the dialogic approach proposed by Stam assumes that an adaptation occurs in dialogue with its literary model, even if it is not meant to be an exact rendition of it. Stam takes the notion of dialogue between "original" and "copy" even further, positing multiple sources for film adaptations, "caught up in the ongoing whirl of intertextual reference and transformation, of texts generating other texts in an endless process of recycling, transformation, and transmutation with no clear point of origin" (66). Even Matheson's novel, then, may be seen as an adaptation of various source materials ranging from Bram Stoker's *Dracula* (1897) and its 1931 film adaptation, which he admits to being his inspiration (Dawidziak 11). Similarly, the film adaptations of *I Am Legend* reference not only Matheson's novel, but also other films in the apocalyptic genre. That said, *The Last Man on Earth* can justifiably referred to as a "relatively faithful" adaptation for a number of reasons, not the least of which is Matheson's role in the initial drafts of its scenario.

By the film's 1964 release date, in addition to his television work, most notably on *The Twilight Zone*, Richard Matheson's reputation had also been made in the field of Hollywood horror with the now classic production of *The Incredible Shrinking Man* and his scripting of Poe for Corman's American International Pictures productions. Indeed, Matheson scenarized other films for low-budget producer AIP, including *Night of the Eagle* (1962), a collaborative adaptation with Charles Beaumont of Fritz Leiber's *Conjure Wife* (1943), and *De Sade* (1969); that firm would also be responsible for the U.S. distribution of the first film adaptation of *I Am Legend*. Matthew R. Bradley recounts the film's genesis as "a saga that began in the late 1950s with Val Guest slated to direct the film, retitled *The Night Creatures*, for Hammer [Films]" (120), which had acquired the rights. Matheson was then sent to England to work on the screenplay himself (Weaver 306), but foreseeing trouble with the then strict British censor's office, Hammer soon sold the rights to American producer Robert L. Lippert (Bradley 120–21). Matheson did write two successful screenplays for Hammer (Astic; Bradley 123–26; 130–37): *Fanatic* (1965) based on Anne Blaisdell's *Nightmare* (1961), and *The Devil Rides Out* (1968), based on Dennis Wheatley's novel, effectively directed by Terence Fisher.

Lippert continued to work with Matheson, telling the latter that Fritz Lang would direct the film (Weaver 306); Matheson produced what he felt was a spot on adaptation, but then William F. Leicester was asked to revise it (Bradley 120–21). As he told Tom Weaver in an interview: "*The Last Man on Earth* followed [the novel] most closely, but it was inept—in fact, I put my pen name, Logan Swanson, on it" (307). In the end, the film became an Italian co-production, with "Sicilian-born Ubaldo Ragona [...] hired to direct the film, while Sidney Salkow was charged with overseeing an 'Americanised' version" (Meikle 105). Jonathan Lampley also asserts that Salkow's "primary responsibility was to reshape the material shot by Ragona in Rome" (97), further suggesting that the Italian director wielded the greater creative responsibility. We do know that Price was sent to Italy for location shots, and the remainder of the cast is Italian, but some exteriors with American cars complicate the task of assigning directorial responsibilities. Ariana Casali asserts that Ragona actually worked with Matheson on the script, but does not provide documentation for this (434).

The film retains the basic plotline and narrative structure, as well as many details from Matheson's novel, using image and sound effectively to convey the novel's atmosphere of desperation, recount the backstory of the pandemic, and depict the emotional rollercoaster of its protagonist's struggle for survival. Structured loosely in three parts, with the first third of the film devoted to Robert Morgan's (as Neville is renamed) daily routine for survival, the middle third a long flashback about his pre-apocalyptic private and professional lives coupled with the origins of the vampire plague that has devastated humanity, and a final third, in which Morgan's hopes are raised and then dashed before the film's conclusion with his ultimate demise at the hands of the new society.

Largely shot on location in Italy, *LMoE* only partially reproduces Matheson's suburban American tract-home setting, an aspect of the film often subjected to critique (e.g., Mitchell 95), including by Matheson himself (Bradley 122–23). As in many horror films of the period and through the 1980s, a conventional opening sequence establishes the film's location, tracking in from an initial panoramic shot which then tapers down incrementally in scope to finally arrive at the protagonist's dwelling, the particular site of horror. Shot by Franco Delli Colli whose 30-year career included a number of Western and horror films, *LMoE* opens, then, as the camera pans across an abandoned cityscape signaled by apparently empty, ultra-modern, concrete apartment complexes. These images are accompanied by Paul Sawtell and Bert Shefter's "haunting score" (Mitchell 96), an appropriately eerie minimalist musical soundtrack, the wind blowing through the grass underscoring the utter silence of the city. The camera pulls in to show abandoned vehicles, empty streets strewn with blowing trash, and then closes in on a view of dead bodies lying in the street and across the steps of a church. The montage concludes by tracking in to a less than subtle marker of the apocalypse's advent, a sign reading "Community Church: The End Has Come," thus maintaining references to Christianity found in Matheson's novel.

The camera then tracks to Morgan's house, on to his bedroom window, moves inside, and stops on the dial of an alarm clock. Sound clearly assists in telling the story as his alarm rings, and a voice-over narrative, which will eventually reveal the dark void of his loneliness, introduces us to his daily routine, the ritualistic activities that keep him alive and relatively sane. The use of voiceover affords the viewer a similar sense of intimacy to that we have felt while reading Matheson's novel, narrated in the third person but completely focalized through Neville's point of view. Price thus unenthusiastically utters his first lines off-screen: "Another day to live through. Well, better get started." Inside the bungalow, as the camera follows Vincent Price— we still have no name for the protagonist, so viewers may mentally refer to the individual on screen with the actor's name—from his bedroom into the kitchen for coffee, we see the breakdown of social norms in the form of a bare light bulb hanging from the ceiling, the dwelling's clutter and disarray signaling that things are not all right with this world. The immediate visual contrast between this disorder and the conventionally immaculate studio interiors of 1950s and 1960s television instantly relates to the viewer the same information it took Matheson several pages to narrate: here is a man in a state of crisis.

Just as the novel specifically identifies the future date of its events, we next see Morgan marking a calendar, uttering (still in voice-over): "December, 1965. Is that all it has been since I inherited the world, only three years? It seems like a million." With the film's release occurring on March 8, 1964, its events are thus moved to the viewer's very near future, dramatically reducing Matheson's two decades ahead. This change reflects the increasing urgency of apocalyptic fears for audiences habituated to the sense of impending doom by the spate of atomic bomb films produced between 1950 and 1963 (see Shapiro, chapters 3 and 4). As he exits the kitchen to go outside, we notice the boarded up windows; he then walks to the garage. Sound again signals activity as we hear the generator that provides electricity for his home, a recurring visual and aural trope signaling the Last Man's efforts singlehandedly to keep a technological civilization running. He unbars the garage doors, opening them and stepping outside, to observe in voice-over: "The eye on the world. An empty, dead, silent world." As he nonchalantly kicks over one corpse and inspects another lying in the yard, his blasé manner reveals that he has become inured to death; "Every day there are more of them." As in Matheson's novel, the lone protagonist refers to "them" and "they," leaving the audience temporarily in the dark as to what his antagonists are, although the crucifix, mirror, and garlic hanging from the door—on which the camera now zooms—offer clues as to the nature of the monsters that will assail the lone hero each night.

Indeed, the opening sequence of *LMoE* follows that of Matheson's novel almost word-for-word, involving Price's examination of the bunker-like reinforcements to his home and the need to replace a broken mirror. Both protagonists appear unkempt, wearing the basic wardrobe of rumpled shirt and slacks during the present crisis; viewers participate in their daily survival routines as they foray out of the home, Morgan driving a station wagon reminiscent of Neville's Willys, to scavenge for food and fuel. During a "shopping" sequence, Morgan contemplates a flashy white convertible, but unlike the Neville of later films who choses snappy sports cars, he realizes that "[t]here was a time I went shopping for a car; now I'm looking for a hearse." Like his literary model, he is thus inextricably linked to the death he metes out as a vampire slayer. Ironically, now that he no longer has a family, he selects the ultimate family mobile in the pre-van/SUV days, replacing his wrecked 1956 Chevrolet Two-Ten Townsman with a 1958 Ford Country Sedan.[8]

The film introduces an element absent from Matheson's novel, in which Neville appears initially certain that he is the sole survivor. In contrast, Morgan's first diegetic speech occurs as he searches for signs of other human life. Like Ralph Burton in the earlier *The World, the Flesh and the Devil*, Price's character ritualistically spends time on the radio, changing frequencies, and compulsively repeating his call signs. Although ham radio hobbyists had been communicating with each other since the first decade of the twentieth century (Haring ix), these protagonists' possession of a radio transmitter reflects the increasing technologization of the average American home in the decade since Matheson's novel and the Cold War development of the Civil Defense movement. Kristen Haring cites statistics for radio licenses at 100,000 in the early 1950s as doubling by the early 1960s (xii). Evidence for a surge in the medium's popularity can also be seen in Herman's (Fred Gwynne) adopting the hobby in an episode of the iconic horror parody series, *The Munsters* (1964–1966).

These early sequences prefigure core activities and coping mechanisms for today's zombie-apocalypse survivors similar to those featured in AMC's *The Walking Dead* (2010–). Like Neville, Morgan drinks, sometimes to excess, and listens to music (although he prefers jazz), and both protagonists are obsessed with time and space, frequently checking their watches. Morgan marks off the days on a calendar and keeps a gridded map of his systematic slaughter. Like his model, Morgan clears his front lawn of the dead and brings them to the burning pit, thus triggering a flashback to his wife and daughter. He also interacts with the "vampires"; including tracking down and staking them.

The lengthy flashback in the middle of the film reveals Morgan's former apparently happy family life and establishes his links to institutionalized science, thus offering a pre-pandemic characterization of its Last Man figure somewhat different than that of Matheson's novel. In keeping with Price's middle-aged, cultivated image, Robert Morgan is a prosperous, middle-class scientist, unlike the original Neville, an average American without the education needed to be even an officer during the war in which he served and who must teach himself to use the scientific method. This move away from Matheson's working-class model reflects perhaps the social trend toward the formation of an America in which everyone perceives themselves as belonging to the middle class. Whereas the SF and horror films of the 1940s, according to David Skal, tended to demonize the mad scientist as a marginal "egghead" (18–19), by the mid–1960s the Cold War campaign for American scientific development had somewhat diminished the early anti-intellectualism. While in 1954, Matheson's Everyman needed to be working-class and not a scientist by training, by 1964 the image of "every man" in America had become that of the white collar, middle-class, and the conventions of Cold War SF-horror had normalized the scientist protagonist.

At this point in the film, dialogue—as opposed to voice-over narration—becomes necessary to engage the discourse about scientific reason versus irrational superstition, typical of the horror film since the 1930s, but particularly of Cold War SF-horror. Morgan's friend and colleague at the Mercer Institute of Chemical Research, Ben Cortman (Giacomo Rossi-Stuart)—the viewer now realizes he is the same man as the "leader" of the vampires that assault Morgan's home each night—shows him news clippings. Along with Morgan's wife Virginia (Emma Danieli), they discuss the early phases of a plague in Europe. Headlines describe it as a "Disease Borne on the Wind." The film efficiently invokes, then, both the notion of an epidemic and fears of wind-borne atomic fallout; what "Europe's disease" is remains for Morgan: "[e]ntirely theoretical, Ben." In the conventional monster film, scientists dismiss—to their later peril—the invocation of vampires or werewolves as mere superstition; similarly, *LMoE*'s scientific discourse blithely explains away the horrible events that have been occurring. Here, too, the scientist Morgan refuses to believe his younger partner: "I cannot accept half-baked theories that sell newspapers; I'm a scientist, not an alarmist."[9] In an eerily premonitory caution, Ben states: "You're whistling past the graveyard."

Cortman's macabre assertion proves true, as leaves blowing across the lawn indicate a change of seasons within the same flashback sequence, and we jump inside the Morgan's home. Here, the visual and aural imagery of epidemic and massive death typical of the apocalyptic sub-genre come into play. From the recurring transitional motif of Morgan looking out the window, the camera turns inside toward a gauze-tented bed in what is clearly a child's room. This tent of sheer fabric evokes the mosquito-netting employed to protect Westerners at risk of contracting insect-borne diseases in tropical climates, a reference to the novel's proposed etiology of the plague. The wind blowing outside continues to signal the "air-borne" menace. He touches the gauze, but then—perhaps in an unconscious effort to avoid any contamination—wipes his hands on his trousers, as if to clean off any infection. After a glance at the little girl asleep under the netting, Morgan passes one closed door and enters the next, adjusting his tie apparently about to say good-bye to his—soon also apparently ill—wife before leaving for work. As the couple look in on their child together, Virginia wishes "somebody would find a vaccine"; Robert reveals that that is precisely his task.

At the lab, Cortman informs viewers of the increasingly desperate state of affairs: "the streets are swarming with tons of bodies that they're throwing into that godawful pit." Finally, the term "plague" is used, as the media—also a recurring trope in apocalyptic films—reveal the extent of the disaster via the governor announcing a state of emergency. Its personal impact appears as we hear Morgan's daughter Kathy saying, bathetically, "Mommy, where are you? Mommy, I can't see? [...] Mommy, help me. [...] Mommy where are you?" To the traditional vampire lore, the film introduces the element of blindness, ostensibly as a metaphor for the public's failure to "see" what has been happening around them in order to react or prevent the disease from spreading. As Morgan leaves home for the lab on a second occasion, he explicitly forbids Virginia to let anyone in their home; he knows by now that Kathy's body will be thrown into a mass grave. To underscore the brutality of the situation, as Morgan leaves his home, he witnesses a neighbor screaming at uniform-clad men who throw a sheet-wrapped boy into the back of a truck. We thus see the dehumanizing effects of massive death and infection, a trope now extremely familiar since the twenty-first century glut of zombie apocalypse films.

At the same time, scenes of the protagonist and his family's plight humanize the pain and devastation the plague causes by returning to their personal tragedy. Thus, "Bob" returns home from the lab at night; he sees a truck pull away, enters a silent home, runs upstairs to find Kathy's bed empty, and then confronts the grieving Virginia who failed to obey his orders and called a doctor, suggesting her feminine weakness and inability to resist the temptation. In contrast, he acts, chasing down the vehicle he believes holds his daughter's corpse allowing the film to reprise the hellish imagery of the burning pits Morgan uses to dispose of slain vampires already functioning while humanity still reigned. We see uniformed men now removing bodies from the trucks, and out of the chaos of the sirens we hear a voice saying tersely, "Sorry, lady, there's nothing I can do," signaling the inhumanity of the disposal machine, as do the gas masks worn by the trucks' staff. Again, sound underscores the growing urgency of the film's imagery during the flashback, as a uniformed motorcycle cop uses his sirens, escorting a caravan of trucks loaded with the dead.

The film's final third returns to Morgan's postapocalyptic present-day situation. As in the novel, encounters with a stray dog—a somewhat bathetic poodle, in this case—and with Ruth both raise Morgan's hopes and dash them to the ground. After he has managed to tame the dog and bring him inside, joyful at the promise of a companion, the animal sickens and dies, clearly infected. Similarly, when a chance encounter reveals the presence of perhaps another human survivor, although he learns she is also infected, the scientist synthesizes a cure from his own blood. But Ruth's revelation of the existence of a new order, which again closely tracks that of the novel, and the fact that they want to kill him, throw Morgan into a state of despair. Unlike his literary model, however, Morgan is not completely ready to give up his life, grabbing a gun and fleeing; a dramatic chase sequence, in which he is followed by black-shirted men, leads him back to a church where black-dressed women have also gathered. He dies on the altar, accusing them: "You're freaks. I'm a man. The last man!" He lands in a Christ-like position, thus setting the stage for subsequent reinterpretations of Neville not as an outdated vestige of an old order, but as a martyr and, in later films, even the savior of humanity.

In *A Theory of Adaptation* (2006), cultural critic Linda Hutcheon eschews the criterion of fidelity, invoking the dictionary definition of "to adapt" as "to adjust, to alter, to make suitable" (7). While subsequent film adaptations of Matheson's novel will make more radical alterations and adjustments to suit their times, one of the reasons that *The Last Man on Earth* remains relatively faithful is due to its similar socio-historical climate. Many of the Cold War conditions under which Matheson composed his novel prevailed in the late 1950s and early 1960s, the period of the first film's conception.

The Last Man on Earth *as Cold War Allegory: Robert Morgan, Survivor and Slayer*

While *LMoE* represents an early "Last Man" film,[10] a number of postapocalyptic fantasies had shared its more obvious and ongoing Cold War concerns about the chances of humanity's survival should a nuclear conflagration occur. Indeed, the period in question marks a definite peak in what Jerome F. Shapiro terms *Atomic Bomb Cinema*. Through the 1950s, director Roger Corman, among others, produced a number of low-budget exploitation films with postapocalyptic settings, including *The Day the World Ended*, *Teenage Caveman* (1957) and *The Last Woman on Earth*. Arch Oboler's *Five*, *The World, The Flesh and The Devil*, and Ray Milland's *Panic in the Year Zero!* (1962) also explore the survival of a small group of humans after an apocalyptic event. Like *I Am Legend*, *The Last Man on Earth* exploits Cold War anxieties about the potentially destructive force of science and technology, but unlike most of these other apocalyptic fantasies, instead of the renewal identified by Shapiro, it concludes on a dead end for humanity. Furthermore, the protagonist's role of vampire slayer sets him apart from other postapocalyptic heroes.

Robert Morgan: Vampire Hunter

Morgan's efforts to survive echo the real-life Civil Defense movement intricately tied to Cold War fears of a nuclear apocalypse, but his role as a vampire slayer ties this first film adaptation specifically back to Matheson's novel and the Gothic horror genre, in general. Unlike other postapocalyptic SF-horror films of the time, Morgan faces a threat from the legends of the past, wielding both the scientific methods and the just wrath of a Van Helsing to battle it. Morgan's "vampire maintenance" includes restocking his garlic supply, hanging crucifixes on his door, and checking the mirrors hanging outside his door because "[t]hey can't bear to see their image."

This assertion follows Matheson's novel in its revision of the lore of the traditional film vampire, which cannot see its reflection in the mirror at all (28). It also operates a transference from the novel, in which Neville saw his own distorted reflection (13), a harbinger of his moral ambiguity; the film

Two. Visualizing Apocalypse Through Compromised Masculinity   71

"They can't bear to see their image." The determined slayer, Robert Morgan (Vincent Price, right), wards off his vampire nemesis, Ben Cortman (Giacomo Rossi Stuart). *The Last Man on Earth*, Legend Films. DVD.

has already begun to revise Matheson's questionable hero, casting instead aspersion onto the vampires.

Like Neville, Morgan must invoke reason and science in his fight to survive. Echoing Neville's need to control his emotions, he asserts: "I can't afford the luxury of anger. Anger can make me vulnerable. It can destroy my reason and reason's the only advantage I have over them. I've got to find where they hide during the day. Uncover every one of them." Morgan walks over to another recurring visual motif; just as the calendar signaled the lapse of time, so a map allows him to situate himself—and his enemies—in space. Both reveal the protagonist's efforts to use instrumental reason to exert control in an increasingly precarious existence. Significantly, whereas in *The World, the Flesh and the Devil* Ralph Burton consulted a map to aid his search for other humans, Robert Morgan uses it methodically to hunt down his antagonists, and the voiceover reveals his genocidal desire to exterminate "every one of them." As a vampire slayer, he is unrepentant, and the film suggests that his drive to kill is justified, a matter of his life or death.

Sound intrudes again, echoing the generator of before, as another machine, an electric lathe this time, clatters along; these few machines represent the last sounds of a civilization Morgan desperately tries to maintain. Once again, the film revises the traditional lore of the vampire regarding the stake. As he inspects his handiwork, Morgan's voice-over adds a new detail: "They're perfect; just wide enough so their body seal won't operate." This "body seal" begins to situate the supernatural monster in the realm of the scientific with a vague explanation of why a wooden stake—rather than bullets—is necessary to destroy his enemies. Finally, what the viewer has been waiting for, the ultimate sign that we are indeed watching a vampire film: "They want my blood."

As he drives off on a slaying mission, Morgan realizes that he is almost out of gas. One of the aspects of Matheson's story and its filmic interpretations that makes it so successful as a post–World War II myth is precisely its engagement with daily routine, our strategies to survive in the contemporary urban world. Although for Robert Neville/Morgan the stakes—pardon the irresistible pun—are so much higher, viewers sympathize with this constant and unending routine to re-stock our cupboards, get gas, perform home maintenance, all of the little chores which, mean for us, too, the difference between Giorgio Agamben's *zoē* and *bios*, the bare life of animals versus a fully human life in society, outlined in *Homo Sacer* (1995).[11] In any case, Morgan's "to-do" list brings the viewer back through the postapocalyptic city, hammering home its sheer emptiness, coupled with the omnipresence of death in the corpses that Morgan encounters not only in his driveway, but all along the route to get gas—which he must siphon from a tanker, since no attendant, of course, remains at the service station—to stop at the grocery store, restock his supply of mirrors, and so on. *LMoE* closely reflects here the focus on routine and domesticity of *I Am Legend*: an individual facing with varying levels of courage and discipline a dehumanizing daily routine, filled with repetitive domestic and consumerist tasks, in a world that seems completely hostile. On one level, minus the vampires, does this regime not prevail for us all?

After this point, however, Morgan's situation clearly diverges from viewers' as the film engages two central visual images from *I Am Legend*: the disposal of the numerous bodies resulting from the plague and the protagonist's hunt for more monsters to slay. In *LMoE*, the burning pits lie outside the city, as the viewer surmises from the desolate countryside through which Morgan must drive, as well as from the apartment complexes seen from a distance in the background. A motif that will recur in flashback sequences as well, the great pits into which he dumps the corpses he finds (and creates) invoke a Dantesque Inferno, hell being a location explicitly invoked in his voice-over. They also suggest the mass graves of the World War II Holocaust. As Morgan dons a gas mask before leaving his car, the multiple associations evoked by this single visual signifier range from the use of mustard gas in World War I, to the gas showers of Nazi concentration camps, to then contemporary fears of nuclear fallout, chemical or biological warfare during the Cold War, and even the growing UFO phenomenon and concerns about an extraterrestrial attack on earth. With the alien-looking mask covering his human features, Price's physical image here foreshadows his eventual identification as the actual monster at the narrative's conclusion.

In order to dispose of the bodies he has picked up en route, Morgan drives his station wagon up to the very rim of a smoking pit, surrounded by abandoned military trucks; partially obscured by the smoke, with the music rising to a quicker, more tense than melancholy tempo, Morgan begins diabolically to throw bodies into the pit. Later, flashback sequences further align these mass graves with images of the Shoah, as men in military uniforms police the area during the original plague, ordering bodies to be thrown into the pit and burned. Indeed, the black and white imagery of this hellish sequence recalls no other film so much as French filmmaker Alain Resnais' documentary about the Holocaust, *Nuit et brouillard/Night and Fog* (1955), which it is likely that the Italian crew responsible for shooting the actual film may have seen even if the U.S. pre- and post-production crews had not.

Having resupplied and disposed of yesterday's corpses, Morgan now sets himself the methodical task of extermination. He breaks into a building, indicating the marginal, potentially illicit nature of his activities; as the music waxes more menacing, he opens an apartment door where we see what at first looks like a normal woman in bed. Morgan's silhouette blocks the door, an ominous figure as he wields a phallic stake and as he hammers it into her, we now see the unhealthy dark rings around her eyes. He grimaces in disgust as he performs what Gregory Waller refers to as the "wild work" of the vampire slayer. Checking off an address in the car, he heads to the next site, carrying his equipment in a suitcase somewhat larger than a doctor's bag, but perhaps signifying the professional nature of his work. His subsequent victims appear to be men, as a dissolve superimposes the image of his enlarged torso over an entire block of apartment buildings, with further superimposed dissolves as he sees a male figure writhing on the floor, then of his car en route

"Morgan, come out!" Ben Cortman (Giacomo Rossi Stuart) offers a queer invocation to Morgan. Although the victims of the plague are described as vampires in the novel and film, we see here the inspiration for George A. Romero's undead in *Night of the Living Dead*. *The Last Man on Earth*, Legend Films. DVD.

to the burial pits, suggesting rather than strictly depicting the repetitive and methodical nature of his work. Finally, in front of the backdrop of a Ferris Wheel, suggestive of the wheel of fortune, of the lost happiness and frivolity of a decadent society that has deserved its demise, he notices the setting sun and returns home to prepare for the long night ahead, "the twelve long hours before the sun will rise."

Given the violence of his days, it seems almost justified that Morgan cannot sleep well at night, but Price's ability to convey that his slaying is carried out not with sadistic glee, but rather a sense of duty and a will to survive maintains the viewer's sympathy. As night falls, the monsters' assault on his home begins, and with it our first glance of the iconic, now familiar imagery of the stiff-limbed, shambling creatures which, over time, will be transformed in the popular imagination from the vampires of Matheson's model into today's burgeoning zombie apocalypse genre via Romero's *Living Dead* cycle.[12]

Their leader, Morgan's former colleague and personal friend, Cortman, signals to his companions, many of whom carry two-by-fours, broomsticks, or some other mob-type weapon. In hindsight, this mob converging on Morgan's home prefigures his own identification as the monster, recalling the peasant mobs requisite to the classic 1930s Universal Studios horror films, like *Bride of Frankenstein* (1935). Once again sound serves as much a purpose as the visual imagery, first, as the leader of the horde directly addresses "Morgan" in an ominous monotone thus introducing the protagonist to the audience. Then, heightening the sense of assault, as his assailants clatter their makeshift weapons against the boards of the house, effectively conveying the sense that Morgan can know no peace while these beings haunt him outside.

Robert Morgan and Institutional Science

Prior to his transformation into a ruthless vampire slayer, Morgan had tried to use the tools of science in an effort to understand and possibly control the pandemic. Unlike the self-taught Neville, however, he has a sophisticated laboratory and institutional support, all depicted in flashback. Diligently working for a cure, Morgan indicates that "the bacilli are multiplying" to the lab's founder, Dr. Mercer (Umberto Rau), who responds: "That kicks the bone marrow theory in the head." The film audience is even treated to an image of the germs under the microscope accompanied by more pseudo-scientific babble about "white counts." The extent of the epidemic becomes clear as Mercer asserts that "all communications are ended outside the continental limit." On cue, as Mercer asks, "Where's Cortman," the latter arrives, donning his lab coat. Robert and Ben are told by their superior to "stay on this virus theory until I say it's exhausted," revealing the low-budget film's lack of concern for scientific consistency since bacilli are bacteria, not viruses.

Ben's growing contempt, however, for the efforts of science appear clearly as he sarcastically asks Morgan what the "great man of science," Mercer, had to say. While Robert summarizes the situation—"an unknown germ is being blown around the world. It's highly contagious and it's reached plague proportions"—Ben accuses Mercer's approach as unimaginative and asks the ever-logical Robert: "And you don't believe that some of the dead have come back? [...]. And why are they burning the bodies, not burying them?" This allows Robert both to provide a logical explanation for containing the contagion, while also explicitly invoking for the first time the trope of the vampire: "Do you prefer us to believe in vampires?" As he denies Cortman's allegations, invoking the "legends" of Matheson's original novel, Morgan emphatically asserts: "They're stories, Ben! Stories!" The tragic results of Robert's failure to believe in the possibility that the dead can return will later be revealed. In the end, only Morgan and Mercer remain in the once busy lab. Even Morgan's confidence is shaken as he asks his authority figure, "What's going to happen, doctor, is everybody going to die before someone finds the answer?" Mercer admits that "I don't deny that there's some strange evolutionary process going on, but mankind won't be destroyed." Of course, he's only partially correct, and Morgan's refusal to believe such stories coupled with his desire to cling to a rational explanation changes nothing: he finds himself to be the Last Man of the film's title. The film thus engages the novel's epistemological quest for an answer, similarly concluding on the impossibility of stemming the tides of change, of reversing humanity's demise, a demise brought on precisely by Western man's hubristic pursuit of techno-science without considering the ethical implications of each discovery.

Not only did Morgan fail to keep his daughter and wife safe from the pandemic, science's failure is underscored again as he fails to cure Ruth near the film's conclusion. Laid on the couch, which has been covered with a white sheet reminiscent of Virginia's shroud, Ruth's fate hangs in the balance, as does Morgan's, when she wakes and asks, "What are you doing?" With the hubris typical of the Western male, believing that his intervention is wanted and removing the choice of accepting his help from those he comes into contact with, Morgan replies, "It's already done. Look!" He gleefully shows her the results in a mirror, where she sees that the incipient fangs, which had been growing because she had not been able to take the pills devised by the new society while in Morgan's company, have disappeared. Almost repeating word-for-word Christ's speech to the apostles at the Last Supper, repeated by Catholic priests and Protestant ministers every time they offer the sacrament of Communion to their flock, he asserts: "My blood has saved you, Ruth." For him this means that "[y]ou and I can save all the others. We won't be alone, we'll never be alone again!" Ruth's loyalties, however, lie with her own people, but she nonetheless wants to save Robert by warning him of her colleagues' impending arrival.

In the end, science utterly fails Morgan. Although he does share a detailed account of his theory about the bat bite in Panama, like his model Neville, he undermines it as "only a guess." He leaves Ruth and the viewer with another explanation, which falls back on metaphysics: "Perhaps I was chosen. That's a laugh." Furthermore, the film closes on the religious imagery that reverses the conclusion of Matheson's novel, in which Neville himself was the monstrous legend. Dying upon the altar, speared by the black-shirted men, Morgan appears as (an albeit failed) savior, a Christ-like martyr to the cause of human civilization, a trope this film hands down to the adaptations which follow.

Ideological Battles of the Cold War

Numerous analyses of SF-horror films of this period focus on American ambivalence to science during the Cold War, but let us briefly recall that the Cold War was as much an ideological conflict as a technological one. Constructed as a domestic problem as much as it was one of foreign policy, the sociological aspects of the accompanying Red Scare have been less readily explored in the secondary literature on *I Am Legend*, its first film adaptation, and similar works. As early as the late 1940s, the House Committee on Un-American Activities investigated Hollywood's ties to communism, holding hearings at which the likes of Ronald Reagan and Walt Disney testified (Walker 22–23). Blacklisting continued through the early 1950s, and just as tensions rose between the U.S. and the USSR in the early years of the 1950s, so, too, "concerns over internal subversion in the United States continued to mount" (Walker 39). Senator Joseph McCarthy's February 9, 1950, speech in Wheeling, West Virginia, in which he announced his knowledge of "205 State Department employees who were members of the Communist Party" (Walker 39), sparked the fire that culminated in the execution of Julius and Ethel Rosenberg in 1953. Price himself was not untouched by the Red Scare, as his daughter Victoria explains in his biography: "In the summer of 1953, Vincent's career suddenly and inexplicably appeared to stall" (173). He soon learned that his name was "on the list of McCarthy's Premature Anti-Nazi Sympathizers" (Price 173). Panicked about how to support his family without work, on the advice of his agent and a former assistant U.S. Attorney General, he voluntarily submitted to an interview with the FBI and signed an affidavit in order to be removed from the gray list (Price 173–74).

Matheson's depiction of the "new society"—read as African Americans by Kathy Patterson, but just as easily read as communists, or even the conformism of Americans in the 1950s ready to give their neighbors up as Reds to save their own skins—remains vague enough to allow for multiple interpretations. For Americans watching *LMoE* in 1964, the black-shirted men and women portrayed in the film also remain largely open to interpretation, recalling perhaps Hitler's SS, revealing a lingering threat of fascism—which could be read as a subversive message about the nature of the previous decade's witch hunt for communists—or as the ongoing fear of communists themselves. John Joseph Gladchuk prefaces his reappraisal, which works to expose the committee itself as un–American by comparing it to Nazism, of the impact of HUAC on Hollywood:

> When looking at the House Committee on Un-American Activities, its history, its people, and the environment within which it operated, it is not too difficult to draw a faint parallel between its evolution and the development of the arm of repression that perpetrated near apocalypse in Nazi Germany [vii].

With "[a]rticles produced by *Life, Look, Reader's Digest,* and *The Saturday Evening Post* [which] spoke of the imminent confrontation between communism and capitalism. The world would become an ideological battleground and a race for nuclear superiority would determine the balance of global power" (Gladchuk 162). In such a climate HUAC and McCarthy flogged the Red Scare for their own personal power and reputations, but given their direct attacks on Hollywood, it seems just as likely that a script like *LMoE*'s could reflect liberals' fear of their conservative, anti-democratic witch hunt as it could be read by conservative audiences as fear of communism.

In addition to expressing and playing on these vague American anxieties, the film's Italian setting and its imagery of the new society to which Ruth belongs give it a nuanced resonance for European viewers. Italian scholar Arianna Casali explains:

> In [...] Ubaldo Ragona's Italian adaptation, the need to ideologically condemn and exorcise Italy's still recent political past in the early 1960s is manifest. In this connection the shooting location is highly significant: it is the stunning futuristic setting of EUR in Rome, a district designed in the late 1930s by the fascist regime. The new mankind hunting and then shooting the protagonist to death on a church altar is represented by black-shirted men, clearly suggesting a direct reference to the fascist dictatorship that dominated Italy for two decades, persecuting its opponents and then ending with the ruination brought about by WW II. The trauma of those years is thus represented and relived with horror particularly in the last sequences of Ragona's film, where the emphasis on the political and historical message completely eclipses the protagonist's inner private tragedy which is, on the contrary, the pivotal meaning of the novel itself [435].

Casali's reading of the first film adaptation, interestingly, recalls my own discussion of Matheson's novel as a text dealing as well with the trauma left over from the World War II era.

After the black-shirts track Morgan to his home, an action-packed chase and gunfight sequence follows as, unlike his literary model, he refuses to surrender. Using grenades and smoke bombs, he escapes to the church for his last stand, like the filmic *Hunchback of Notre Dame* (1939), played by another Hollywood queer, Charles Laughton (Benshoff 14), to seek "sanctuary."

Wounded and trapped, he climbs up the altar; Ruth arrives to try to stop the execution, but she's too late. He cries out, his last words of contempt, "You're freaks. All of you. All of you, freaks! Mutations," words that essentially annul Matheson's conclusion as they leave the besieged white man, who *could* have saved the world with his blood, to die for nothing. Standing at the altar, surrounded by black-clad men and women, Price is finally slain not by a bullet, but significantly by an iron stake through the heart. "You're freaks. I'm a man! The last man." His last words express his complete incomprehension, "They were afraid of me. They were afraid of me," as he dies in Ruth's arms. She walks out accompanied by the cries of an infant, signaling a new species' reign on earth.

The first film adaptation of Matheson's novel, then, maintains intact the reversal in which the hero becomes the monster, but only up to a point. Through its religious imagery and Price's dialogue, it clearly paints Morgan in far more positive colors than the original Neville, making him out to be a misunderstood savior. Jeffrey A. Weinstock correctly contrasts the novel's conclusion with Morgan's last words:

> What Matheson's ending vividly illustrates is that normalcy is entirely a social construction. If everyone drinks blood and sleeps during the day, drinking blood and sleeping during the day become the norm. It is not the vampires who are freaks in *The Last Man on Earth*, but Morgan, the only non-vampire left [61].

By positioning Morgan as a misunderstood altruist, the film's ideology departs from the novel's "progressive" viewpoint (Hantke 182). This is not necessarily surprising. It has become a general truism that Hollywood films "dummy down" the social criticisms that might occur in works of literature or even in original screenplays in order to reach the widest common denominator. For this reason, too, popular films often seem highly ambivalent, as various messages intersect, appear to contradict each other, and then ultimately cancel each other out, leaving the film open to each viewer's interpretation.

The sympathetic conversion of Robert Neville, vampire slaying legend, into Robert Morgan, a lonely scientist looking for a cure, can also be attributed in part to the casting choice and performance of Vincent Price in this role. Although the vampire slaying sequence early in the film is quite effectively shot, showing Morgan capable of the cold-blooded "wild work" necessary to rid the earth of a scourge, it is edited as a montage and thus there is no diegetic dialogue. Because of Price's highly recognizable voice and audience familiarity with his previous screen performances, removing his mellifluous voice enhances his severity. Indeed, Morgan becomes increasingly sympathetic to the viewer as we learn of his tragic losses and his unfailing efforts to find a cure. In the final sequence, his inability to believe that the Others could be afraid of *him*, the guy who tried to save the dog and who "cured" Ruth, is more convincing than a sequence that might have been more faithful to Matheson's steely-toned irony as Neville faces his end in the novel.

Before examining in greater detail how the casting of Vincent Price specifically altered viewers' interpretations of the various threats faced by *The Last Man on Earth*, an examination of post-war masculinity under threat as found in Matheson's other iconic SF-horror novel, *The Shrinking Man* helps establish a pre-existing condition of queer anxiety in these works.

Shrinking Men: Scott Carey and Fear of the Queer

Robert Neville is not Matheson's only veteran protagonist to suffer such trauma that survival itself represents a questionable gift. Returned veteran Scott Carey realizes that he has become *The Shrinking Man*, victim of a freak combination of exposure to a radiation cloud and inhalation of an insecticide (96–97). While Neville has been enshrined in his suburban California home for some time, and his wartime experiences seem to have occurred several years prior, Carey's story in contemporary readers' present tense more clearly signals the post-war context. Invoking Cyndy Hendershot's assertion that height was "one of the measures of masculine confidence in the 1950s" (81), Christopher M. Moreman argues that Carey's shrinking status graphically "illustrates the problems of a reconstitution of post-war male identity" (140). Furthermore, whereas *The Beardless Warriors* explored the actual combat experience, this novel explicitly references the difficulties faced by the ex-GI trying to reinsert himself into society, as the narrator relates Carey's thoughts:

> He was thinking about his application for life insurance. It had been part of the plan in coming East. First working for his brother, then applying for a GI loan with the idea of becoming a partner in Marty's business. Acquiring life and medical insurance, a bank account, a decent car, clothes, eventually a house. Building a structure of security around himself and his family [9].

Indeed, Carey's gradually shrinking stature, of course, renders these plans impossible and negatively impacts his status as a man, as Pulliam and Fonseca observe (78–83). While little critical energy has been expended upon Matheson's novel, its screen adaptation has been frequently suggested as symptomatic of the 1950s crisis in masculinity (Foster, "Monstrosity" 50; Hendershot 81, 139–40; Jancovich, *Rational* 129 ill.; Shapiro 115).

The novel gradually undermines its protagonist's image as a heterosexual male in the patriarchal society of the 1950s; as he shrinks in size, he shrinks in potency, and he becomes unable to provide materially for his family. Like many a fairy tale, Matheson's SF novel literalizes the metaphor, as its protagonist physically shrinks along with his figurative social status: "When it had begun, he was a six-footer. Now he looked straight across into his wife's eyes; and his wife was five feet, eight inches tall" (8). A few weeks later, she is "unable to hide her shock at seeing him four inches shorter than herself" (13). While he feels that "[t]his is the bottom, he thought, the very bottom. There is nothing lower than for a man to become an object of pity" (77), he realizes that it can get worse as his daughter loses her respect for him as he reaches her size. Eventually his wife, who has remained supportive—although no longer sexually interested in her boy-sized husband (30–32; 75)—finally snaps under the strain at his childish tantrums: "He'd yelled and ranted, his little face red, stamped his cunning high-topped shoes, glared up at her, until suddenly she'd turned from the sink and shouted back, 'Oh, stop squeaking at me!'" (92–93)

Not only is he called "kid" (21), and his wife strokes his cheek "as if he were a boy" (29), he mocks himself as he tries on his now oversized adult clothing—"He snickered hollowly at the child playing grownup" (43). Carey finally breaks down at the strain.

> He began to cry.
> It was not a man's crying, not a man's despairing sobs. It was a little boy sitting there in the cold, wet darkness, hurt and frightened and crying because there was no hope for him in the world; he was beaten and lost in a strange, unloving place [86].

As he loses the stature of a man, he loses his very manhood, as suggested by a scene of childhood cruelty. This time, the diminutive Carey leaves the house for a stroll and is cornered by a group of bullies. Their taunting takes an ambivalently homoerotic/homophobic turn:

> "Hey. The kid thinks we're funny," said the boy with the baseball cap on. "D'ya hear that, fellas. He thinks we're funny." His voice lost its banter. "Maybe we oughta show 'im how funny we are," he said.
> Scott felt a crawling sensation in his groin and lower stomach. He looked around at the boys, unable to keep down the fear [...].
> "We wouldn't wanna hurt a kid. Would we, fellas?"
> "Naw, we wouldn't want do *that*," said another [82].

The scene concludes as they call him "Freako" and threaten to "pull down his pants and see if *all* of him shrunk!" (84). While aggression trumps eroticism here, Scott's manhood is explicitly questioned; but a truly queer encounter—one apparently considered too risqué for inclusion in the novel's film adaptation *The Incredible Shrinking Man*—occurs in another episode.

Again, outside the safety of his home, a childlike Scott is confronted by a grown man who offers him a ride. "You alone, my boy? [...]. You alone, young fellow?" (52) Carey accepts the ride, and inadvertently sits on the man's hand in the car; going a step further, the man touches his leg (52–53). The passage's queer undertones are clear and the grown male driver's misogyny and his ethnic origins reinforce the sense of an encounter with a non-normative Other. The man reveals his minority status through his Cajun French interjections, *"mon cher"* and *"Mon dieu"* (53). He asks Carey, "You understand French, my boy. An excellent boy, a most seemly boy" (53), commenting on his physical attractiveness ("seemly"). The French coding, too, raises ambivalent flags linked to sexuality; on the one hand, for Anglo-Americans, French is the language of heterosexual love, as we refer to "French kisses" and condoms used to be called "French letters." At the same time, however, Frenchness also appears linked to effeminacy in the UK and the U.S., a foreign language for sissies spoken by effete intellectuals in berets and boat-neck striped jerseys. The driver's attitudes about women further undermine his heterosexuality, as he bewails the fate of a friend, Vincent (could Matheson have been thinking of Price as he wrote in the mid–1950s?), after his marriage, describing him as hen-pecked, emasculated:

> "And what," the man said, "was a *man*, dear boy, became, you see, a creature of degradation, a lackey, a serf, an automaton. A—in short—lost and shriveled soul [....] Women. Who come into a man's life a breath from the sewer." He belched. "A pox on the she [....] And dear Vincent," said the man, "lost to the eye of man. Swallowed in the spiritual quicksands of—" [54].

The ride comes to an abrupt halt as the unnamed driver asks Scott, "You like girls, my boy?"(55), and the shrinking man proffers a non-reply with an exemplary Freudian slip: "I get off here" (56).

Harry Benshoff invokes this incident in *Monsters in the Closet*, referring to Matheson's novel to make his case about the omnipresence of queer anxiety in the 1950s: "In many films of this period, young men were at risk from deviant sexual feelings [...] even the diminutive hero of Richard Matheson's famous science fiction novel *The Shrinking Man* finds himself the recipient of a drunken homosexual's attentions" (138–40). What Benshoff could not have known in the late 1990s is that, once again, the writer was inspired by events in his own life to stage this scene of a male sexual predator. In Matheson's fictionalized memoir *Generations* (2012), published only a year before his death, he exorcizes a number of personal and family demons, imagining his real-life family members therapeutically airing their dirty laundry in an imaginary gathering after his father's funeral. During this process, Matheson's fictional avatar confronts his mother with the unpleasant truth that he had been sexually abused at age 15 by a music teacher, reproaching her for her naïveté or her willingly blind refusal to see the danger she had put him in (111–15).

At the novel's conclusion, Carey has become imprisoned in his home's cellar having shrunk to the size of about two inches tall. At this point, not only his manhood, but his very existence is consistently under threat as he struggles to obtain food, water, shelter and safety from a variety of threats, the most notable of which is a black widow spider. Carey points out the symbolic nature of the beast, echoing the misogyny of the Cajun pedophile: "Black widow. Men called it that because the female destroyed and ate the male, if she got the chance, after one mating act" (15). But the third-person narrator also recalls Carey's military service after an initial battle with the (to him) oversized arachnid: "It reminded him of a time, long before, when he had been with the Infantry in Germany. He'd been so tired that he'd gone to sleep without digging a foxhole, knowing it might mean his death" (73). Readers will recall that the novel concludes with Carey's utter disappearance as he has shrunk down to molecular, even atomic size. In spite of his courageous battles to survive, the forces at work putting him in this perilous situation eventually win out.

Queering Robert Neville: Vincent Price as the Last Man on Earth

Whereas *The Shrinking Man* clearly explores the problem of masculine angst, Jamil Y. Khader builds a similar case regarding *I Am Legend* in a 2013 essay, "Will the Real Robert Neville Please, Come Out?: Vampirism, the Ethics of Queer Monstrosity, and Capitalism in Richard Matheson's *I Am Legend*." His work can be fruitfully applied to the casting choice of Vincent Price for the *Last Man on Earth* as participating in the perception of a crisis in masculinity fueling apocalyptic fears in the long 1950s. It is important to note here that the "queer" in queer theory is broadly defined as applying to any non-normative sexualities or gender performances and not limited to representations of homosexuality itself. Rather, as Benshoff explains,

> queer seeks to go beyond these and all such categories based on the concepts of normative heterosexuality and traditional gender roles to encompass a more inclusive, amorphous, and ambiguous contra-heterosexuality [...]. Queer is also insistent that issues of race, gender, disability, and class be addressed within its politics, making interracial sex and sex between two physically challenged people dimensions of queer sex also, and further linking the queer corpus with the figure of the Other as it has been theorized by [Robin] Wood in the horror film [5].

Given this broad definition and Chapter One's discussion of Robert Neville's battles with sexual desire in a world of the walking dead, the fact that it raises the specter of necrophilia opens Matheson's novel up to a queer reading, fully detailed in Khader's analysis. With the consummately queer actor Vincent Price cast in its lead role, *The Last Man on Earth* suggests as well an alternate reading of this film as not just another expression of Cold War anxiety about communism's threat to America, but as symptomatic of the gravity of the national crisis in white masculinity and its traditionally perceived prerogatives.

Two. Visualizing Apocalypse Through Compromised Masculinity 83

The previous chapter identified how Matheson's fiction engages the various anxieties of the returning World War II veteran, including among these a sense of compromised masculinity. Khader also links Matheson's "invocation of vampirism as a metaphor to embody the unspeakability of forbidden queer sexual desire [... to] Neville's military past" ("Will the Real" 537). Let us recall that Neville acquired his immunity to the vampire plague bacillus because he was inoculated by a bat bite during the war in Panama. Among other compelling indices, Khader rests his arguments on an intriguing, and repeated, invocation that neighbor-turned-vampire Ben Cortman uses to interpellate the bunkered Robert Neville: "Come out, Neville" (Matheson, *Legend* 18, 20, 148). Whereas Khader concludes that in Matheson's novel Neville never answers Cortman's calls, ultimately disavowing any homosexual desire, its first film adaptation allows Neville to take a few steps out of his closet, so to speak, precisely because of its casting of Vincent Price as Robert Morgan.

Khader considers the usual contextualization of *I Am Legend* within the anxieties produced by its Cold War setting, but he also makes an original connection between the anti-communist witch hunt initiated by Senator Joe McCarthy and its anti-homosexual paranoia. In addition, the 1948 publication of Alfred Kinsey's report on *Sexual Behavior in the Human Male*, "the emergent gay liberation politics of the early 1950s" which occurred precisely in the novel's Los Angeles setting (Khader, "Will the Real" 540), and Matheson's engagement with critical discourses about the persecution of a group identified as a threatening Other, all allow Khader to flesh out a more specific context for his queer reading of *I Am Legend*. He thus argues that not only is Robert Neville's sexual frustration "ambiguously coded to surpass and subvert the heteronormative ideals of suburban masculinity" (533), his bunker-like home can be read as a metaphor for the closet (535).

From the moment it introduces its protagonist, we can read *LMoE* queerly, as the camera voyeuristically peers into the bedroom window of a fully dressed, but disheveled man lying prone in his bed, it signals Morgan's vulnerability, but the viewer also sees Price's delicately mustachioed good looks. Still asleep, he becomes the passive object of the camera's gaze, rather than the active subject a mid-twentieth-century American man should be. Prone, he seems younger than in the following sequence, where he appears as a hunched-over, frumpy middle-aged man. Further hints of his compromised masculinity appear in his less-than-ironclad stomach as he both expresses what is at stake here, but also declares his lack of readiness for it: "They want my blood; their lives are mine; I still get squeamish." As the object of the vampires' desires, Morgan is feminized, his nausea a reaction to their boundary-violating, abject lust.

As a vampire hunter, Morgan's agency is restored; the film displaces, however, the original Neville's frustrated sexual desire for the female walkers he encounters with more explicit aggression. Morgan has clearly overcome his nausea during the montage extermination sequence, his first execution vividly depicted as a rape. The slaying montage suggestively depicts Morgan as a serial rapist and murderer, indiscriminately attacking men and women, an active predator—thus perhaps more "masculine" since he has become an aggressive agent—but certainly not "normal."

Various changes made to Matheson's original storyline further allow for a ludic queer reading of *LMoE*'s characterization of Morgan. For example, rather than the classical music that Neville collects, he prefers jazz. Not only does his musical taste suggest perhaps an openness to the Other, jazz being a musical form that originated in African American culture, it also associates him with the Beat Generation open to more alternative, bohemian lifestyles. Its tense rhythms, rather than soothe him or the savage beasts outside, however, simply agitate. As an exterior shot reveals the shuffling, stumbling horde approaching his door, it individualizes a single figure capable of verbal communication: a youngish, formerly handsome blonde man in a suit, who signals the others to follow him. Carrying a (phallic?) two-by-four, he repeatedly calls out: "Morgan, come out, out [....] Morgan, out, come out." This repetition, almost word-for-word, of the passage that Khader singles out to begin making his case for a queer reading of Matheson's novel, also functions in this queer reading of *LMoE* as it introduces Ben Cortman, as a rough equivalent of Pharr's "king vampire."

Following Benshoff, it is tempting to read Cortman as involved with Morgan in a homoerotic triangle like those he analyzes in a number of horror films from the 1930s through the 1960s. Not only does Ben introduce the protagonist to the audience by giving him a name ("Morgan"), he takes affective priority over Morgan's wife since the film introduces Ben both visually and audibly *before* Virginia is shown to the audience. Not only does *LMoE* thus underscore the relationship between Robert and Ben, it also represents the *only* filmic text to maintain intact this significant secondary character from the original novel. Subsequent adaptations thus largely evacuate the text of similar possibilities for a queer reading. By effacing the connection between these two men, *The Omega Man*, *I Am Legend* and *I Am Omega* foreclose slash interpretations like the one that follows.

We learn the backstory for the odd couple, Morgan-Cortman, via home movies that allow the viewer a glimpse of life before the apocalypse. The first image is that of a beautiful young woman and infant, our first visual for "Virge"; the very next clip reveals the same woman, paired with a handsome young blonde man. At first, we presume that he is her husband and the little girl with them, their daughter. The conventions of heteronormative Hollywood cinema allow the viewer to interpret this image shot from Morgan's viewpoint, as he both took the home movies and watches them in the post-apocalypse. On one level, we know that this is Morgan's wife and daughter, and that he is filming them at a social gathering with a family friend. Read queerly, however, this image begins to suggest that Ben and Virginia would form a more appropriate couple than the middle-aged Morgan and Virginia. But by placing the handsome young Ben in the center of the frame the image focuses visual desire on him rather than on the woman. The home movie then cuts to the family attending a circus, and in flashback as Morgan begins to laugh at the clowns, his laughter dissolves into a present-day fit of hysteria. As the vampires' thumping outside begins again, he breaks down sobbing, exhibiting a clearly "feminine" lack of control over his emotions.

To complete the homosocial horror triangle, however, Morgan's two love interests are juxtaposed as the very next speech heard after Cortman's hollow-voiced invocation, "Come out," are Virginia's cries of suffering in her husband's dream. Yet she appears masculinized; not only are her cries uttered in a startlingly low voice for a woman, the first time that Morgan addresses her in memory, he uses a masculine-sounding diminutive of her name, crying over her tomb, "Virge, Virge? By gosh I miss you!"[13] Furthermore, our first images of the married couple's relationship—as in Price's interpretations of both Locke in "Morella" (*Tales of Terror*) and Verden Fell in *The Tomb of Ligeia*—verge on the necrophiliac. After his night-long assault from Ben and his undead buddies, Morgan drives out to the cemetery to visit his wife's tomb; much like Roderick Usher and the other Poe characters Price had recently and will continue to play for the rest of the decade, he has placed her casket in an elaborate chapel mausoleum. Unable to move forward emotionally, he remains tied to the past; he ritualistically lights the candles he has carefully placed there, touches the coffin, sitting beside it to talk to "Virge." The only witness to this monologue is Christ on a crucifix hanging over the altar, signaling the sadomasochistic aspects of the Passion and foreshadowing Morgan's later death in a similar, ecclesiastical location. He confusingly addresses someone whom we do not yet know to be his wife with this masculine sounding nickname; physically and emotionally exhausted, he falls asleep, suggestively draped over the marble casket.

The central flashback sequences recount how Virginia has died and Robert's post-mortem treatment of her. Having seen his daughter's corpse dumped into a mass grave and burned, Morgan refuses a similar fate for his wife. Defying the state of emergency regulations, the theme of necrophilia returns, overtly signaled as the woman always referred to as "Virge" utters her last cries, as Morgan looks out the window, surveying the street—checking, we realize, for signs of the authorities. Upstairs, like so many of Price's other film wives in the Corman-Poe Cycle, the deceased Virginia is laid on the master bed. In denial about this, as about all of his other perversions, Morgan says, "No. No, I won't let them put you there, Virge." He carries her out of the house in a white shroud-like bed sheet; accompanied by the sounds of the blowing wind, he places her not in the back of the hearse-like station wagon but rather in the front, where she rides next to him like a still living passenger, although her face remains covered by the shroud. Borrowing other types of imagery from horror films, reversing the work of the body snatchers, or imitating the work of a serial killer, he takes her body out to the moors for a clandestine burial. The film thus effectively begins blurring the lines between the man and the monster. Morgan returns to their still immaculate home and pours himself a drink. As if he had killed her with his own hands, the trope of the revenant avenging herself on her murderer is invoked, as Virginia returns from the grave to claim her rightful husband. Just as Matheson's novel relied on the sounds of the vampires outside clattering away at Neville's bunker, *LMoE* also uses sound to effect, as Morgan hears a vague, but clearly feminine whispering before he sees the doorknob being turned from outside, the ultimate horror cliché. In a reversal of Cortman's call to "come out," the now phallic corpse bride penetrates her husband's haven, groaning in an ever louder and more insistent voice, "Let me in." Price inscribes Morgan's growing sense of horror and realization on his face, asking, uselessly, for we all already *know*: "Who is it?"

Morgan steels his courage by demanding more aggressively, "Who's there?" As he turns the knob, the music swells and we first see only a haloed silhouette, the outline of Virginia's distinctive hairstyle. As she walks into the room, however, her disheveled state and Price's expression of pop-eyed terror signal her predatory nature; mouth open, hands up and opening toward him, Virginia-the-vampire—whom we read today as the proto-zombie—advances relentlessly toward Morgan, as the female vocal chorus of the soundtrack swells menacingly. She croaks out his name, "Robert, Robert," as he retreats, shadow now covering his eyes. As if a scene too horrible to bear, at this point of high tension, the shot, reverse-shot images begin to blur, transitioning the viewer out of the flashback and back to Morgan's present existence as the *Last Man on Earth*.

Prior to the flashback sequence, viewers had already seen Virginia's rival for Morgan's affections, an as yet unidentified Ben Cortman, lead the nightly assault on Morgan's home, repeatedly banging at its door with his phallic two-by-four. In earlier sequences, he utters the iconic, "Come out, Morgan, come out!" later making the exact nature of the horde's threat more explicit: "We're going to kill you, Morgan [...]. Do you hear, Morgan? Do you hear?" Returning home late from the cemetery, Morgan engages in one of a handful of hand-to-hand struggles with the vampires. Cortman wields his phallic two-by-four, a caveman's equivalent of Morgan's precisely lathed stakes, but Morgan uses a mirror to fend the creature off. Unable to bear the image of his no-longer handsome self, Cortman cringes as Morgan reaches the house.

Not completely inarticulate, another walker cries "Ow! Ow!" as Morgan brutally slams his arm in the closing door. Ben's nightly assaults target not just Morgan's life and blood, but also his heterosexual virtue, as he calls him out again, "Morgan, do you hear, Morgan; Morgan, do you hear, Morgan?" The camera tracks in for a close-up, Price's voice-over, "Three years," indicates how long he has had to bear up under these conditions, as the image goes out of focus to transition to the first actual flashback.

These flashbacks fill in the details about Morgan's relationship to Ben Cortman. Reprising the birthday party featured in the home movie, a blurred dissolve technique reveals Morgan filming the party below in the garden, with Virginia standing next to him. This fluid imagery undermines the solidity of the couple's relationship. As the birthday girl finishes counting her seven candles, Morgan turns the camera on "Virge." Aping her role as modest housewife, she cries, "Oh, no. My make-up, my hair," words which belie her pleasure as she smiles for the camera and fluffs up her perfectly smooth sixties helmet-hair. At this moment, we hear a deep voice, "Hey, where is everybody," and see a figure laden with presents cross the threshold into this domestic scene. As he mentions that he can hear the party, but "I can't see any children," he eerily predicts one of the final symptoms of the illness that causes the transformation of humanity into a horde of vampires. The birthday girl's cries of, "Uncle Ben, Uncle Ben," both signal his familiarity to the household, but also add an incestuous spin to this queer reading. It is not made clear if he is a literal Uncle, thus Virginia's brother—the two are both stunning blonde beauties—or simply a figurative one. Just as he had filmed Virge, Morgan films the handsome new arrival with his daughter, creating a parallel with his beautiful wife. The frame returns to the trio of Virginia, Ben, and Kathy, underscoring the May-November nature of Morgan's marriage, again suggesting that a pairing between Ben and Virginia would be more appropriate. Thus, whereas Rebecca Janicker remarks that "Matheson's fiction expresses a general unease with regard to gender relations, which is especially pronounced as far as the subject of sex is concerned" (117), an assertion which clearly includes *I Am Legend*, its first film adaptation reveals that this "general unease" has developed into a full-blown crisis.

The viewer is clearly struck by the warm relationship between Ben and Virginia and the disequilibrium in age and conventional attractiveness between Virginia and her husband; the film suggests not only the queer possibility that Robert should "come out" about his relationship with Ben, but that Ben and Virginia may have had an affair. In stark contrast with the children's joyful play in the large suburban yard, complete with a merry-go-round, the adults' conversation turns grim. Now Morgan and Ben are framed together; the older man standing, the younger seated, suggestive of their hierarchal professional relationship. As Morgan clears away the gift boxes and paper, literally setting aside childish things, Ben pulls a newspaper clipping out of his breast pocket: "Take a look at this." Morgan reads the headlines revealing the nature of the disaster that has occurred, leading to the circumstances of his present tense. His tone of voice and gestures toward Ben are somewhat condescending; as Morgan sits on the table at which Ben is seated, Virginia arrives and takes the paper from her husband's hand. At one point, he almost completely obscures her, asserting his authority, which is immediately undermined as she asks not her husband, but Ben for his opinion.

The headline reads, "Is Europe's disease carried on the wind?" At this point, we still wonder, just what can Europe's disease be? Of course, we will soon learn about the vampire plague, but a queer reading suggests perhaps decadent perversions and accompanying venereal diseases coming from an effeminate "Europe" which had been reduced to a shambles during World War II, recovering only through U.S. aid with the Marshall Plan, now playing second fiddle to the U.S. as the torch-bearer of Western civilization. Furthermore, GIs on duty in Europe were repeatedly warned against contracting venereal diseases while stationed in Europe. In denial, Morgan refuses to believe the headlines, yet he utters these in Price's quintessentially fey voice. The three adults appear interestingly framed, not literally as a triangle, but certainly making a clear angle, with Ben still seated on the left, Virginia standing and so a bit higher and in the center of the frame, with the tall Morgan at the right.

During their conversation, not heated or an argument, but rather a concerned discussion involving divergent points of view, Morgan takes exception to Ben's insinuation that he is in denial about the nature of the plague, asking "Is that a comment on my work at the lab?" Ben replies, "We all know how hard you've been working." Again, we read into this innocent comment, wondering if Morgan has been working too hard and thus perhaps losing his grip on the facts. We might wonder if he has been away at the office too much, who is taking care of Virginia and Kathy (is it Ben?); or, conversely, does he fit the trope of the 1960s husband covering up an extramarital affair with the excuse of work? Still the doubting Thomas, Morgan ends the conversation, "I just can't accept the idea of universal disease." This denial points both to societal unpreparedness for most major historical epidemics and the actual difficulties of fighting such contagions. Again, reading the disease queerly, in this pre–AIDS film, homosexuality itself maybe the decadence coming from Europe, or even the internal threat as the Kinsey report had so recently provided statistics for the much more widespread prevalence of homosexual activity even among men considered "straight," suggesting a continuum of desire rather than a black and white hetero-/homo- dichotomy. At this point Kathy interrupts the adults placing her own claims on Uncle Ben's attention; "Who can resist that face?" he asks. "Virge" moves to Ben's vacated chair, and

Two. Visualizing Apocalypse Through Compromised Masculinity 89

Robert literally talks down to her, the silly woman, in an avuncular rather than husbandly manner, emphasized by the 25 year disparity in age between the two actors, Price (1911–1993) and Danieli (1936–1998). For only the second time—the first perhaps when she mugged it up for her husband's camera— we see the married couple act as such. As Virginia rises to answer Kathy's calls to cut the cake, Robert takes her hand, pulls him toward her and gives her a kiss on the cheek. This expression of affection, however, is not done in close-up as a romantic scene would have been filmed, but rather in a medium shot from a relative distance.

As a later flashback reveals that the contagion has struck his family, Morgan leaves his sick wife and daughter at home; the laboratory thus becomes an excuse for dodging his responsibilities as a husband and father, as much perhaps a commentary on the 1950s and 1960s professional pressures placed on men to excel in the public sphere, leaving the private to their wives. Reading queerly, however, he significantly has come to pick up Ben on the way to the lab; his handsome young colleague proves more attractive and interesting than the heteronormative household he escapes. Indeed, Ben comes to the door in a bathrobe, again placing him in parallel with Virginia, still in pajamas at a time of day that respectable people would be immaculately dressed. "What's the matter with you?" asks Morgan; "Nothing, and I'm going to keep it that way." Having stayed home from work to avoid the contagion, Ben's paranoia will later prove justified, but the men's discussion soon engages the time-worn clichés of a lover's break up. "Look, let's talk about this," pleads Morgan. "There's nothing to talk about," insists Ben: "You think I'm out of my mind; you laughed at me and my theory." "You might be one of them," says Ben, ironically, as we know he will become the vampire, but also introducing a certain homophobia, fearing that Morgan may be "one of them." Furthermore, still prevailing discourses identifying homosexuality as an illness are engaged, as Morgan says, "You ought to see a doctor." Angrily, Ben responds: "You take care of your life; I'll take care of mine. Get away from here!" Thus ends their relationship in life, with Cortman angrily rejecting a hurt and confused Morgan, in a clichéd version of a lover's spat. As in Matheson's novel, dialogue easily allows for a *double-entendre* reading, in which the vampire contagion doubles for non-normative sexualities.

Besides his non-normative relationships with a much younger wife which develops into a Poe-esque form of necrophilia and his closeted homosexual desire for his colleague, Morgan's relationship with Ruth, the new society's ambassadress further supports a queer reading of the film. His initial aggression appears almost "normal" in its hegemonic masculinity; amazed at the sight of another "human" being, he chases her across an expanse of grass, a park or a golf course. Once they enter his home, however, Morgan appears emasculated and their interactions are largely evacuated of the sexual tension that subtends this encounter in Matheson's novel. The now mild-mannered Dr. Morgan gently expresses his concern, offers coffee, like a good pre-apocalyptic host (or hostess?). Indeed, Neville's sexual angst is replaced in this film by Ruth Collins' sexual aggression toward Morgan: she plans to use sexuality, like a Mata Hari, in the interest of her mission. She makes it clear, "I was married. I lost my husband," immediately signaling her availability. She tells him, "You are alone. You were married? Children?" This invocation of his wife reminds Morgan; he goes to the kitchen to test her with garlic; she startles, rising, now feeling threatened, "What are you doing?" He appears to gain sadistic pleasure from her discomforted aversion to the iconic bulb, insistently asking, "Why do you turn away?" She uses her feminine wiles to convince him otherwise, asking, "Facts? What facts?" Offering an alternate explanation for her aversion, "I've had a sensitive stomach all my life," Ruth builds a fabric of lies to gain Morgan's trust, to learn about him for her own society's purposes. Despite her late-coming warning to Morgan, she is a *femme fatale*.

Other signs link Ruth to a different contemporary social concern, the 1950s beatniks evolving into hippies by the end of the 1960s. Partially seen as emulating the style and mores of the Beat Generation of writers, referenced in the title of a 1959 serial killer film scripted by Matheson, these forerunners of the counterculture were portrayed to comic effect in the popular media. Episodes of *The Munsters* (1964–1966) and *The Addams Family* (1964–1966) mocked artsy beatnik types, and even Sissy falls in with such a crowd to Uncle Bill's consternation in *Family Affair* (1966–1971). Frequent Matheson collaborator Roger Corman also exploited social fears of these nonconformists in films like *A Bucket of Blood* (1959) and *Little Shop of Horrors* (1960). With her disheveled hair, short skirt, paired with calf-high boots, and Virginia's black sweater, Ruth resembles an artsy marginal. Furthermore her "infection," which Morgan of course discovers, may be read as a venereal disease, since Morgan wants to clear up any confusion about her status by giving her a blood test. As he calms down after her cries of "don't touch me!" and offers to fix her some dinner, the fact that she is hiding something returns. Morgan should be more perceptive when she "can't" eat, ostensibly nervous as we hear once again the nightly assault begins outside. When he is distracted by the horde outside, Ruth grabs her throat, as if the garlic had caused an anaphylactic reaction making it difficult for her to breathe; we later discover she needs an injection—like a heroin addict—a drug linked to the jazz Robert listens to and her beatnik look. Hearing her groans, which resemble depictions of withdrawal, Neville bursts in on her as she is about to shoot up; she hides her face in shame. "You are one of them!" "I was, and without that injection I'll be one again." She tells the truth and explains the existence of the new society. She takes "defebrinated blood plus vaccine; the blood feeds the germ, the vaccine keeps it isolated" (155). As they discuss the possibility of finding a cure, the dialogue subtly invokes not only the notion of a venereal disease, but also then contemporary discourses of the pathologization of homosexuality (see Benshoff and Griffin 86–88). While Ruth claims to fear her malady is incurable, Morgan hopes again, thinking he can create a serum.

Their conversation reveals a turning point in the film and its identifications of normalcy and monstrosity, as she asks how he can get used to "them," revealing that the "new society" shares Morgan's prejudices. He answers: "I'm not frightened of them anymore if that's what you mean. I protect myself against them, but only because there's so many." As Cortman again cries, "Come out, Morgan," we're again tempted to ask what kind of "protection" Morgan means. His words and actions belie, perhaps, Morgan's assertion that, "intellectually, they're weak. Mentally incompetent, like animals, after all." He actually explains his relationship: "Hear that. That's Ben Cortman. He was my friend [...]. He was like a kid brother." But he then insists, "When I find him, I'll drive a stake through him, just like all the others." Morgan expresses an ambivalence to the queer-coded Cortman similar to Neville's dialogue about prejudice toward vampires; he is sympathetic to and at the same time unwilling fully to embrace the Other.

What Morgan is more shocked or excited about is Ruth's indication that "we've had it for some time now." "We! We!" he shakes her, disillusioned about her status as lone damsel in distress. Now realizing the extent of her deception, he demands the truth, growing bitter: "And I was going to cure you. Does that amuse you?" She explains: "We're alive. Infected yes, but alive. We're going to reorganize society." The camera, which had been shooting their conversation in a medium two-shot, with both actors partially in profile, now changes angles, showing Ruth alone and in close-up to describe the new order of humanity. As she expresses the wish to "[g]et rid of all those loathsome creatures who are neither alive nor dead," we see the rings under her eyes, and she appears less human, her skin slightly darkened. A reaction shot reveals a concerned Neville, as she asserts: "Start everything all over again." When he proposes that they want him to join them, she relies on an essentialist vision of society as racial or ethnically based, retorting, "You can't join us. You're a monster to them. Why do you think I ran when I saw you, even though I was assigned to spy on you. Because I was so terrified." In this sequence of shot/reverse shots, Price's face reveals Morgan's growing shock as Ruth invokes the conclusion of Matheson's novel, "You're a legend in the city. Moving by day instead of night. Leaving the evidence of your existence behind. Bloodless corpses. Many of the people you destroyed were still alive! Many were the loved ones of people in my group." *LMoE* thus allows Ruth's accusation to undermine the righteousness of Morgan's campaign, following Matheson's novel. Through the casting of Vincent Price as the Last Man on Earth, though, and underscoring the potentially queer nature of his relationship with Cortman, it also points toward new concerns and anxieties for the 1960s. As we have seen, while it continues to evoke the trauma of World War II—particularly through its location shooting in Rome—it expresses great anxieties about male sexuality. Although it does not go so far as to suggest that the apocalypse has occurred because of the scourge of homosexuality, read through the lens of queer theory, it provides a vehicle for the exploration of a number of non-normative gender performances and non-heteronormative sexual desires.

Matheson's "The Night Creatures"

Unhappy with the changes made to his screenplay for the AIP production, Matheson used his pen name for co-credit with William F. Leicester, as seen in the opening credits for *LMoE*. Matheson's recently published script for the original Hammer project titled "The Night Creatures" reveals that a good proportion of his own adaptation was respected. His mark remains on the film from the unproduced screenplay's description of the opening sequence, to various motifs like the "dark and greasy pall of smoke" (Matheson, "Night" 33), through tidbits of dialogue, such as Cortman's gift-laden arrival at Kathy's birthday party. A brief examination of the differences between "The Night Creatures" and *LMoE*, however, sheds further light on how the film reflects the contemporary climate and how the writer's words were altered to suit producers' ideas of what filmgoers wanted.

First and foremost, it should be mentioned that the precise reason that Matheson's script was not used either by Hammer or by AIP can be traced to conservative mores in the UK and the U.S. in the late 1950s and early 1960s. After Hammer Films had rejected the script due to fears of censorship by the British board in 1957, it was submitted to the Motion Picture Association of America (MPAA) (Dawidziak 14–15). *Visions Deferred: Three Unfilmed Screenplays by Richard Matheson* (2009) includes their letter, which objects to the language and violence of the project. At that time words like "bastards," "hell," "damn," and references to "God" (violations of the fourth commandment not to take the Lord's name in vain) were unacceptable on American screens. The letter cites instances of "[b]rutality and gruesomeness" during Neville's battles with the vampires as also inappropriate (Dawidziak 29); even an instance of "retching" is considered potentially "troublesome" (Dawidziak 30). The sanitized script by Leicester for *LMoE* contains, of course, none of this objectionable material; Price's dialogue is appropriate for all audiences, and the actual staking of vampires during slaying sequences, for example, occurs off camera. But apart from measures taken to please the censors, what else was changed?

Two. Visualizing Apocalypse Through Compromised Masculinity

Some alterations appear rather anodyne and probably enhanced the film's aesthetic quality; for example, Price's voice-over narration replaces Matheson's device of a written journal in which his Neville (he did not, of course, change his protagonist's name in "Night Creatures") relates the backstory for his current circumstances. Rather than blowing across the Pacific from Europe, headlines read that the "ASIAN PLAGUE [IS] SPREADING" (43); this early geography of the menace may have originally made more sense when it was written for Hammer Films in England. Other changes, however, appear more significant; some may be related to the casting of Price, but the most dramatic and surprising change of all remains puzzling. For, Matheson himself radically altered the conclusion of his novel as he conceived its adaptation to the screen.

In keeping with the present interpretation's discussion of Price's problematic sexuality as a star persona, it makes sense that William F. Leicester removed all references to a sexual relationship between Morgan and Ruth in the final version of *LMoE*. In Matheson's "Night Creatures," however, although the film's conclusion suggests that Ruth has developed sympathy for Neville her role as a Mata Hari–like *femme fatale* is taken even further than in the novel. Indeed, Ruth and Neville kiss (164) and the morning-after sequence—chaste by today's standards—implies that they have slept together (164–65). Matheson's script suggests rather than shows in a manner appropriate to the time period so it is unclear that this change was made in anticipation of censors' objections. In fact, Leicester's decision to cut references to a sexualized relationship between Morgan and Ruth alters viewers' perceptions of the character. Furthermore, Matheson's Neville in "Night Creatures" retains his working class status (indeed, he has to borrow Cortman's car to bury Virginia, not owning one of his own until after the apocalypse).

As does his literary model, the unfilmed Neville must learn the scientific method on his own, consulting books in the library and painfully learning how to use a microscope. It is thus clear that for Matheson Neville's working-class status and his self-taught approach to science were core elements of the character and his story as originally conceived. Perhaps Leicester thought these sequences held little dramatic potential or that a middle-class scientist protagonist better fit audience expectations, but these changes further alter the nature of the ambiguous hero.

Yet, the most dramatic change to his original story introduced by Matheson in "The Night Creatures" did *not* seem appropriate to Leicester who maintained the novel's key event: Neville's/Morgan's demise. In contrast, at the conclusion of Matheson's screenplay Neville does not die, but rather Ruth has convinced the "new society" (168) of his potential value to them. When the black-clad men arrive at Neville's home, slaying Cortman and his cohorts, the protagonist is convinced that he will be killed next. Instead, Ruth explains:

"you're too valuable to kill. You [sic] immunity to the germ is worth more to us that [sic]—" (174). She then leads a "dazed, still not completely aware" Neville away from his home and to the new society's compound (175); his last concerns are for his home, as he utters the final words of the script in "a sorrowful whisper": "My *house* ..." (175). Matheson's conclusion seems puzzling for a number of reasons. Although he maintains a certain level of rugged masculinity, including sexual desire for what he believes to be another human woman, Matheson completely emasculates his character with this pitiful conclusion. Instead of the novel's Neville who bravely accepts his fate as inevitable, extinguishing humanity with his death, leaving the Earth to the new order of beings, "The Night Creatures" Neville becomes a befuddled victim. At the same time his survival appears to signal humanity's renewal as Ruth's words suggest that his blood will be used to cure her people.

In the end, although it largely exonerated Morgan's slaying activities through its depiction of the brutality of the black-shirted men, in its conclusion *The Last Man on Earth* thus remains truer to Matheson's novel than the author's own scenario. With Morgan's death, accompanied by his parting shot, "You're freaks, all of you. I am the last man," the Vincent Price vehicle makes clear that humanity as we know it will not survive this pandemic, an "evolutionary process," as Dr. Mercer described it in the lab, is at work. The filmed version thus offers a more faithful rendition of the nihilistic conclusion of Matheson's novel than the author's own unproduced scenario did. It is, then, not insignificant that Matheson altered the title, shifting the focus away from Neville and his acceptance of his fate in the novel's title and final lines, "I am legend," and onto those who will inherit the earth, "The Night Creatures."

Conclusion

In addition to their exploration of the fate of the ex-GI attempting to reinsert himself into society, Matheson's novels *The Shrinking Man* and *I Am Legend* engage the contemporary crisis in masculinity. This kernel of angst becomes magnified in the novel's first film adaptation through the casting of Vincent Price—an actor frequently coded as queer—in the lead role of *LMoE*. That film, in addition to its expression of contemporary apocalyptic anxieties and concerns about fascism/communism, can also fruitfully be read as an expression of the intensity of the crisis in American masculinity. Its association of the vampire plague with non-normative forms of sexuality, including Ben Cortman's homosexual desire for Morgan and Morgan's own effeminacy, can only be read in hindsight in association with how the AIDS epidemic will be spun as divine punishment for a decadence infecting Western civilization. In the meantime, however, the seeds planted with World War II's function as a catalyst for the Civil Rights movement, the forced integration of public schools, and race riots in major urban centers in the late 1960s will bring race to the fore as America's primary concern. This, then, will be the preoccupying subtext of the next film adaptation of Matheson's novel, *The Omega Man*, which—by the overtly rugged Charlton Heston in the role of Neville and reframing its critical discourse to address the apparently more immediate concern of race relations—seems to indicate that the crisis in masculinity has at least partially been addressed by the year of its release, 1971.

Three

The Last White Man on Earth
Charlton Heston in *The Omega Man*

> *"The very foundations of civilization are beginning to crumble under that adversary long feared: germ warfare"* (News anchor Jonathan Mathias in *The Omega Man*).
>
> *"There's never a cop around when you need one."*
> *"Bah, not my color"* (Col. Robert Neville).
>
> *"It's okay, Tommy, this is the man, and I mean the man, but he's cool"* (Lisa).

Apart from its conclusion, which repositions its lone human as norm and the new race of mutants as "freaks," *The Last Man on Earth* offered a relatively faithful rendering of *I Am Legend*. *The Omega Man*, however, the next big screen version of Matheson's 1954 novel, reworks the core narrative to such an extent that it at first appears almost no longer an adaptation, but rather, in Ryan Baker's words, "only mildly similar" (197). Matheson describes it as having "*no* resemblance to the book" (Dawidziak 18). Aside from the main character's name, restored to Matheson's original (Robert Neville) and the core plot driver (a plague has left him as the last man on earth), almost everything in Boris Sagal's film is different. One explanation for this great gap between the original and its second film adaptation lies in the extent to which American society had changed in the intervening years. Whereas Matheson's novel and *LMoE* were both produced in the period referred to as the "long 1950s" (Booker 25), a time of post-war economic prosperity dampened only by the vague menace of the Cold War, historians have seen the dates 1965 and 1968 as hinge years, plunging the U.S. into the immediate uncertainties of racial violence, student protest, and the divisive military intervention in Vietnam. The socio-historical context of *The Omega Man* (henceforth *TOM*), released in 1971, then, is arguably exponentially different than that of Matheson's novel and its first screen adaptation. After outlining some of the major changes introduced to the film cycle, including a new identity for its monsters, this chapter unpacks how the casting of Charlton Heston repositions the film in relation to evolving images of masculinity. Above all, it analyzes the film's engagement with this period's most divisive social issues, "race and civil rights" (Patterson, *Eve* 3), as well as the military conflict that "divided American society at every level" (Dumbrell 1), the Vietnam War. Before concluding, it takes a brief look at several precursor films' treatment of race and interracial romance, and how they contributed to this film's visual depiction of the apocalypse and the last humans on earth.

Matheson's novel and Boris Sagal's film have been read respectively as allegories of white anxiety about Civil Rights and integration (K. Patterson) and the Black Power movement and the race riots of the late 1960s (Baker; Nama), as well as more generalized class anxiety about the hungry, urban hordes (Pharr). The novella's protagonist, Robert Neville, has been interpreted as a manly pioneer figure (Krulik), and certainly the casting of Charlton Heston, read as a model of virility with integrity (Raymond; Jancovich), appears to reinforce this view of the tale as an allegory of heroism (Brooks). If we scratch below the surface, placing it under closer scrutiny, *TOM* presents a much more ambivalent treatment of these issues.

"I Am the Beginning and the End": Charlton Heston and The Omega Man

Until the major success of Francis Lawrence's 2007 eponymous adaptation of Matheson's *I Am Legend*, *The Omega Man*, a free adaptation partially spear-headed by its star Charlton Heston, had received the most critical attention of the film versions. Considered a cult classic in the postapocalyptic genre, the film's script—drafted by married couple John William Corrington and Joyce Hooper Corrington—maintains relatively few of the novel's key elements. Here, Robert Neville has become an all-out action hero, his nemesis a cult of mutants with a mastermind leader, and a group of apparently normal human survivors replaces the infected "new society." The greatest change of all was, of course, to drain the life's blood from the novel's brilliantly subversive ending, allowing Heston's Neville to become the unambiguously Christ-like savior of humanity. And yet, like the other texts examined here, it offered a parable for its time that resonated with a mass audience far greater than that of its original story or the limited release low-budget feature, which had starred Vincent Price.

Released August 1, 1971, *TOM* engaged recent events such as the urban race riots of the late 1960s, Charles Manson and his Family's murder spree, urban flight, and the Vietnam War. Taking full advantage of its big-budget, Technicolor production values, its look and tone drew upon recent trends in film and fashion, including Blaxploitation action films, socially conscious SF films, and the counterculture. No wonder many fans of Matheson's work felt betrayed by what his claustrophobic little novel had become in the hands of the Corringtons, Charlton Heston, director Boris Sagal, and the entire Warner Bros. studio apparatus. As was the case with Vincent Price, this film's leading man steals what is in any case largely a one-man show; indeed, Jeff Rovin asserts that "it was Heston who was responsible for the film's being made" (204).

In his autobiography Charlton Heston (1923–2008)[1] recounts that in the late sixties, he "stumbled across, *I Am Legend*" (*Arena* 433); Jeff Rovin says that he learned of Matheson's novel from Orson Welles (204). In any case, he decided that

> there was surely a film [there]. It rested on a familiar but evergreen concept, a universal fantasy that seems to have invaded everyone's imagination and launched a thousand speculations: What would you do if you were the last man on earth? It's the dark side of the Genesis story of the creation of Adam, the first man—the end instead of the beginning [Heston, *Arena* 434].

He brought the novel to the attention of producer Walter Seltzer and the two apparently collaborated throughout the project's development (Heston, *Arena* 433–35). Because of his seminal role in bringing this new adaptation of *I Am Legend* to the big screen and the fact that his star persona—so very different from that of Vincent Price, although both had become typecast—plays a key role in how the novel was adapted to become *TOM*, a discussion of his career is pertinent here.

Heston was born in backwoods Michigan in 1923, but his parents' "traumatic" (Raymond 10) divorce brought him to Illinois where his stepfather worked in a steel plant. Having arrived as a hick and a loner, the teenage Heston got involved in extracurricular activities like drama and sports to fit in and eventually excel (Raymond 9–12). Of a generation with Matheson, Heston served in World War II as a sergeant in the Eleventh Air Force and was posted to Alaska (Raymond 13). Heston's "lower-middle-class or working-class" origins (Raymond 2) would later be reflected in the types of roles he played, roles which typically featured his rugged masculinity; it would also perhaps serve as a point of identification in his later political-activist career for the National Rifle Association. However, as Emilie Raymond observes in her perceptive study *From My Cold Dead Hands: Charlton Heston and American Politics* (2006), Heston did not become a registered Republican until 1987. Instead, during the 1950s and 1960s Heston had "used his celebrity status to promote causes and programs generally associated with the Democrats" (Raymond 1). Indeed, Heston walked in the Civil Rights March on Washington as part of the "Arts Group," actors committed to passage of the civil rights bill, and he gave limited support to the political campaigns of Lyndon Johnson (1964), Hubert Humphrey (1968), and—changing party allegiance—Richard Nixon (1972). He also served on the National Council on the Arts and the NEA under Johnson and Nixon (Raymond 5).

Heston's career as an actor began in high school, which earned him a drama scholarship to Northwestern University, where he met his future wife Lydia Marie Clarke. After the war, the couple moved to New York City, working as artist's models until their theatrical careers took off. In contrast with his later image as a rugged action hero, Heston frequently performed in Shakespeare productions. His appearance in the film noir *Dark City* (1950) launched his Hollywood career, but he became a household name after the biblical epics, *The Ten Commandments* (1956), *Ben-Hur* (1959), and *The Greatest Story Ever Told* (1965). Both Steven Cohan and Mark Jancovich ("Charlton Heston") analyze Heston's career within the context of a 1950s crisis in masculinity, attributing his popularity to a reaction to the somewhat effete image of the man in the gray flannel suit personified by Cary Grant. Heston, like Burt Lancaster and Kirk Douglas, offered a more rugged image of masculinity, an aspect that links *TOM*'s Neville back to Matheson's. Through the 1960s, the actor continued to work regularly as a leading man. At this time he also starred in a series of futuristic message films, including *Planet of the Apes* (1968), *Beneath the Planet of the Apes* (1970), and *Soylent Green* (1973).

Heston's journal dated February 6, 1970, reveals that he was initially unaware of the existence of *LMoE*, as he writes: "there are now some problems on the rights for LEGEND" (*Actor's* 331). He later clarifies:

> We got strong early interest from Warner Bros., almost simultaneously with word that an Italian company had already filmed the novel. They hadn't released their film in the U.S., but if we announced I was doing it, they'd certainly try to sell their version here. We got hold of a print; fortunately for us, though it starred my friend Vincent Price, it was a pretty torpid piece [*Arena* 434].

Heston's clout was sufficient for Warner Bros. to clear up the rights issues and move forward with a project with which, at least by his own accounts in both *The Actor's Life* (1978) and *In the Arena* (1995), Heston remained integrally involved in the decision making processes. For example, not only does he suggest that he was in on the decision to hire John William Corrington, the latter also took some of his suggestions during the writing process (*Arena* 435). Heston attributes Joyce with a secondary role (*Arena* 438) and also notes that William Peter Blatty—later famed for his novel, *The Exorcist* (1971)—was hired for some dialogue cleanup (*Actor's* 340–41). He credits producer Walter Seltzer with the name change to *The Omega Man* (*Arena* 438).

Similarly, through the use of a vague "we," Heston suggests he was also involved in casting decisions, such as the choices of Rosalind Cash (*Actor's* 343–45) and Anthony Zerbe: "Warner's are reluctant to move on Tony Zerbe. I hate to use muscle, but I'm convinced he's the best actor for the part" (*Actor's* 343). The Russian-born director Boris Sagal (1923–1981) was a journeyman who had largely worked in television, including directing some episodes of *The Twilight Zone* and *Alfred Hitchcock Presents*; his feature film credits include seventeen works, none of whose titles are recognizable today. Indeed, his most famous production may have been as a father rather than a director: his actress daughter Katey Sagal has garnered more publicity than her father received for any of his films for her lead in the pioneering Fox television series *Married With Children* (1987–1997), then voicing Turanga Leela on the long-lived animated SF series *Futurama* (1999–2013), and her more recent casting in a secondary role in the *Twilight Zone*-esque series *Lost* (2004–2010).

Transforming the Legend: The Omega Man

Set in 1977, thus in the viewers' very near future, *The Omega Man* (henceforth *TOM*) retains the scientist status attributed to Robert Morgan in *LMoE*, but militarizes its *Colonel* Robert Neville, ruggedly characterized by Heston, and thus counteracting any of the effete-ness sometimes attributed to the scientist or intellectual in American popular culture. In this Vietnam-era production, the military title also lends a certain right-wing air to a film whose aesthetics reflect more clearly the counterculture. Indeed, Steffen Hantke sees the film as "[a] product of the United States' coming to terms with its 1960s counterculture" and rewriting "the themes of evolutionary and cultural progress in Matheson's novel in the register of generational change" (178). Taking place in Los Angeles proper, it transforms Matheson's suburban setting to a completely urban one, the more effectively to convey its evocative imagery of urban emptiness and decay,[2] which can be translated into a number of messages about race, class, and the urban landscape. In addition, most domestic aspects of Matheson's and Price's Last Men have been exorcized, as well; while we do join the colonel on his daily routine, this is glamourized as he drives a Ford Mustang convertible, a military jeep, or a Land Rover instead of a station wagon. Indeed, Pulliam and Fonseca describe the sporty bachelor as "the traditional action hero fused with the *Playboy* version of manhood" (123). The film's opening sequence shows him racing through the empty city streets, pausing occasionally (in an oddly cheesy fast-motion) to shoot at shadowy figures in ground floor windows. In spite of his violence this Neville is, however, a rather cultivated brute; alone at home he listens to classical music, plays chess, drinks brandy in his smoking jacket, and discourses with a bust of Julius Caesar.

Three. The Last White Man on Earth 101

"It's your move, imperator [....] You used to be a nice guy." The playboy machismo of Colonel Robert Neville (Charlton Heston) reflects an ambivalent approach to the institutions and icons of Western civilization. *The Omega Man*, Warner Bros. DVD.

TOM links humanity's apocalyptic transformation directly to biological warfare; it also radically changes the nature of Neville's nemesis. The protagonist has survived an epidemic caused by a bacterial agent purposely released during the (obviously fictional) Sino-Russian War of 1975 by injecting himself with an experimental vaccine he had been developing. Those infected—i.e., the rest of humanity, he believes—develop an intense sensitivity to light and extremely pasty white skin (which, via make-up, looks like a really bad white-face job). Many in the Los Angeles area, at least, have joined a cult-like organization called The Family led by Brother Mathias (Anthony Zerbe), a direct reference to Charles Manson's group and their notorious murders only a few years earlier. Mathias' followers wear long black robes, resembling a bizarre cross between Spanish Inquisitors and the Ku Klux Klan; a former television journalist, he preaches a Luddite message of anti-technology, blaming it for the straits in which humanity now finds itself. Because of Neville's crusade against them, the Family's members have staged an ambush attack as Neville returns to his urban bunker, in one of many action sequences. The film is thus evacuated of all reference to traditional supernatural creatures like vampires, although the Family members with their artificially white faces actually resemble the zombies of Haitian folklore.[3] This is particularly true of Zachary, Mathias' second-in-command, played by African American actor Lincoln Kilpatrick (1931–2004).

TOM further breaks with the narrative structure of Matheson's novel and Price's film, diminishing the significance of the flashback, eliminating the hero's family in favor of explaining the pandemic's origin, and providing a backstory for Mathias. While it also removes the dog sequence, it adds details that will be retained in the 2007 remake, items possibly inspired by an earlier Last Man film *The World, The Flesh and The Devil*. Transferring Neville into a downtown setting exploits the dramatic visual imagery of the sole survivor dwarfed by the skyscrapers that surround him, but also allows his appropriation of the entire city.

As Neville searches an apparently empty department store, the mannequins take on an uncanny significance, particularly when another survivor that he is about to encounter attempts to hide her presence by mimicking a storefront dummy. By introducing Lisa, another living, seemingly normal, and female human *TOM* complicates the problem of survivors, eventually opening up the film's conclusion to the continuation of humanity in a manner completely foreclosed in Matheson's novel. Unlike Matheson's Ruth who is infected, but in a different manner than the mindless vampires, the sassy, afro'd Lisa (Rosalind Cash) appears healthy. As he gains the trust of Lisa, her brother Richie (Eric Laneuville), and the counter-culture figure Dutch (Paul Kelso), Neville learns that they have formed a small colony of child and adolescent survivors in the hills outside the city, but they believe the children will transform once they reach puberty. Having developed an antidote, Neville battles the Family once again, but this time unsuccessfully. The film's climax reveals Neville, bleeding into a fountain, via an overhead shot which features his spread-eagled body, the very image of Christ on the cross, sacrificing himself to save humanity and making the biblical reference in the film's title to Jesus' famous utterance, "I am the Alpha and the Omega, the beginning and the end" (Revelations 21:6), crystal clear as Robert Neville was the last

"I see him living high in the light, while we struggle in the dark." Brother Zachary (Lincoln Kilpatrick, right) to the leader of the Family, Mathias (Anthony Zerbe) about the last white man, Neville. *The Omega Man*, Warner Bros. DVD.

man on earth, but also its hope for a new beginning, as his blood holds the antibodies for a cure.

The film's treatment of race and race relations is ambiguous and at the same time cutting edge, drawing heavily on the stylish sassiness of the Blaxpoitation film. It also returns to a central concept of Matheson's novel almost completely lost in the Price vehicle: the sexual tensions experienced by the lonely protagonist. However, whereas *TOM* allows an interracial romance to occur between Neville and Lisa, this romance is, of course, doomed. Furthermore, since both Richie and Lisa fall victim to the disease and to Mathias' cult, although the latter survives, and the film's conclusion suggests that she will be cured, the film reduces the injection of much color into the gene pool of humanity's future, thus undoing some of the potential in its superficially progressive treatment of race. Its "happy" ending, which offers hope of survival for humanity through the children Dutch carries off in a jeep, along with Neville's blood as an antidote, completely reverses that of the novel.

A Different Story for a Different World: The Omega Man *and the End of the Sixties*

Award-winning historian James T. Patterson makes a compelling argument in *The Eve of Destruction: How 1965 Transformed America* (2012) for 1965—the year *after* the first film adaptation of *I Am Legend* was released—as the "Hinge for the Sixties" (xi). Viewing "1965 as a year of exceptionally rapid and widespread change" (*Eve* xiii), Patterson opines that key events that year set the stage for the period of racial and student unrest, changing sexual mores, and the increasingly oppositional nature of popular culture (music, film, fashion, and so on), which we now refer to as the "Sixties." Acknowledging the significance of John F. Kennedy's assassination in November 1963 and the passage of the Civil Rights Act in June 1964, Patterson nonetheless privileges the sweeping social programs instituted by President Lyndon Baines Johnson's Great Society platform and the increasingly violent racial conflict sparked by the failure of *Brown v. Board of Education* (already over a decade old) or the Civil Rights Act in changing the reality of segregation in the south or the overwhelming disadvantages faced by blacks across America. 1965 also saw the beginning of student activism beyond the Civil Rights movement as the nation became increasingly divided over the U.S.'s escalating engagement in Vietnam, an intervention initially downplayed by Johnson himself. The perception of "a credibility gap" (Patterson, *Eve* 125) fueled the developing sentiment of a generation gap between the first baby boomers now entering university and the nation's social, economic, and political leaders.

The impact of events that occurred in 1965 was even greater by 1968, more commonly viewed as a moment when "a great divide began to open up in American life" (Wyatt 1). After the violence outside the 1968 Democratic Convention in Chicago, the election of Republican candidate Richard M. Nixon marked a turn toward conservatism, ending the great social vision for change inaugurated by Kennedy and built upon by Johnson. The assassinations of Robert F. Kennedy and Martin Luther King, Jr., snuffed out the flame of hope for civil rights and the movement turned more radical in the form of Black Power and the Black Panthers. The Tet Offensive scandal and the My Lai massacre of a civilian village in Vietnam would add even more fuel to the anti-war movement that would soon force Nixon to decrease the number of American troops. In the years leading up to *TOM*'s début, the nation had witnessed the assassination of several visionary leaders, violent and destructive race riots in major American cities, bombing and defoliation by U.S. troops in southeast Asia, and the National Guard turn its weapons on American students at Kent State University, the culmination of "the escalating level of political violence" in "the divisive year of 1970" (Heineman 9).

Whether we accept James Patterson's thesis that 1965 was the hinge year or we follow Jules Witcover and David Wyatt in embracing 1968 as the turning point, there is no doubt that American society at the dawn of the 1970s was radically different than it had been in 1954 or even in 1964. The following comparison of *TOM* to its literary and filmic precursors reveals some of the extent of that change, confirming Ryan Baker's assertion that it is "[f]irmly grounded in the early 1970s" (197).

In her effort to develop a theory of criticism that goes beyond the criterion of faithfulness to the original, Linda Hutcheon proposes that adaptations need to be considered as works in their own right. Without completely eschewing the analytical tool of comparison, she describes the adaptation as

- an acknowledged transposition of a recognizable other work or works;
- a creative *and* an interpretive act of appropriation/salvaging; and
- an extended intertextual engagement with the adapted work [Hutcheon 8].

As acknowledged *transpositions* of an earlier work, adaptations thus avow their sources while at the same time transposing these into a different medium (literature to film), genre (SF-horror to action adventure), and/or context (1954 to 1971). Adaptors thus do not seek servile imitation, but rather propose a creative appropriation, which is certainly engaged with the original, but interpreted for a new audience. Rather than relating the two texts as original and (inferior) copy, she adopts the metaphor of the palimpsest, a piece of vellum or paper from which the original manuscript text has been scraped off so that a new work can be inscribed upon it. Borrowing a term that combines the palimpsest with incest in order to underscore the closeness of the relationship between source text and adaptation, Hutcheon argues that:

> To deal with adaptations *as adaptations* is to think of them as [...] inherently "palimpsestuous" works, haunted at all times by their adapted texts. If we know that prior text, we always feel its presence shadowing the one we are experiencing directly [6].

As applied here, this theory allows us to view Matheson's novel and its earlier film adaptations as continuing to haunt subsequent ones, while at the same time it allows us to judge these films independently of their fidelity to this source text(s) without wholly abandoning the tool of comparison. Unfortunately, not all critics are ready completely to relinquish this criterion.

For later critics, then, the film's rootedness in its contemporary time has typically been seen as more of a curse than a blessing, and *TOM* has garnered the same mixed critical responses that *The Last Man on Earth* (*LMoE*) received. Baker opines that it is "as dated as its fashion sense" (197); Jeff Rovin asserts that "as an adaptation it's rather poor" but "in and of itself it is good, sturdy entertainment" (198). As a major studio production, the Charlton Heston vehicle nonetheless had many advantages over *LMoE*; in contrast with the latter's AIP "shoestring" budget (Silver and Ursini), which allowed only for black and white photography and was partially shot in Italy in some half-dozen sets and locations, *TOM* was filmed on the streets of Los Angeles, the Hollywood hills, and a number of interior sets in Technicolor and Panavision. Instead of *LMoE*'s tiny cast comprised of one American genre star, with only three other speaking roles cast by Italian actors and a handful of extras, *TOM*'s cast was led by a major Hollywood figure since the 1950s and it introduced a number of new secondary characters with speaking roles. Furthermore, it developed special make-up and costumes for its updated version of Matheson's vampire hordes. Finally, not content with the status of a low-budget horror flick, *TOM* and its male lead aspired to make it an action blockbuster, building up the fight and flight scenes, allowing Robert Neville to drive the sexy cars that Robert Morgan had denied himself in the earlier film, and pitting him against more violent and more intelligent foes.

Significantly, while *TOM* introduces more action sequences—in particular car and motorcycle chases, but also pyrotechnics, explosions, and an array of weapons, both high tech and low—for its adventure hero, it downplays the systematic slaying sequences central to both Matheson's novel and Price's film. As we shall see, it goes even further than *LMoE* did in rehabilitating Neville and reversing the dark conclusion of Matheson's novel, instead elevating its last white man on earth into a full-fledged hero, a sacrificial savior for the human race. In addition, its far higher production values allowed *TOM* to indulge in more sophisticated art and costume design, giving it a distinctive look that very much situates the film in the original viewers' very near future. Finally, its screenwriters, clearly given a free hand to update Matheson's story, indulged in frequent cultural references that situated the film as both fashionably "hip" and to be read as "a parable for our times." As adaptors, the Corringtons thus creatively appropriate and interpret Matheson's novel, extensively engaging with its core narrative tropes, transposing these from its original Cold War context to that of a new generation, while at the same time refusing to exorcise the ghosts haunting this American myth.

The Counterculture Aesthetics of *The Omega Man*

TOM aligns itself with the counterculture fashion and politics of the late 1960s and early 1970s in a number of ways, clearly distinguishing itself from its more sober and mainstream models with its colorful, glossy, sometimes psychedelic look. It begins racily, with Robert Neville speeding through the empty city streets in a red 1970 Ford XL convertible, pausing to put an 8-track tape into the car's stereo system. A calendar in a car dealership tells us that time has stopped in March 1975—the very near future, a device used in *LMoE*, but closer to the actual dates in which Matheson set his novel. Later we learn that the film's present is dated August 1977. Although the hero wears a rather impeccable safari jacket, a fashion statement that aligns him with an oppressive colonial elite (an aspect of his identity addressed later), he then enters a movie theater where he turns on a generator and screens Michael Wadleigh's rockumentary *Woodstock* (1970). Many viewers will miss the burning irony that Warner Bros. studios shamelessly plugs here one of its own productions, filmed at a key demonstration of the youth counterculture's rejection of the commercialism, consumerism, and capitalism that such a move emblematizes. That this viewing has become a ritualized activity for Neville is made clear in the dialogue, as he quips to himself, "Great show! Held on for a third straight year." He repeats significant dialogue in sync with an interviewee at the concert: "What's really important is that if we can't all live together and be happy, if you can't go out and smile at somebody, what kind of life is that?" *TOM* thus appears to adopt the oppositional values of the "summer of love" just a few years prior, while at the same time revealing that given the present postapocalyptic state of affairs, any such utopian hopes have been completely shattered.

TOM's protagonist, despite his square threads, seems at times, then, to share the critical attitude and liberal values of the late 1960s and early 1970s youth movements. In addition to appreciating the performance of "rocket soul music" by Country Joe and the Fish in *Woodstock*, he greets his own high-tech surveillance system glibly, "Hi, Big Brother; how's your ass?" At the same time, however, he remains implicated in consumer culture; maintaining a high standard of living even at the end of the world as we know it. Unlike the unkempt Robert Morgan in *LMoE*, who leaves home to obtain gas and garlic in the same rumpled clothes he slept in and eschews a fancy car in favor of a practical one, Heston's character drives snazzy convertibles, and "shops" for a new track suit when the one he's wearing gets a bit too sweaty. Instead of a suburban tract house, his uptown bachelor pad, equipped with a state-of-the art television and sound system, brings Neville up-to-date, as well. But he also works hard to preserve a "civilized" lifestyle by maintaining certain traditions: not only has he filled his apartment with antiques and artworks, he keeps up appearances by always dressing for dinner on Sundays. Yet his frilly shirt and a green velvet jacket remain in keeping with the cutting-edge of male fashion at the dawn of the glam rock era. Thus, conservative elements distance him somewhat from the counterculture and implicate him in the power structures of contemporary capitalist consumerism and its roots in the European traditions of Western civilization.

The film's cast of secondary characters actually goes further in terms of identifying with oppositional ideologies than its clearly middle-aged, authority-figure protagonist. First, by casting several African Americans in speaking roles, *TOM* reflects the 1970s media's progressive desire to represent the U.S. as a multicultural society. Rosalind Cash, cast as Neville's love interest, Lisa—a greatly transformed analogue for the novel's Ruth—prefigures the black action heroines played by Pam Grier in the early 1970s Blaxploitation films *Coffy* (1973) and *Foxy Brown* (1974)[4] with her sassy attitude, afro-styled hair, leather pantsuit, and paisley caftan, which link her to current fashion trends. Eric Laneuville, who plays her younger brother Richie, appeared on the trendy and popular *Room 222* television series (1970–1973). Finally, their friend Dutch (Paul Koslo), rides a motorcycle and, in spite of his medical training, is clearly coded as an anti-authoritarian figure with his quirky aviator's helmet and leather jacket sporting a bright red hand giving the world a finger painted on its back. The other (as yet uninfected) survivors of the pandemic that has wiped out most of humanity are a handful of children and teenagers; most of these are white, although there is one Asian and one Latino boy. Embodying both God the Father and Jesus Christ, his more radical son, Robert Neville wields both the Old Testament wrath of Jehovah and the New Testament activism of the Messiah and, like the latter, will eventually save these still fully human survivors with his blood.

The Vietnam Context

In 1971, the U.S. was still entangled in its Vietnam intervention, although public opinion had largely shifted against it, calling for an end to the conflict (Dumbrell 140). *TOM* references contemporary concerns about military action in its revised backstory for the plague epidemic that has left Neville to presume that he is the last man on earth. Just as flashbacks in *LMoE* revealed the origins of the vampire plague, *TOM* uses a memory-montage superimposed over Neville's face of explosions, a rocket shooting off, a hammer and sickle drawn across a map, and Chinese demonstrations, cutting to a pre-apocalypse television studio where news anchor Jonathan Mathias refers to the use of biological weapons as the "Sino-Russian border war" escalates. The fears of Maoist China's influence in southeast Asia that were at the root of Johnson's insistence on following Kennedy's advisors and intervening in Vietnam (Patterson, *Eve* 22–29) are referenced here along with the more immediately contemporary Nixon-era concerns over "the emerging Sino-Soviet split" (Dumbrell 27). Neville himself is revealed to have been a military officer *and* a scientist engaged in research precisely exploring ways to respond to biological weapons.

This backstory is told using the device of pseudo-media coverage, a common element in apocalyptic visual narratives from the 1950s to today; *LMoE* included frames of both newsprint headlines and a televised emergency address from the governor. Similarly, the news anchorman, Mathias—prior to his transformation into Neville's nemesis, a greatly revised analogue for Ben Cortman—describes the breakdown of law and order, the destruction of property, and the declaration of martial law over stock footage montages of plague victims falling dead in the streets. These images, of course, to the 1971 viewer will feel all too familiar, a reflection of the televised violence of the "living-room war" in Vietnam (Chong 127) and of the recent years' urban riots in nearby Watts (1965), Detroit (1967), and the "Days of Rage" in Chicago (1969) (Chong 28).

A New Monster for a New Time: From Vampire to Religious Fanatic

Just as the film updates the cars, fashion, and political situation current in 1971, it also updates Matheson's epidemic and the monsters it creates. Whereas Matheson's novel and the Vincent Price vehicle both explicitly invoked vampires, nonetheless offering a science-fictional explanation for them, the Heston film takes a step away from the classic monsters of Gothic and Hollywood horror, evacuating any references to such mythical creatures. With their black robes, white skin and hair, and white irises, the plague's victims certainly appear as uncanny as any classic vampire. Indeed, their physical transformation (via make-up artistry) is much more dramatic than that of *LMoE*'s vampires or the revenants (not yet officially referred to as zombies) more recently featured in George A. Romero's *Night of the Living Dead*. But the cause of their disease—biological weapons—and its symptoms, are all logically explained; these include "blindness in light, albinism, [...] occasional stages of torpor," traits linking them to vampires, but they also suffer from "psychotic delusions." Thus, while they have been undeniably physically transformed into something *other* than humanity as we currently know it, some of their strangeness derives from insane behavior, as well. But the film also implies that their way of life—and their persecution of Neville—includes the possibility of choice and, at least for some individuals, free will. Not only do critics disagree as to how to interpret these *inhuman* beings, the film itself remains coy in its terminology. Jeff Rovin, following Matheson's original, refers to them as "vampires" (198), but Heston refers to them as zombies in his autobiography (*Actor's* 347). Like his literary counterpart, the filmic Neville first refers to them simply as "they"; Dutch calls them "tertiary cases"; but they call themselves the Family.

For—in yet another reference to contemporary society—the strangely pale, hooded figures that pursue Neville every night actually belong to a sort of cult, led by the former newsman, Mathias. The Corringtons drew on a threatening phenomenon not at all available to Matheson or the first adapters of his film: the rise of religious cults led by unstable sociopaths, such as the Family led by Charles Manson. Their murderous spree, resulting in the highly publicized death (among others) of the pregnant wife of director Roman Polanski, model-actress Sharon Tate, had occurred on August 8, 1969 (Bugliosi). To mainstream America such cults may not have appeared too different—in part because their leaders often propounded values of collective love and property appropriating the utopian discourses of communal societies—from the other forms of "hippy" communes cropping up around the nation, but particularly in northern California, in the late 1960s (Boal *et al.*; Case and Taylor). Later critics, though, have most frequently interpreted the Family as an allegory for the Black Power movement—a view nuanced here.

Mathias' Family is also linked to fundamentalist religious movements of varying types through their belief system, which he expounds at length in several monologues. Mathias is far more articulate—indeed, he is an apparently charismatic figure given the number of his followers—than Ben Cortman or even the new society members described by Ruth in Matheson's novel. Except in one detail: *TOM* maintains and even plays with the by now almost iconic line, "Come out, Neville." Not only do we hear it at several points in the film, prior to Neville's ultimate downfall Mathias predicts, "I think Neville is going to come out tonight." The cult-like aspect of the group allows the introduction of the religious elements partially evacuated from the film with the removal of the vampires, but present in many earlier apocalyptic films.[5] Mathias' overt message is clearly a Luddite critique of where science and technology have led humanity: to the brink of extinction.

Already as a journalist, in the flashback sequence, Zerbe's character avers: "We were warned of judgement; well, here it is, here, now. In the form of microscopic bacilli. This is the end." *TOM* develops much further the religious imagery intimated at more obliquely in both Matheson's novella and *LMoE*. The novel includes a brief flashback reference to a religious tent revival

(112–13); the Price film signals the plague as divine judgment with the opening sequence's shot of a church sign ("The end has come"), and Morgan dies upon the altar stairs. Not only do Mathias' teachings include the explicit message that humanity has been punished by God for its hubris with this pandemic, locating "evil" in Neville as a scientist and a "man of the wheel," he and his followers' costumes and behavior invoke much older forms of religious intolerance. Indeed, their long mostly black, but some brown, robes resemble nothing so much as the garb of monks. They gather to hear Mathias preach, and their capture and parading of Neville through the city streets in a hand-made cart, placing a white conical hat on his head, further resembles the treatment of those condemned to the *auto de fe* by the Spanish Inquisition (Kamen 204–12). Rather than hunting down Neville because they are driven by instinctual cravings like vampires or zombies, it is instead their beliefs that cause them to act violently and irrationally. Mathias madly proclaims, "With fire my brothers, we have purified all that lives with zeal; we shall cleanse the world," and their use of fire, of course, makes for brilliant special effects. Their overt characterization paints them as deranged zealots, enemies of humanity and its civilization, "vermin"—in Neville's words—that he is justified in exterminating.

Like Matheson's novel and its first film adaptation, *TOM* maintains the division between different types of plague victims, although it eventually denies its Neville the unique status of last human being on earth. In addition to the hooded zombie-like monsters, who have been completely transformed by the plague into something posthuman, another group of human survivors exists. Comprised mostly of young children and teens, cared for by the young adults Dutch and Lisa, the latter have been studying the disease and trying to find a cure, for they believe it is inevitable for the children to eventually fall victim to it, and that only their youth has preserved them. Indeed, the fact that Lisa's brother Richie is already showing symptoms of the "advanced secondary" stage motivates them to seek Neville out, since Dutch is familiar with his pre-war research. Not realizing that he is immune, they believe he can nonetheless help them find a cure.

From Low-Budget Horror to SF Blockbuster

This transformation of Matheson's vampires, which retained a direct link to the classic supernatural monsters of Gothic fiction and the Universal Studios monsters of the 1930s and 1940s, into a new form of being operates a radical updating of the story appropriate for the dawn of the 1970s. Matheson had innovated the vampire genre by offering a scientific explanation for a monster dating from the Middle Ages, but he refuses to evacuate the supernatural from his tale. His vampires still shrink unexplainably from religious artifacts. In part due to the presence of Vincent Price, an icon of the horror cinema, the 1964 film adaptation of Matheson's story remained true to genre, just one of the many apocalyptic films of the 1950s and 1960s that blurred the lines between SF and horror. It did include a few action sequences, as Price struggles with first the vampire horde led by Cortman and then with the black-shirted men of the new society. But *TOM*'s more "scientific" approach to the monsters and heightened level of physical action, with stunts and special effects takes a big step toward moving the SF blockbuster out of the horror ghetto. Although it retains certain inevitable horror elements of the visual narrative of apocalypse, such as Heston's frequent discovery of mummified and skeletonized plague victims, and in spite of the fact that the studio saw *TOM* as "a high-class horror film" (Heston, *Arena* 444), by appropriating the tropes of the action-adventure film and casting a blockbuster star, *TOM* moved Matheson's legend into the mainstream.

Mark Jancovich sees Heston's work with producer Franklin J. Schaffner in *Planet of the Apes*, along with his roles in several other science-fiction films of the period, including *Beneath the Planet of the Apes*, *The Omega Man*, and *Soylent Green*, as marking "a point of transition between the SF film as it emerged in the 1950s" as low-budget and B-series fare and into the Hollywood mainstream (55). Heston's presence helped smooth the transition for SF film from low-budget black and white fodder for teenagers, into its culmination in the 1970s blockbuster, *Star Wars* (1977) (55), the precursor for all of today's major SF films. Following on the huge popularity of *Planet of the Apes*, but also building on a past body of work known to film audiences in the early 1970s, *TOM* ensures that its hero will be perceived by audiences as righteous. It takes even further the revisions to Matheson's original narrative, which ultimately questions the hero's moral status, begun in *LMoE*. More than a mere casting decision, he was involved in the very development of the project from its earliest stages—Heston's interpretation of the character of Colonel Robert Neville brings a whole new array of meaning to the film, in terms of models of masculinity, ideology, and race.

Charlton Heston as the Last Man on Earth: Masculinity in The Omega Man

In the late 1960s and early 1970s, a number of films had begun to revise images of the hero in traditional genre films. At this time, we saw the rise of the revisionist Western, such as *Butch Cassidy and the Sundance Kid* (1969) and *McCabe and Mrs. Miller* (1971), which rewrote the narrative of black and white distinctions between good and evil in America's so-called destined expansion west (Herzberg). Although not quite the oppositional figure found in *Little Big Man* (1970) or *Jeremiah Johnson* (1972), Heston's role as the vulnerable, aging cowboy *Will Penny* (1967) begins to point toward America's questioning of its master narratives and its growing disrespect for traditional authority. Superficially, as discussed above, some aspects of Robert Neville's characterization in *TOM* align him with such anti-authority figures, attributing him with some of the oppositional values of the counterculture, making him an appealing lead to a younger generation of filmgoers. His sardonic quips, his openness to racial Others (an affair with Lisa, a paternal desire to help Richie), his acceptance of Dutch, and so on, code him as "hip." A far greater number of elements, however, actually allow us to read him as a kinder, gentler, but still traditional figure of Judeo-Christian patriarchal authority.

A key piece of dialogue occurs as Neville, a gun in his back, drives Lisa into the hills on a motorcycle; as they reach the human survivors' enclave she tells the Asian youth on guard duty: "It's okay, Tommy, this is the man, and I mean the man, but he's cool." There is no denying that, although he is "cool," Colonel Robert Neville is *the man*, beginning with the screen presence of Charlton Heston himself. In addition to Heston's age—almost fifty by the time of the film's release, he is clearly the oldest member of the film's cast—and the character's military promotion to the rank of colonel (this without losing the scientist status he had gained in *LMoE*), all of the baggage the star brings with him to this role must be considered. Once again, Richard Dyer's *Stars* elucidates the added meaning that the choice of a particular actor in a particular role brings to a film, and Heston brings important material in relation to masculinity and patriarchal authority, ostensibly confirming the moral imperatives of America as torch-bearer for the Western, Judeo-Christian civilization.

Heston's Hegemonic Masculinity

The casting of Vincent Price in the role of Robert Morgan introduced—or perhaps, rather, reinforced, if we accept Jamil Y. Khader's arguments about Matheson's original novel ("Will the Real")—a queer subtext to *LMoE*. Price's star baggage as a campy figure of compromised masculinity situated that film within a crisis of masculinity occurring in the 1950s and 1960s. The casting of he-man figure Charlton Heston swings the pendulum in the other direction. Almost overcompensating for Price's weak, effeminate inefficacy, Colonel Robert Neville as portrayed by Heston becomes an icon of burly, effective masculine authority, of what R. W. Connell refers to as "hegemonic masculinity" (77).

In *Masculinities*, Connell offers the following explanation of the concept he has been largely responsible for popularizing:

> Hegemonic masculinity can be defined as the configuration of gender practice which embodies the currently accepted answer to the problem of the legitimacy of patri-

archy, which guarantees (or is taken to guarantee) the dominant position of men and the subordination of women [77].

Applying Connell's notion to film, Nick Trujillo summarizes that "media critics and scholars of gender ideology have described at least five features of hegemonic masculinity in American culture: (1) physical force and control, (2) occupational achievement, (3) familial patriarchy, (4) frontiersmanship, and (5) heterosexuality" (15).

Heston's portrayal of Dr./Col. Robert Neville in *The Omega Man* reflects all of these traits. We see his physical force and control immediately as he drives skillfully, athletically fights groups of plague victims, jogs, and reveals his trim, but muscular form, removing his shirt and wearing rather tight-fighting tracksuits and jumpsuits. As a research scientist whose publications are known to others, a medical doctor, and a military officer, his professional achievements are self-evident. Although he is not attributed with a family of his own—indeed, Heston's is the only Neville who is a confirmed bachelor—he clearly assumes a paternal role with Richie and the other children cared for by Dutch and Lisa. His frontiersmanship, although indirect, is also demonstrated through his survival skills during the apocalypse, including skillful shooting, but also his intended goal of leaving the city to found a new colony with Lisa, Dutch, and the children once he has distilled a cure. Finally, his consummated attraction to Lisa confirms his heterosexuality. But all of these traits are compounded when we add Heston's star persona to this characterization. Let us recall that,

> as Dyer explains in *Stars*, the "star image" is an institutional product, a construction resulting from a complex, often overdetermined, sometimes undermined, interplay of biological details, film roles, body codes, and media coverage, and extending, often in contradictory ways, across the duration of a performer's career [Cohan 26].

The discussion of "Charlton Heston" that follows refers not to an actual person, but rather to the star image that has been constructed around him by all of these factors.

In *Masked Men: Masculinity and the Movies in the Fifties*, Steven Cohan describes the then dominant model for masculinity on screen as "the domesticated breadwinner, commonly identified in the media as the Man in the Gray Flannel Suit"; this model "was responsible for legitimating the hegemony of the professional-managerial class" (38). This figure was embodied on screen by cultivated, slender, economically successful, suit-wearing professionals played by Cary Grant, Gregory Peck, and Rock Hudson.[6] However, by the late 1950s and early 1960s, this domesticated male model fed into a perceived national crisis in manhood, explicitly stated in Arthur Schlesinger, Jr.'s article "The Crisis of American Masculinity" published in *Esquire* magazine in 1958 (Wyatt 18). In popular culture terms, this crisis appears visible in the repeated representations of compromised masculinity in several Alfred Hitchcock films including *Rear Window* (1954), *The Man Who Knew Too Much* (1956), and *Vertigo* (1958), in which formerly dominant male leads like Jimmy Stewart are depicted as symbolically castrated, unstable, and threatened (see Modleski). In partial response, says Cohan, studios began casting an alternate, more rugged type of male lead. Incarnated by Burt Lancaster, Victor Mature, and Robert Mitchum these manly men aligned with more traditional images of masculinity, exerting physical power and dominance over others, rather than economic privilege.

Heston's Biblical Authority

Of course, among these more hegemonically masculine stars, the figure of Charlton Heston looms large. Cohan devotes an entire chapter, "The Body in the Blockbuster" to an analysis of the images of masculinity conveyed by depictions of the male body in the biblical blockbusters of the 1950s, several of which featured Heston. Mark Jancovich makes similar arguments in "'Charlton Heston is an axiom': Spectacle and Performance in the Development of the Blockbuster" (2004). Cohan's and Jancovich's analyses of Heston's earlier films are pertinent to this examination of Heston's casting in the role of Robert Neville through the lens of Dyer's *Stars*, which asserts that viewers will consciously or unconsciously consider the actor's prior films while watching him on screen.

As Jancovich posits, "Charlton Heston is probably the best known star of biblical or historical epics" (51); audiences in 1971 would be completely familiar with his films from the 1950s, which were played regularly on television, particularly during religious holiday periods like Christmas and Easter. In 1956, Heston was cast as Moses in *The Ten Commandments*, an iconic figure of patriarchal authority. Analyzing that film, Cohan observes that "[b]y repeatedly placing Heston's tall body in the foreground, the camera process brings out the actor's physical connotations of moral and racial superiority as embodied in his height" (158). Furthermore, Cohan contextualizes this image of white male power within the Cold War climate of the era. In its juxtaposition of the exotic, racialized Yul Brynner—recently cast as the King of Siam (Thailand) in *The King and I* (1956)—as the Egyptian pharaoh Ramses side-by-side with Heston, "[t]he poster for *The Ten Commandments* follows the logic by which the film itself reproduces the central binarism of cold war ideology: the opposition of the American and the alien" (Cohan 124). Further breaking down this imagery, Cohan argues that, in contrast with the partially naked and bald "Oriental" Brynner,

> fully if simply clothed and thickly bearded so as to resemble Michelangelo's famous sculpture of the prophet, the white-haired Heston contextualizes the film's title, representing *the authority of the Judeo-Christian law that holds Western civilization together in a continuous tradition* [127; emphasis added].

Following his performance as Moses with lead roles in the academy award winning *Ben-Hur*, in which he plays the persecuted Christian turned champion gladiator Judah Ben-Hur,[7] and John the Baptist in *The Greatest Story Ever Told*, Heston consolidated his image as a figure of patriarchal, Judeo-Christian authority. As Cohan asserts: "Heston's close identification with the epic genre solidified his emerging star image as a patriarchal male," embodying "moral forthrightness" (156). Whereas the religious conservatism of the 1950s and early 1960s had clearly eroded by 1970, viewers of *TOM* could not help but associate Heston's Robert Neville with the moral authority of the biblical heroes he had portrayed in his youth.

The Omega Man's conclusion, which overrides subtler characterizations that might have questioned Neville's hero status and his moral imperatives (and they do occur as outlined below), also reverses the original novel's conclusion, which interrogated both of those elements. Not only does the film close on a freeze-frame of Heston in an unsubtle Christ-like position, an imagery reinforced by Heston's earlier roles in biblical epics, it also constructs direct associations between his Neville and God the Father. The film is thus peppered with visual and verbal references linking Neville with the moral authority of the Bible, Old and New Testaments, but also foreshadowing his final sacrifice to save humanity. His eventual martyrdom at the hands of the Family is prefigured several times as he is tied to a pyre to be burned at the stake, then tied down spread-eagled to a table in a courtroom. After he has found Lisa and Richie, and they discuss their efforts to find a cure, Neville reveals that he does not have the plague. Flashback sequences had revealed that like his literary model his immunity can be traced back to a military situation. He had been researching a vaccine and while transporting it his helicopter had crashed, destroying all but the injection he gave himself. It worked, meaning that now, as he explains to Lisa, "My blood might be a serum." The apostrophe in Richie's exclamation at this good news unsubtly identifies Neville with humanity's biblical savior: "Christ! You could save the world." His less-than-pious sister retorts, "Screw the world, let's save Richie." Later, a little girl from the colony asks Neville, "Are you God?" reinforcing his patriarchal status, but also harking back with a self-conscious wink to Heston's earlier roles. Not only did he play Moses in *The Ten Commandments*, but also his voice—slowed down—was used for that of God in the film (Cohan 145).

Added to the physical screen presence of Heston and his star persona, we have in addition the screenplay's characterization of Robert Neville; *TOM* restores the character's original name and military background, but promotes him socially into the scientific and military elite. His wardrobe distances him from the counterculture image fostered as he watched *Woodstock*, including a safari jacket, athletic wear, and in the final sequences he dons his colonel's military hat and a nylon jumpsuit, reminiscent of a pilot's flight suit. In addition to the antiques and fine art in his apartment, a bust of Julius Caesar, a founding father of Western civilization, features prominently in his home décor. Admittedly, he addresses it a bit disrespectfully while playing chess, "It's your move, imperator," and accuses the bust, "You used to be a nice guy." Yet, these icons of European imperial power clearly link this Neville to the establishment, vaguely defined, but also to the military-industrial complex: one room of his apartment is devoted to a state-of-the-art scientific lab.

Like many popular films appealing to a broad commercial audience, *TOM* constructs Neville somewhat ambivalently, hoping to please both more conservative adults ("he's the man"), as well as a younger audience ("but he's cool"). Just as Heston's screen presence allows viewers to link Neville to earlier biblical heroes, the opening and flashback sequences' identification of Neville as a former military officer, now toting a gun, and shooting at shady figures through the figurative urban jungle in a safari suit, aligns him with the forces of Western colonial and imperial order. Furthermore, his sardonic complaint that in his postapocalyptic world, "There's never a cop around when you need one," codes on the side of law and order. That he is a man of action, certainly no peacenik, appears in numerous sequences, as he drives rapidly and skillfully in red, then powder blue, convertibles, as well as various paramilitary vehicles. His prowess as a fighter are unmatched; both as a sniper (in the opening slaying sequence) and in hand-to-hand combat with the mutants, coming home to an ambush early in the film.

In this vein, Heston's frequent quips can be read as double-entendres, both complicit with the society he remembers and somehow wishes to preserve, but also critical of it. This appears most particularly in his relationship to the lost economy. On the one hand, "shopping" sequences and Neville's home align him with middle-class values of consumerism and the privileging of high quality, as well as fashionable, consumer goods. Yet critiques of that system appear as well, as he returns home to utter ironically, "Fine, another day, another dollar." In a car dealership, he accuses an imaginary salesman of being a "cheating bastard." Later he echoes the sentiments of the Beatles' hit "Taxman" (*Revolver*, 1966) asking Mathias and his crew when captured, "Are you fellows really with the Internal Revenue Service?" But it should also be remembered that Neville's appropriations of consumer goods in the interest of survival might all be construed as looting in another context. Elsewhere, Neville's use of colloquial language, suggests that he is not square, as he tells Mathias: "You are full of crap."

Although Heston's sheer physical presence attributes Neville with a certain form of hegemonic masculinity, he also must assert his heterosexuality. In contrast with *LMoE*, which overtly avoided questions of sexuality and covertly queered its Neville as played by Price, the 1971 film returns to the original novel's discussions of sexuality. But whereas the novel denaturalized those desires, focusing on Neville's torment from the vampire women, *TOM*'s protagonist is a healthy American male, interested only in a living female.

Lisa's Femininity

On the one hand, the film offers a subtle feminist critique of the 1950s and early 1960s image of the model woman as passive, silent, and domesticated through its characterization of the sassy Lisa. Indeed, she is introduced as a new kind of woman; uncertain of Neville's status as good or evil, when their paths cross in a department store she freezes, pretending to be a mannequin. This passive, "model" behavior does not last for long, though, as she moves and runs, taking action. Up to this point, the encounter similarly follows that in *LMoE* when Morgan discovers Ruth, chasing after her; Heston's Neville calls out, "Hey, come back!" Fearing that perhaps she was yet another hallucination he proffers yet another quip: "Is this how it starts? With a trip to the laughing academy?" Admittedly, the film does not portray Neville as completely invulnerable, as it depicts the negative effects that his solitude has on his mental health, not just through frequent one-liners addressed to himself, skeletonized victims, or inanimate objects, he also experiences an auditory hallucination of phones ringing (directly borrowed from *The World, the Flesh and the Devil*). His ability to overcome this vulnerability, however, simply reinforces his hero-status; he stops the ringing by sheer force of will, commanding them to be still: "There are no phones!"

When the two meet again, Lisa comes to Neville's rescue, wearing a tight leather pant suit; her slender figure barely reveals any secondary sexual characteristics, rendering Cash somewhat androgynous with her unisex hairstyle, a longish afro. Neville has been captured by Mathias and—in one of the film's best action sequences—she and Dutch arrive at a football stadium, the former Los Angeles Colosseum (Rovin 201). The locale for Neville's planned *auto de fe* by the Family winks yet again to Heston's star persona, referencing his role as a gladiator in *Ben-Hur*. Whereas Neville politely introduces himself, "My name's Robert," still unsure of his intentions Lisa dominatingly retorts, "Your name's mud," and punches him, knocking him unconscious. When he awakens, she refers back to their encounter in the mannequin sequence, but also critiquing traditional images of femininity, introducing herself sarcastically as his "living Playtex doll." The film thus enacts the changing nature of femininity as the Women's Liberation movement sought more active roles for women in society and in the media. Her ironic reference to men's desire for women to be like mannequins and rubber dolls obviously belies her true agency and signals her refusal to be his passive toy. Not only does Lisa assume position of subject, refusing to be a mere object of male desire, her assertiveness relieves the potentially problematic associations of this sexually charged interracial situation. It removes Lisa from the black woman's historical position as victim of white male power prevalent under slavery (see Randall 177–78). Here and in the interracial romance, the film adopts a progressive stance about race and race relations, as Lisa desires Neville as much as vice versa.

But, of course, Neville must desire her in order to perform his heterosexual masculinity; already allusions to the more open sexual mores of the 1970s appeared in Neville's bachelor pad and his Hugh Hefner–like smoking jacket. Once he is brought into close working contact with Lisa, her beauty cannot fail to seduce him. While Virginia Slims cigarettes had recently coined the phrase, "You've come a long way, baby," in 1968, Lisa has not quite come all the way, yet. She is black and beautiful, but in order really to capture Neville's interest, she has to remove her pants and don a dress. Indeed, the scenario somewhat undoes these images of feminist and black militancy it initially constructs around Lisa. In the later seduction scene, although she "makes [her] move," putting smooth jazz on the stereo system, thus, again, actively expressing her desire for Neville, she has also dressed in a more "womanly" fashion, donning an elegant caftan with gold threads. Furthermore, she is restored to the position of object as she rises naked from the bed the next morning, whereas Neville is already fully clothed. Finally, her wardrobe becomes increasingly conservative as her relationship with Neville develops, as she later sports a midi skirt and high-necked blouse, even asking, "Honey, can I borrow your credit card?" The racy interracial affair is thus contained, becoming a parody of a mundane, middle-class marriage.[8] Significantly, just before she "turns" into a tertiary case and briefly rejoins the Family, Lisa's wardrobe becomes more marked in racial terms, as she wraps a scarf around her hair in an African-like manner.

Neville's Moral Righteousness

Thus far, the case has been made that, in spite of a veneer of counterculture "cool," Neville represents a heroic patriarchal figure whose moral rectitude appears unquestioned, thus reversing Matheson's more ambiguous ending to the novel. Before turning to how a detailed analysis of the film's treatment of race relations might challenge that reading, it should be observed that, in fact, his role as a slayer does *not* go unquestioned by other characters in the film. Generally speaking, Neville's on-screen killing always appears to be in self-defense, in response to a direct threat on his life, with the exception perhaps of the opening sequence when he stops his red convertible to shoot up at a shadowy figure in a window. Indeed, when he has the opportunity to use a high-powered scope systematically to shoot down a horde gathered outside his town home, he simply destroys the medieval catapult the Family has built to firebomb his home. Although he is depicted, like his precursors, mapping the city, looking for their hide-out, this Neville is never shown to slay systematically, thus maintaining for the audience his moral imperative.

Yet other characters explicitly question Neville's behavior; Dutch refers to him as an "exterminator"; in a distinct echo of Ruth's accusations in *IAL*, Lisa accuses him of "shooting at everything that moves," putting their own lives at safety. But the most condemning attack comes from the idealist Richie who, once he has been cured, wants to share the serum with the Family:

> RICHIE: You know you ought to do something about those people. Come on, you going to give them the serum?
> ROBERT: Fat chance, how come?
> RICHIE: You know they're humans.
> ROBERT. They're vermin.
> RICHIE: If you're not going to cure them, then just kill 'em. ... Well go on, ain't you going to go down there and zap 'em? Either kill 'em or cure 'em dammit.

When Neville ultimately refuses, Richie accuses him: "You're hostile! You just don't belong!" This exchange not only identifies the Family as fellow human beings, it posits their condition as curable. In addition to his explicit expression of racism (vermin), Neville is condemned for his earlier killings and his current refusal to help. Finally, Richie utters here the equivalent of Matheson's conclusion, in which *Neville* admits that he is the monster, "I am legend" (170): "You don't belong." In the end, however, Richie's benevolence proves to be ill-placed, and Neville's characterization of the Family as "homicidal maniacs" true: the youth is brutally killed by Mathias who rejects his offer of becoming as they were before. They prefer their current abjection.

The film's less-than-subtle final image, in which Heston appears spread-eagled, having given his blood to save the world, thus figuring Christ as a sacrificial redeemer (Jancovich, "Heston" 60–61) further aligns with his career in biblical blockbusters. What is significant, however, is that although Neville has been presented throughout the film as an arbiter of good, his motives and moral rectitude largely unchallenged, he is killed off at its conclusion. The survivors are not the icon of Judeo-Christian, Western, patriarchal society, but the counter-culture Dutch and a bunch of children. So, as Jancovich concludes:

> Heston's body [...] may be presented as a powerful and positive image of masculinity but, in these cases, it is usually through its capacity to suffer, not to conquer, or through the sense that the masculine public persona is itself a painful and self-destructive one to maintain ["Heston" 66–67].

So, in spite of so many details that construct Heston's Neville as an unambiguous hero, a defender of civilization and humanity, the film makes its final appeal to a young, countercultural, idealistic audience. When we reexamine it through the lens of critical race theory, we will see that its messages about race are even more mixed than its ambivalent portrayal of Neville as "the man" but "cool."

Dead White Men: The Omega Man's Confused Racial Allegory

In an essay titled simply "White," Richard Dyer effectively argues that George Romero's *Night of the Living Dead* and its sequels offer allegories of the U.S., its consumerism, and its "military-industrial complex, with its underpinnings in masculine supremacy" (159). Its zombies are dead white men, preying inexorably upon the living, while the film's hero is a black man, often armed with Molotov cocktails (157–58), struggling to survive. This section offers a similarly racialized reading of *TOM*. As we shall see, traditional race readings underscore Neville's performed whiteness, a figure of the last white man on earth under siege by urban black hordes represented by the Family. A more sustained application of critical race theory, however, reveals that *TOM*'s racial allegories are not quite as neatly tied up as critics have presented. Indeed, Janina Subramanian asserts that "[t]he film's racial dynamics are as muddled as its politics" (47).

Performing White: Neville's and Heston's Race Identity

Heston's star persona attributed him with the ultimate moral authority invoked throughout history as Europeans sought to dominate other peoples in colonial settings around the world: the Judeo-Christian religious tradition. In Heston's later life he became famous for his role as spokesman for the conservative gun rights organization, the National Rifle Association (NRA), so viewers of *TOM* today have additional baggage to add to their reception of his casting as the last man on earth. In addition to this ideological baggage, his sandy blonde hair, pale skin, hairy torso, and blue eyes inevitably code Heston as "white." Why, then, would he need to "perform" his racial identity? Is whiteness as the norm not a given?

The answer to this question is a complex "yes, but no." Critical race theory tells us that while "white" may be the dominant, majority "race" in America, the first audience to which a mainstream popular culture text like a Hollywood blockbuster will play, even whiteness is a performed identity (see Chideya for an overview of the complexity of race categories and their varied meanings in America; 3–32). This notion is implicit in the preceding discussion of Lisa's changing portrayal of her femininity, from a more androgynous assertive role to a more traditional feminine role. Similarly, her hair and fashion choices, along with her dialogue also allow her to perform her "blackness." In discussions of film roles this performed aspect of race or gender is more obvious because actors play roles that were written for them and directed in certain ways by the filmmaking team, but the theory extends to individuals in real life, as well.

Furthermore, there are different kinds of whiteness that can be performed, linked to class, educational-level, profession, ethnicity, and nationality, among other things. Heston's biography reveals an interesting trajectory of whiteness for the actor. Heston's rural, working-class origins bring him closer to Matheson's original Robert Neville than any of the character's screen iterations. During his childhood in backwoods Michigan, his parents' divorce and his mother's remarriage brought him to urban Illinois. Through high school extracurricular activities like sports and drama, he transformed this uncultivated, rural image (Raymond 9–12). Readers may be surprised to learn that his early roles were frequently in theater classics, so that as a young adult, "Heston had transformed from a 'backward hick' into a sophisticated Shakespearean" (Raymond 16). Heston's own biography, then, reveals how an individual can work actively to change an aspect of identity that at first view might seem innate and immutable through active choices and performances.

With Heston cast in the role of Robert Neville, the character's whiteness appears unquestionable. First, in 1971, as a leading man in a Hollywood blockbuster it is essentially a given that he is white since *all* leading men were white. Then, we have discussed at length the actor's career-long association with biblical figures of "white" authority (never mind that in reality these individuals were historically Semitic peoples). In addition, Neville's own characterization creates associations with Julius Caesar, the military-industrial complex, leisure athletics like jogging, and his taste in home décor, all of which further code him as white. What is interesting is that his whiteness becomes overdetermined the minute he has explicitly to perform that whiteness while giving blood to Richie with the assertion that his is "160 proof good old Anglo-Saxon." By calling attention to his racial alignment at this moment of intimacy, Neville appears to ward off any potential contamination that might pass back from Richie to himself.

White Fear of a Black Planet: The Family as Black Power

Both Ryan Baker and Adilifu Nama read *TOM* as reflecting white anxiety about the Black Power movement and the race riots of the late 1960s. In his Jungian analysis, Ryan Baker offers a straightforward allegory: "the Family is a monolithic shadow to Neville, expressing deep-seated technological and racial anxieties. Neville represents science, civilization, and order, whereas the Family eschews these artifacts of society in lieu of destruction, religion, and mass identity" (200). In *Black Space*, his pioneering study of race in SF film, Adilifu Nama soundly condemns the film's depictions of black identity:

> With its visual coding of blackness, *The Omega Man* was a thinly veiled attack against the black nationalist stage of the black freedom movement [.... It] reflected the real-world racial paranoia over black militancy's spread to urban centers across

America. The film communicates the message that traditional white males are under attack. The bleak image of Neville, the failed military officer, as crucified victim foreshadows the fatalistic impulse of white masculinity and the narcissistic self-pity of white male martyrdom [51].

The film undoubtedly exploits racial anxieties in its depiction of the urban apocalypse, but the following analysis demonstrates that these allegories are much more blurred and confused than these critics would have.

TOM's images of the streets of Los Angeles littered with trash, upturned vehicles, broken storefronts, and fires burning at night as crowds hoot and holler may have seemed familiar to contemporary viewers as echoes of those seen in relatively recent media coverage of race riots in Watts—not far from the novel's original setting—in 1965, in Detroit in 1967, and Chicago in 1968, among others. It seems difficult to argue against the interpretation that the Family's white-face make-up and the pre-apocalypse white identification of their leader, Mathias, is a simple race reversal that only thinly disguises the group's metaphorical role as a symbol of black urban unrest. The portrayal of Mathias' right-hand-man Zachary by African American actor Lincoln Kilpatrick, with his sunglasses, afro, and references to Neville's "honkey paradise," particularly likens him to radical leaders of Black Power. Mathias refers to his followers as "brothers and sisters," invoking stereotypical black discourse, a practice derived from religious communities, but also used in the Black Power movement and black student activist groups (Heineman 245). Physically, Nama's description is on target:

> First, like the Black Power activists of the era, the mutants wear dark sunglasses as they provide soapbox speeches to the followers regarding the evil of "the Man" (Neville). Second the mutants wear only black robes and hoods, which work to code the colorless mutants as "black." Third, the mutants use Molotov cocktails to attack Neville at night, clearly signifying the racial unrest of the late sixties that erupted across the nation [....] Finally, in their condemnation of Neville, the mutants' rhetoric mirrors the Nation of Islam's extremist articulation of black nationalism. The Nation of Islam, a black nationalist, quasi-cult organization, advocated the idea that whites were "devils" united in systematically oppressing black people [48–49].

The Family, according to this reading, is symbolically coded as the disaffected black masses blamed for the destructive riots in urban centers across the 1960s. While this reading is compelling, there are a number of oppositional messages conveyed by the film that might invoke sympathy for the Family's cause in some viewers who see a certain justice in their accusations of oppression.

Despite explicitly contextualized images of the urban apocalypse, which play directly upon white concerns about the increasingly impoverished nature of America's major inner-cities developing across the 1960s and into the 1970s, *TOM* retains other images that align it more positively with certain aspects of the Black Power movement. Furthermore, these may also signal racially-motivated violence *by whites*, such as the cross-burnings of the Ku Klux Klan and other forms of intimidation involved in the southern white backlash to the *Brown v. Board of Education* decision on school integration. Indeed, one of the root causes of the urban riots of the late 1960s was the sense of black frustration at the lack of progress made in the social, political, and economic situation of African Americans since 1954, as documented by James T. Patterson in *Brown v. Board of Education: A Civil Rights Milestone and its Troubled Legacy* (2001).

First, let's re-examine the white make-up the actors portraying members of the Family so obviously wear.[9] It seems to be merely a thinly disguised reversal of blackface make-up used first by white, and later also black, minstrel show performers (Carlin 9; Bean *et al.* xiii; Southern 43). Through its deployment of this controversial practice, the film clearly calls attention to the question of race and asks viewers to interrogate how we interpret such supposedly simple and obvious social codes as skin color. Annemarie Bean, James V. Hatch, and Brooks McNamara write in the introduction to *Inside the Minstrel Mask: Readings in Nineteenth-Century Blackface Minstrelsy* (1996) that "minstrelsy is a gigantic mirror, reflecting America's struggle and policies on issues of race, class, and gender" (xi). Eric Lott's essay in that volume unpacks the ambivalence behind the practice of white performers darkening their skin with burnt cork, and then appropriating slave culture for the entertainment of white audiences, seeing "an instability and a contradiction in the form itself" (3).

In the dominant interpretation of blackface entertainment today, many scholars and the general public view it as a racist practice which, by lampooning the supposed behavior of, at first enslaved, and later free African Americans, was meant to reassert the myth of white superiority. Let's not forget that the term Jim Crow to describe the body of southern segregation law came precisely from a popular blackface character devised by white performer T. D. Rice in the 1830s (Carlin 10). Lott explains, however, how blackface has been reinterpreted by certain scholars as "a celebration of an authentic people's culture, the dissemination of black arts with potentially liberating results" (5). The sheer popularity of the form in the nineteenth century reveals "a profound white investment in black culture" (Lott 6) and simply represents one of the first instances in U.S. history in which white entertainers have appropriated and popularized black cultural forms, such as jazz, the blues, and rap, because of their liberating potential. The ambiguities behind such a practice become even clearer when black performers don blackface make-up, further underscoring how "[b]lackness, then, is not innate but produced, a cultural construction" (Lott 25–26). For, in addition to the naïve and gullible characters, there were also black dandy and trickster figures in the blackface repertoire, who, as they clowned, also flaunted the power of the black body and expressed the desire for freedom (Lott 12–13). Such analyses of the complex meanings behind the original use of blackface support this reading of the use of whiteface in *TOM* as more than a simple reversal, coding the Family as black and only black, as bad and only bad.

A similar color reversal occurs at the film's conclusion, perhaps suggested precisely by the type of polyvalent meanings such reversals can take on, as the "crucified" Neville's "white" skin becomes "black" in the negative reversal of the image before final credits role (admittedly, because the film is in color, the effect is less obvious). What does it mean when the film's hero is shown with a skin color other than white? Is it a subtle acknowledgment of the ethical ambiguities of his behavior as the last white man, an unrepentant, indiscriminate slayer, paying subtle homage to the myth's original ending in Matheson's novel? Does it allow that a "colored" man could be humanity's savior? Does it point ironically to Heston's own earlier career starring in biblical epics, in which the blonde haired, blue-eyed actor played Jewish characters? Again, rather than a simplistic black-for-white reversal, these characterizations foreground the question of race and skin color in order to underscore the fact that race is not a simple issue. They reveal that "race is socially constructed and its boundaries fluid in almost every case—except for the ambiguously located 'color line' in America between blacks and everyone else, which has proven slightly permeable" (Abu-Lughod 11). Even so, individuals have repeatedly violated it through various acts of passing, or been permitted to cross it because of tokenism, quotas, and exceptional success. Ultimately, *TOM*'s treatment of skin color blurs the issue, suggesting that no one's behavior in these situations is all black or all white.

Similarly, in addition to invoking medieval Christianity, the Family's black robes obviously reverse the Ku Klux Klan's white robes, as does their behavior: they want to burn things in order to purify, with sequences evocative of cross-burnings. Might some viewers not recognize the Family's nighttime gatherings around bonfires, and their relentless persecution of Neville as the preludes to a lynching? Indeed, this characterization invokes a comment by Lyndon Baines Johnson during the 1965 Watts riots, likening rioters to Klan members (Patterson, *Eve* 183). Conversely, a black GI returning from World War II had likened racist southerners to "the Alabama version of the Germans" (Patterson, *Brown* 1), others referred to Jim Crow laws as "Hitler's Creed" (Patterson, *Brown* 54).

Besides Mathias, the white man in white face, Zachary, a black man in white face, bears further scrutiny. In his Jungian interpretation, Ryan Baker unconvincingly argues that Zachary represents "an aspect of Neville's repressed self" (202). He uses this argument to fuel a traditional reading of the film as an expression of white fear:

> Zachary represents the ushering in of a new era, a new society, and Neville is a staunch symbol of the remnants of old society. It is the embodiment of America's fear, societal usurpation through violence—specifically, a black uprising that would "infect" American society [203].

In fact, Zachary's significance lies in the manner in which he undermines the black-and-white allegories that analysts like Baker and Nama set out to make, but also because of his links to the Haitian zombie. It is not clear if the Corringtons or the film's make-up designer were at all familiar with the actual lore of the Haitian zombie, but this figure of the oppression of black workers at the hands of white (or later mulatto) planters is claimed to be identifiable by his whitened skin (Ransom, "Black Zombie"). The choice of a black actor for the role of Zachary becomes significant when read through this lens, as his whiteface reflects a form of zombification, whether it be a literal reference to the Haitian zombie or a metaphorical one of black oppression. It also invokes the assimilation of black Americans to the dominant white culture, a form of inauthenticity, perceived by some as even a race betrayal.

Another example of confusing race reversal occurs as the Family—physically ultra-white but allegorically supposedly coded as black—are accused of a certain form of racism. Lisa explains how she and Richie had attempted to stay with the Family immediately after the apocalypse, but that they soon had to leave, explaining that "[t]hey began to see how different we were, our skin, our eyes." Here, as now the white-faced Family resembles white racists rejecting the African American Lisa and Richie as different and so unacceptable, the racial allegory appears jumbled.

Rereading the Family's Message

Viewers in 1971 would certainly have more recent memories of black violence during the urban riots of the 1960s. But it is important to remember that black rage stemmed from an overwhelming sense of frustration that the non-violent Civil Rights Movement had failed to achieve real changes, which had been expected for well over a decade since the Supreme Court ruled that school segregation was unconstitutional in *Brown v. Board of Education* in 1954. A decade after the ruling, "virtually all southern black children who had entered first grade in 1954 and who remained in southern schools graduated from all-black schools twelve years later" (Patterson, *Board* 113). In the mid–1960s, the median family income of blacks remained about half that of whites (Patterson, *Board* 131). Furthermore, all too often forgotten are the waves of *white* violence in the south that erupted in backlash after *Brown*, culminating in the "Mississippi Burning" summer of 1964. As James T. Patterson reminds us, "[l]ong before the 1960s and 1970s, when battles over busing of children to schools erupted in violence, white people in these cities resorted to firebombings and other intimidating tactics" (*Brown* 4). In the late 1950s and early 1960s, the Ku Klux Klan reasserted itself, bringing white on black violence to new highs since its peak between 1890 and 1920 (Patterson, *Brown* 96; 87). If we use this lens to reexamine the Family in *TOM* as a representation of the Black Power movement, we can read the Family's preaching as oppositional references to the inequalities of material prosperity between blacks and whites which were at the heart of the largely justified black rage at poverty and injustice that fueled the urban race riots of the late 1960s.

For example, Zachary describes Neville as follows: "I see him living high in the light, while we struggle in the dark." Read metaphorically, this literal expression of the mutated Family's inability to support the sun's light (itself an ambivalent expression of their unenlightened status) echoes the anger of residents of Watts or Detroit, looking at "the man," specifically, the white man—figured by Neville—and his material prosperity as opposed to their poverty and lack of access to quality education and housing. There is potential here for a subversive reading of *TOM* as actually supporting the Black Power agenda, a reading suggested by Joyce Corrington herself in interviews. The potential for this oppositional reading seems quickly evacuated, though, when later on, Neville—again figuring the white urban dweller threatened by the rioting masses—expresses his resistance to them, a position which many viewers may share because it deals with the sanctity of the American home. When Lisa asks him why he stays in the city, he replies: "That's where I live. That's where I used to live. That's where I'm going to live. And neither Mathias or his family or any other son of a bitch is going to make me leave." He clearly figures here the threatened white, urban or suburban since neighborhood integration dynamics were now changing, righteously defending his property.

The traditional interpretation of the Family as an allegory for Black Power activists, as well as the more voiceless urban poor who rioted in various major cities every year since *Legend*'s first film adaptation in 1964, is partially confirmed by the memories of co-scenarist Joyce H. Corrington, who freely adapted Matheson's novel with her husband John William Corrington. In an interview included in the special features of the DVD release of *The Omega Man*, she directly admits that "this was the 70s and Black Power was very big" (Corrington). When this remark is given more context, however, we understand that her use of that expression was not uttered from a position of threat or of a desire to exploit white fear. Instead, admitting that it was her idea for the last woman on earth to be black, she also fills in some personal history for that inspiration. With a Ph.D. in organic chemistry, she was teaching at Xavier University, a historically black, Catholic institution ("About"). When she praises Rosalind Cash's portrayal of Lisa with "Black Power panache" (Corrington), it is clear from her facial expression and tone of voice that—although she may be trivializing the social activist movement as a fashion statement—this is a positive assertion. In her teaching job at Xavier, Corrington would have had daily interactions with young and idealistic African American students and could not have failed to reach some understanding of the dashed hopes and frustrations leading up to the radicalization of the Civil Rights movement into the Black Power movement. Christopher M. Moreman independently attests to the Corringtons' commitment to progressive social values, noting that John William had left academia after "a yearslong battle over the dismissal of a homosexual colleague with the Jesuit administration of Loyola University" in New Orleans (143).

Just as other works in Matheson's oeuvre elucidate interpretations of *I Am Legend*, it is also useful to revisit the Corringtons' career in support of arguments against those who view *TOM* as *solely* conveying negative, racist images. Eric Greene argues that the Corringtons offer a progressive image of hope for racial harmony in their script for *Battle for the Planet of the Apes* (114). Greene attributes the couple with a significant role in constructing this film's progressive message, contrasting their work with the film's original outline by Paul Dehn (writer for the three previous sequels in the franchise):

> Dehn either could not or would not extricate his characters from that compulsive cycle [of racial violence]. Justice, peace, and reconciliation were denied a place in his *Apes* stories. It took two other writers, John William Corrington and Joyce Hooper Corrington, to introduce even a meager glimpse of hope into the series [115].

Greene asserts how "the Corringtons' *Battle* screenplay empowers the victim to *choose* not to become a victimizer" (139) and "the commitment to 'begin again' is juxtaposed with the dire consequences of failing to achieve racial peace" (141). While *TOM*'s largely negative images of the Family can easily be interpreted as playing upon white fears of the Black Power movement and urban violence, a more in-depth analysis of the film's dialogue and the Corringtons' overall progressive attitudes force us to nuance this analysis.

Critiques of the White Man's World and His Agenda

Having re-examined the film's complex representation of racial violence and re-thought traditional interpretations of it, we can now see that the Corringtons retained the subversive core of Matheson's novel and its interrogation of its white hero and his moral imperative. On the one hand, the film's graphic conclusion overtly depicts Neville as a Christ-like figure of sacrifice, who saves the human race from Mathias and his mutant horde, sending a message that seems to be a conservative victory for the white man over the racialized masses. On the other, the film also emits some of the messages of the Black Power movement that Mathias and his crew appear to figure that supports *IAL*'s oppositional message that questions white might's right. Indeed, the Corringtons preserve Matheson's final message when the original Neville admits that he is the monster, he is the "legend" (170), placing it instead in the mouth of the film's villain, Mathias. Uttered not at the film's conclusion, which admittedly does give the last word to conservative values, but toward its beginning, Mathias alludes to Neville as the monstrous one:

> One creature, caught, caught in a place he cannot stir from in the dark. Nothing to live for but his memories, nothing to live for.... The Family is one. But him, that thing, that creature of the wheel, that lord of the infernal engines, the machines.... The evil forbidden things, the tools that destroy the world.

In addition to referring to Neville as the "creature," this speech also links him to the technology that has destroyed the film's world, placing it in the postapocalyptic situation that prevails. Later, Neville is overtly referred to as "the last of the scientists, of the bankers, the lawyers, users of the wheel. He's part of the dead." Through Mathias' discourse, the film allows a glimpse of countercultural and environmentalist critiques of science and technology and their potentially nefarious impact on the Earth and human life. In the end, Mathias accuses Neville: "How many of us have you killed? You're the angel of death, doctor, not us." This phrasing invokes the ultimate racist doctor and science's role in the Nazi's Final Solution: the head physician at Auschwitz, Josef Mengele, who was nicknamed "the angel of death." Thus, on closer analysis, the Corringtons have in fact maintained a good many details from Matheson's original novel, as these words echo Ruth's justified accusations toward Neville and his acceptance of his guilt.

Whereas Zachary figures a Black Power activist, Mathias may represent instead the white student protest movement that had gained steam since the hinge date of 1965. Whereas the predominantly white vein of the student protest movement is best known for its actions against the Vietnam War, for a time it worked with black activists, much as Mathias and Zachary work together. With the movement, various groups had an array of differing demands, both practical and utopian. Ranging from freedom to behave as adults, unfettered from the paternalistic policy of *in loco parentis* which gave university administrators the authority to police students' sexual behavior, to Marxist and Maoist socialist dreams, members of the movement displayed a wide array of beliefs and positions. One of these, according to Kenneth J. Heineman in *Campus Wars: The Peace Movement at American State Universities in the Vietnam Era* (1993), critiqued the increasing implication of public university research with the military industrial complex, which frequently funded it. This concern links directly back to Mathias' Luddite message, and Heineman's description of Tom Hayden allows the construction of a parallel between these two visionary—but portrayed as symbolically blind—figures. Summarizing Hayden's self-perception in his memoir, *Reunion* (1988), Heineman writes: "Hayden [...] argued that his was a redemptive, not destructive force in American society. Student activists politically empowered blacks, brought peace to Indochina, and exorcised malevolent Cold War spirits from the soul of the Democratic party" (1). While still a news anchorman in the flashback sequence Mathias had warned: "The very foundations of civilization are beginning to crumble under that adversary long feared, germ warfare." Given the current post-apocalyptic situation, his Family's fears about technology and their desire to blame techno-science for power appear justified. As Neville accuses them of being "barbarians," his own alignment with white, Western civilization is reinforced; but Mathias plans to fulfill the promise of his prediction: "We mean to cancel the world you civilized people made."

Positive Images for Future Racial Harmony

In contrast with the ambivalent portrayal of Mathias and Zachary respectively as white and black activists and the less articulate members of the Family as impoverished black citizens expressing rage through rioting, a group whose cause may have some justification but whose means ultimately cannot be tolerated, Lisa and Richie are portrayed clearly as "good colored people." If Lisa's original exterior is at first a bit rough around the edges, she becomes "civilized" under Neville's influence, as we see her identity evolve from that of a hip, urban Black Power activist into that of a suburban (white) housewife. Her jive-talking and the admission that she "hustled" her beautiful dress while making a stylized pimp-step (a clear, self-conscious performance of her blackness) may seem offensively stereotypical today, but for the time period these characteristics may have represented a step forward in the desire to portray "authentic" black characters on screen. Unlike the very straight, white-assimilated black television characters pioneered by Bill Cosby in *I Spy* (1965–1968) or the eponymous nurse in *Julia* (1968–1971) played by Diahann Carroll, Lisa and Richie are allowed to perform their own blackness on screen. And they do so in a powerful and articulate way, representing characters that have some dimension to them, no longer the butlers or drug-dealers of an earlier era of films (Bogle; Fain). Lisa's dialogue, for example, comes straight out of the rising genre of the Blaxploitation flick. While she's still uncertain of Neville's intentions, she puts him in his place: "All right you son of a bitch, you just hold tight, you mother [....] If you just have to play James Bond, I'll bust yo' ass." Her banter also includes the prophetic assertion, "Sure 'nough I'll crucify you, baby," as well as an overt engagement of racism.

When the interracial sexual tension begins to mount between Lisa and Neville, they discuss their meeting and the presence of the children. Neville suggests, "They might get spooked." To which Lisa retorts, "Hey, watch your mouth." While the film's real spooks—in its original meaning of eerie, ghost-like figures—are Mathias and his crew, this assertion allows Lisa to correct Neville who has unintentionally made reference to a contemporary racial slur.

Lisa's afro and colloquial sass seem to suggest the following message: "Look, middle-class white audience, just because she has an afro doesn't mean she's a criminal." Furthermore, Lisa's early suspicion of Neville reveals that racist stereotyping can work both ways; the film's ultimate message appears to be that after some initial misunderstanding based on appearances, once they really begin to talk and get to know each other, people from widely different backgrounds—Lisa and Neville—can get together to solve the world's problems.

Lisa and Dutch thus decide to trust Neville and bring him to their commune outside the city, which represents a utopian microcosm of a—to a limited extent—multicultural human society: in addition to the two African American characters, it includes the Asian Tommy and a perhaps Latino child, called Mario. The rest—the numbers of which vary by scene, but clearly under a dozen total—are all, however white, and Richie will die before the film's conclusion. Neville's position within this group, however, brings us back to his characterization as "the man, but cool"; in the end, he cannot escape his paternalistic image, playing the role of the Great White Savior. And while I agree with Nama's characterization that "[t]he ability of Neville's white blood to reverse the symptoms of a black teenager about to 'go over' is a powerful racial metaphor" (51), as Richie improves, instead of whitening, his skin darkens. The film allows a rather radical association here with whiteness as abnormal and blackness as the norm.

Before concluding any discussion of race in *The Omega Man*, we must, of course, consider its representation of the interracial relationship between Neville and Lisa. Whereas by 1971 it was certainly not the first interracial romance in film or television (Childs; Kennedy 95–96), it was a relatively early and prominent one. In his published journal, *In the Arena*, Heston explicitly invokes both his own iconic status as a patriarchal figure of authority and Rosalind Cash's reaction to their on-screen romance: "It was in the seventies that I realized a generation of actors had grown up who saw me in terms of the iconic roles they remembered from their childhoods. 'It's a spooky feeling,' [Cash] told me, 'to screw Moses'" (443). Even Nama admits that "Neville and Lisa are certainly a couple" (50). The couple does indirectly assert that their formerly taboo relationship has become perhaps permissible because it is the end of the world. As some chemistry comes into play between the man and the woman, the following exchange occurs:

> LISA: Now whatch'ya thinkin?
> ROBERT: Well, you know the old song, if you were the only girl in the world, and I were the only boy.

Neville thus elliptically acknowledges the extraordinary circumstances that have brought together the interracial couple. Later, as they gather supplies in the pharmacy, Lisa picks up a package of contraceptives and asks: "Are you ready for this?" While the frank discussion of contraception is definitely a sign of the changing times (the first birth-control pill had been available since 1960, but the recent sexual revolution had made it more widely available), their hysterical laughter and then awkward silence remains ambiguous. The film thus lightly touches in an overt fashion on the notion of miscegenation, but is unclear on its position. It is ridiculous that they should use birth control since they ought to repopulate the earth. In the end, however, their relationship is revealed to be impossible to sustain. Not only has Lisa begun to turn, joining the Family, Neville, of course, dies.

For Nama, the threat of miscegenation is at the core of *TOM*. His chapter titled "Bad Blood: Fear of Racial Contamination" argues that the film "draw[s] on racial eugenics and reflect[s] America's history of hypersurveillance of racial boundaries" (43–44), and that ultimately it "associates race mixing with dire postapocalyptic consequences" (47). He even sees Richie, with both Neville's and Lisa's (they are siblings and share a "bloodline") blood running through his veins as "represent[ing] the couple's racially mixed child" (50). Although Richie's wide-eyed idealism is naïve and results in his death, his hopes for a utopian solution in which "we could all get along" are at least allowed expression.

Once again, the film's meaning is ambiguous. On the one hand, the paternalistic white man, tolerant of difference up to a point (remember, where he loves Lisa, he's ready to kill Mathias and his crew like vermin), saves the world. However, the logic of the film renders his death necessary for a new human society to develop, founded by Lisa, Dutch, and the children. He must die not for the sins of these innocent survivors, as had Christ, but rather Neville dies for the sins of the white man and the flawed civilization he had built, as Mathias wished all along. As Dutch describes the new world they hope to found: "Just like the beginning of the world. Like we were starting all over again in the Garden of Eden. Only this time we don't trust no friggin' snake." Robert Neville, the Omega Man, the film's title invoking Christ's famous speech "I am the alpha and the omega," cannot be present for the new beginning. The film's conclusion, in which Lisa rides off with Dutch, the children, and Neville's blood to cure them all, then, remains ambiguous in its final racial message. While the numbers would suggest that the majority white population would assimilate the single representatives of African, Asian, and Latino heritage in the group, they are nonetheless subtly acknowledged as included in the mix that will make up America's reconstructed future along new lines and with new values.

The Omega Man *as Vietnam War Allegory*

In his analytical memoir, *When America Turned: Reckoning with 1968* (2014), David Wyatt admits that "I had entered college with a high-school textbook sense of American history, a belief in the righteousness of the country's foreign wars and in the nation's essential purity of intent" (88). The events of 1968, he argues, marked a turning point in that sense of American right; key, of course, in the graying of America's moral purpose was not just the troubling action occurring in Vietnam, but the increasing credibility gap between stated messages by the nation's leaders and their actual behind-the-scenes decisions. With the nation facing such a crisis in its faith in leadership, *I Am Legend* provided a vehicle for yet another popular engagement of the troubling issues facing the nation. And even with—or perhaps because of—Charlton Heston cast in the lead role, Robert Neville's true character as a relic of a bygone era could not help but peep through the cracks in the film's overt messages about the good father sacrificing himself for his children's survival. Also glimpsed through the cracks of a film that largely engaged questions of race are references to the conflict in Vietnam, a conflict in which race played a key role in the scandalous abuses that shocked the public. Thus, Matheson's core story, an expression of survivor's guilt about one conflict (World War II combat) and anxiety about present (Korea) and potential future (Cold War/Soviet Union) wars, leaves itself open to reinterpretation a decade and a half later in the Vietnam context.

Whereas Korea, sometimes viewed as a rehearsal for Vietnam, has been referred to as the "forgotten war," as Sylvia Shin Huey Chong asserts in *The Oriental Obscene: Violence and Racial Fantasies on the Vietnam Era* (2012), "[t]he trope of describing the Vietnam War as a national trauma" has become "omnipresent" (2). Today we are familiar with a number of iconic Hollywood films depicting that war from Francis Ford Coppola's *Apocalypse Now* (1979) to Oliver Stone's *Platoon* (1986) and Stanley Kubrick's *Full Metal Jacket* (1987). While the war was being waged and immediately afterward, Chong tells us, in contrast with World War II, during which "the close collaboration between Hollywood and the government" meant that the film industry became part of the war effort, film executives felt that Vietnam "was too fresh a wound in the American psyche" (127). Thus, "[b]etween 1964 and 1977 only a single Hollywood film [...] attempted to directly represent the Vietnam war" (Chong 127). But Chong admits, "This is not to say that the Vietnam war was completely absent on American movie screens during this time. In fact Vietnam haunted many films made in this era, often through the presence of Vietnam veteran characters" (128).

Although he is not specifically identified as a Vietnam veteran, Robert Neville in *The Omega Man* is a veteran of the "Sino-Russian War," a fictional conflict that had definite resonance with the then contemporary Asian situation. Like the Korean War, the "domino effect" theory was used to justify U.S. intervention in Vietnam to prevent the spread of communism from North to South. The use of a helicopter—a military vehicle made iconic during the Vietnam conflict—and the heavy presence of fire in the film's visual imagery, also invoke the specifics of Vietnam weaponry: the controversial use of Agent Orange and napalm, the burning of civilian villages, and even the self-immolation by burning of Buddhist monks in protest of the war. Just as Matheson's novel represented an allegorical working-through of World War II combat and survivors' guilt *TOM* may represent a collective fantasy engaging indirectly the ongoing war by displacing it onto a postapocalyptic setting not quite a decade before the first realist film productions dealing directly with Vietnam began to appear on American screens in 1978 (Chong 129).

Chong's analysis supports not only this reading, but it helps us understand some of the very mixed messages about race and the images of violence enacted by both Neville and the Family in *The Omega Man*. She argues that prior to the release of films like *The Boys in Company C* (1978), *The Deer Hunter* (1978), and *Coming Home* (1978), numerous metaphors were used to engage American fears and doubts about Vietnam in the media, including street crime, rural poverty, racism, drug dealing, and other wars in history (128). One example of such transference, the mega-hit *Patton* (1970), starring George C. Scott as the famous World War II general, was directed by Frank C. Schaffner, who also directed Heston in *Planet of the Apes*. Not only does *TOM* engage most of these issues, it blurs the lines between them, as seen in the Family's ambivalent portrayal as white but black, representing Black Power/Ku Klux Klan/white student activists all at once. Analyzing novelist David Morrell's recollection of the origins of his iconic Vietnam novel, *First Blood* (1972) which introduced the character of Rambo to the American public in its film adaptation starring Sylvester Stallone in 1982, Chong notices that Morrell falsely remembers a single news report in 1968 that juxtaposed images of Vietnam with images of urban rioting and student protest. She describes this blurred effect of memory which creates "a fascinating and phantasmatic triangulation between traumatized white war veterans, black urban rioters, and oriental guerillas" (36).

Chong sees a similar effect in the language of the January 1969 report of the National Commission on the Causes and Prevention of Violence formed by Johnson after the assassination of Robert F. Kennedy. Once again, we see this phenomenon of different kinds of violence blurring together in the American psyche of the times:

> Assassinations and revolutions are not singular events linked to proper names and specific dates but rather generic instances in a series full of imitations and variations. *The categories of violence also mirror and blur into one another, as the body of the slain leader becomes like the burning city, each a symbol of the nation while boundaries are threatened by dissolution* [34; emphasis added].

TOM reenacts precisely this blurring of the entire array of categories of violence assaulting the American public in the media at the time. Furthermore, as Chong observes "rioting and student unrest suggest a population out of control, its members refusing to stay in their proper roles" (34). Not only does the film blur the lines between urban rioting and student unrest in its depiction of the Family, Robert Neville—with his albeit ironic request for "a policeman when you need one"—also enacts the violent repression by the forces of "order," such as the Chicago Police or the Ohio National Guard, of these mass protests.

Although the indirect references to Vietnam cited above are sparse and there are no direct references to it, the most compelling link between this adaptation of Matheson's novel and the conflict in southeast Asia lies in the nature of Neville's enemies. Although it is a stretch, the Family's black robes might figure "the black 'pajama-clad' Vietnamese peasant guerillas" (Chong 4). Let us recall that one of the biggest moral ambiguities of both the Vietnam War and *I Am Legend* and its adaptations is the fact that the white soldier/slayer cannot distinguish between two different types of racialized Other. Neville indiscriminately kills both mindless and sentient vampires; the American GI in Vietnam kills not just Viet Cong soldiers but also innocent civilians precisely because he cannot distinguish between different types of individuals within a larger category, the racialized Asian Other, the "gook." This basic misunderstanding underlies Matheson's core myth, allowing it to be resuscitated at different times in relation to different groups. Thus, in addition to the obvious engagement of black and white, *The Omega Man* allegorically introduces America's problematic relationship with "yellow," as well, offering a possible elucidation as to why Robert Neville rejects the *yellow* track suit in a shopping scene with the line, "Bah, not my color."

The racial dynamics of *TOM* outlined in the traditional race readings of Baker and Nama with Neville as the last white man on earth trying to survive the onslaught of the black horde are completely overturned in the next big-screen adaptation of Matheson's novel. Francis Lawrence's *I Am Legend* stars African American action hero Will Smith in the role of Neville, himself under siege by a horde of ultra-white monsters. But before we turn to that analysis, some background discussion of how precursor films that directly engage the question of race by including a black man among earth's final survivors will allow us to address any sense of progress (or not) made in representations of race in American film at the dawn of the twenty-first century.

Racing the Last Man on Earth: The Precursor Films Five *and* The World, the Flesh and the Devil

It might seem a bit belated to discuss filmic precursors at this point, but they provide a good transition from *The Omega Man*, with its interracial romance, to our last chapter's discussion of *I Am Legend*, with its black protagonist. Half a century before the most recent film adaptation of Matheson's seminal novel, three films had already envisioned that at least one man in a small group of survivors would be black. Arch Oboler's *Five* and Ranald MacDougall's *The World, the Flesh and the Devil* predate both *LMoE* and *TOM*; in addition, the underappreciated New Zealand film, *The Quiet Earth* (1985) preceded *I Am Legend* (2007).

Filmed in 1951, Arch Oboler's *Five* was a seminal work in the spate of nuclear apocalypse films produced during the next two decades of Cold War scare, a number of which are analyzed by Jerome F. Shapiro in *Atomic Bomb Cinema*. Its sober speculative realism contrasts, however, with subsequent low budget horror fare produced by AIP, such as Roger Corman's *Day the World Ended* and *Attack of the Crab Monsters*, and the slightly more prestigious *Panic in the Year Zero* (1962), which Ray Milland both directed and starred in with teen idol Frankie Avalon. *Five* establishes several visual tropes invoked later in *LMoE* and *TOM*, such as the empty, trash-littered streets, skeletonized victims, and an aerial shot of the lone survivor dwarfed by the expanse of road around her. It also prefigures Corman's *The Last Woman on Earth*, as its focalizing protagonist is a woman, rather than a man: Roseanne Rogers (Susan Douglas Rubes).

Introducing what would become a cliché in such films, *Five*'s opening montage of a mushroom cloud followed by cuts to iconic buildings around the world cites a Bible passage in epigraph. The film follows Roseanne as she wanders alone, calling out "Somebody! Anybody!" Eventually, she reaches a house high in the hills (Oboler's own Frank Lloyd Wright designed home), only to find a young man, Michael (William Phipps)—something of a beatnik figure—already squatting there. They are soon joined by an elderly man, Mr. Barnstaple (Earl Lee), accompanied by a black man, Charles (Charles Lampin), an ex-GI and handyman, now acting as chauffeur. It is clear that Mr. Barnstaple is dying of radiation sickness, but he has one last wish: to see the sea. His new friends take him there, where the fifth and final member of their party joins them: a man immediately coded as foreign by his accent, Eric (James Anderson). Each has a story of how they survived: the pregnant Roseanne was in a doctor's x-ray room, Michael was trapped atop the Empire State Building, Mr. Barnstaple and Charles were locked in a bank vault, and Eric was at the top of Mt. Everest: "I was the only living thing!" He has been traveling the world looking for other survivors until his plane ran out of fuel in the sea.

This path-breaking film not only represents perhaps the first realist representations of a post-nuclear apocalypse, it also daringly addresses the race question through the presence of Charles. Although he maintains the role of a secondary figure, Charles appears to be fully integrated into the circle of survivors. Indeed, he has practical knowledge of agriculture and machinery that will be necessary to the group's survival, and he teaches Michael how to farm. Eric's arrival, accompanied by clear racial hostility, interrupts the utopian potential of this community starting over. Not only does he admit, "Your very presence is distasteful to me. To eat with you, sleep under the same roof with you," but he also finally murders Charles when the latter stumbles on his plan to leave for the city with Roseanne. Something of a Nazi-figure with his Germanic accent, Eric represents a specifically white male form of hubris; although he has conquered Everest, he is content here to idle and watch others work. His obsession with returning to the city to simply take, rather than grow, food, however proves fatal as he dies of radiation sickness. He is also a negative model of masculinity, with his entitlement and aggression; this is contrasted with Michael—who has an English degree from Dartmouth—who, although white, is ready to learn from Charles, to work for his food, and to start a new world, not reproduce the old one. Above all, he treats Roseanne with a respect that Eric—who treats her like a possession—fails to display. In the end, though, Jerome F. Shapiro argues that the film's superficial vision of enacting a liberal dream of racial harmony is foreclosed by the survival of the white couple. He compellingly concludes that

> *Five* is an example of a reactionary apocalyptic film, one in which the "vision" consists of rugged white individualism applied to social maintenance. Thus, typical of the 1950s, beneath the wholesome, optimistic liberalism, which resides on the surface of the film's text, is a great deal of angst about the changes liberalism brings [77].

Although it ultimately refuses to allow its black character to survive, *Five* nonetheless condemns Western technological, capitalist society, offering an alternative back-to-the-soil vision for humanity's future. Even more daring in its approach is *The World, The Flesh and The Devil (WFD)*, "suggested by" M. P. Shiel's Last Man narrative, *The Purple Cloud*. Directed and written by Ranald MacDougall, with a screen story credit to Ferdinand Reyher, this film more explicitly engages the problem of race within an even smaller group of survivors. Focalized largely through the perspective of protagonist Ralph Burton, with Caribbean-American actor Harry Belafonte cast in the lead role, like Robert Neville, he believes himself to be the last man on earth. Trapped by a mine cave-in, he has been isolated from what he and the viewer presume to have been a nuclear holocaust. Having dug his way to the surface, he goes in search of other humans, arriving in New York City and eventually discovering another survivor, Sarah Crandall (Inger Stevens)—or rather, she discovers him.

Director of photography Harold J. Marzorati's camera codifies a central visual trope of the Last Man narrative: the city—not in ruins—but completely empty. Rather than a pile of rubble, the expected result of an atomic explosion, the post–World War II apocalyptic film captures the sinister nature of perhaps an even greater fear than that of the instant death suffered at the epicenter—or even several kilometers from—of the bomb's detonation point: that of nuclear fallout, the "cloud" so presciently evident in the title of Shiel's plague novel (actually invoked in the prologue sequence to *Five*, which shows menacing clouds drifting over the world's capitals). Later, tapes of the last radio broadcast inform us that "tons of radioactive dust released in the upper-atmosphere" by an unknown nation has caused the apocalypse. Thus, the city, still standing in all its grandeur, but without the ant-like hordes of humans that normally populate it, offers a much more disquieting image for Cold War audiences, particularly when a long shot reveals the sole survivor, dwarfed by the skyscrapers, wandering the streets alone. Practically speaking, without the Computer Generated Imaging (CGI) available today filmmakers had no other choice than to leave the city standing, but the empty city has nonetheless become a central trope of the genre, recurring in twenty-first century films like Danny Boyle's *28 Days Later* (2002).

A regular trope in the Last Man genre involves the lone protagonist reaching out to mitigate his solitude by searching for other survivors; in earlier literary models like Jean-Baptiste Cousin de Grainville's *Le Dernier Homme* (1805; trans. anon. *The Last Man*, 1806), Mary Shelley's *The Last Man*, and Shiel's *Purple Cloud* and more recently, George R. Stewart's *Earth Abides*, he had to accomplish this through travel. In *WFD*, Ralph prepares to travel from his West Virginia mining town to New York City; his preparatory activities introduce visual and sound motifs that will recur in later films, from *The Last Man on Earth* through *I Am Legend*. Invoking Cold War fears and society's preparedness for it, he sees a poster for the Civil Defense program, finds their headquarters, and obtains a Geiger counter and a gun. He traces his route on a map from West Virginia to New York City; the iconic image of the Brooklyn Bridge looms large behind him, but jammed with cars he cannot cross it. He finds a boat, and we get a glimpse of the Statue of Liberty before he crosses to Manhattan to land at the New York docks. Although this film apparently owes little or no inspiration to Matheson's 1954 novel, as he wanders the empty streets of New York, Ralph yells in a deeply resonant voice, "Come out! Come out! Are you all crazy? I can feel you all staring at me."

Having left the church, again wandering alone, dwarfed by the skyscrapers, Ralph appears as a Western frontiersman in an interesting parodic sequence. Frustrated by the failure of an answer to his calls, he shoots; at the time, he is pulling a wagon—not a pioneer's covered wagon, obviously, but a child's wagon. Soon, he lights a fire in the middle of the street and heats up a can of beans to eat. Although the "extraordinarily handsome" (Kennedy

96) Belafonte's acting talent does not match that of his more intense contemporary and close friend, Sidney Poitier, the viewer nonetheless senses his isolation and frustration. When he seeks to fill the void, adopting two mannequins whom he names Snodgrass and Betsy, we begin to realize that this film may actually be about race and that the nuclear apocalypse provides an allegorical vehicle for the expression of the isolation of the black man in an American consumer society constructed for the white majority, a notion recently explored in Ralph Ellison's poignant novel *The Invisible Man* (1952).

Like Charles in *Five*, Ralph is the man who "can do things"; perhaps a stereotyped image of George Washington Carver's ideology for blacks to integrate into American society by learning trades at his famous Tuskegee Institute, both of these African American characters are portrayed as *capable* and *knowledgeable* in contrast with their decadent white antagonists, the antipathetic Eric and the cynical Ben. Indeed, Ralph has restored civilization to his luxury apartment, the precursor to that of Heston's Neville; not only has he begun to decorate by saving artwork and books from the ruined libraries and museums, he has hooked up a generator. As he "entertains" Betsy and Snodgrass, white mannequins—yet another visual trope later borrowed by *TOM* and *IAL* (2007)—in elegant clothing, he allows a glimpse of black rage to emerge, accusing Snodgrass: "You look at me, but you don't see me. You don't see me, and you wouldn't care if you did. Do you know what it's like to be lonely?" He then throws the dummy off his upper-floor balcony, triggering the shock that will allow him to meet Sarah, who has been surreptitiously spying on him. Believing Ralph has killed himself, she emerges from the shadows, crying out. The black man and the white woman thus meet, metaphorically, over the white man's dead body.

From the start, the racial difference causes tension. As an amazed Ralph moves to touch the only human being he has seen for months, Sarah shrinks: "Don't touch me!" Ralph replies, "That's great. We're the only two people alive in the world, and all you can say is don't touch me." She admits, "I'm afraid." But after they have introduced themselves according to social convention, before leaving for her own building, Sarah admits, "I need you, Ralph Burton." Although they live in separate buildings, Ralph installs the telephone; through daily interaction and routine, the two form a bond of close friendship and trust. Unlike Neville, they have no enemies to fight; like him, however, they scavenge to fulfill their daily needs, another central trope of the subgenre. The sudden nature of the catastrophe and their location in a cultural mecca, however, allows them to indulge their desires in a manner not available to the literary Neville in his ransacked world, but one adopted by Heston's in *TOM*. With shops and boutiques suddenly abandoned and intact, Ralph and Sarah occupy some of their empty time "shopping" for luxury goods as the entire empty city has become their larder and their wardrobe. Since they have not yet realized the sheer valuelessness of fur coats and designer suits in a world with no humans and thus no economy, the protagonists scavenge luxury items like designer dresses and caviar from the abandoned storefronts.[10]

As two healthy, attractive young adults who are also "good" people, sexual tension inevitably arises, allowing the race question to be explicitly addressed in the film's dialogue. As they have lunch together at Ralph's apartment, Sarah asks, "Ralph, wouldn't it be easier if I moved into this building?" As the image cuts to his black hand reaching to clear her plate in front of her white bosom, he freezes, to answer, "No [...]. People might talk." As they clear the dishes to the kitchen, tension builds; we see that Ralph's industry may derive in part from his need to sublimate his own sexual desire for Sarah, which he continues to control and repress. It is a thoughtless comment on Sarah's part that brings the tacit problem to the fore; as the slightly older Ralph appears to give her advice, she retorts, unthinkingly: "I'm free, white, and 21. I'm going to do what I please!" For the moment, he lets the comment pass, but then Sarah becomes maudlin: "Marriage. I'll never get married now, will I? [...]. But there's nobody left to marry anybody." This last ambiguous statement allows Ralph to attempt to calm her; always the fix-it man, "We'll find somebody for you. Somebody to marry! [...]. I'll do the marriage. I'll be the mayor."

The sequence refuses to end there, building more and more tension as their conversation skirts their desire for each other and its expression/repression. Having defused Sarah's tears by offering hope, Ralph has also deflected desire away from himself and onto a potential other. Yet when Sarah suggests, "We have to keep hoping, don't we?" He can't resist replying, "As long as we're alive, the world's still alive," bringing the conversation back to a "we." Their tango continues, as once Sarah had rejected Ralph's touch, now she asks for his help with a task that requires he touch her: she needs a haircut. This brilliant sequence introduces all of the unspoken taboos about interracial romance of the time; Ralph, conditioned to know that lynching is the consequence for a black man touching a white woman, physically shrinks from the ultrablonde hair of Swedish-American actress Inger Stevens. She must practically force him, and his aggressive chopping with the scissors begins to allow his rage to appear; she asks him to be more careful, and eventually the unspoken words come out:

> SARAH: It's taking you too long to accept things, Ralph. This is the world we live in. We're alone and we have to go on from there.
> RALPH: I don't know what you are talking about.
> SARAH: You know me well enough to be honest with me.
> RALPH: Don't push me. I'll be so honest, it'll burn you.
> SARAH: I know what you are if that's what you're trying to remind me.

RALPH: That's it, all right. If you're squeamish about words, I'm colored. If you're a polite southerner, I'm a nigra—nigger if you're not!
SARAH: I'm none of those things Ralph.
RALPH: Little while ago you said you were free, white, and 21. It doesn't mean anything to you. It's just an expression you've heard for a thousand times. But for me it was an arrow in my gut!
SARAH: Ralph, what do I say? Help me. I know you—you're a fine, decent man. What else is there to know?
RALPH: In that world that we came from, you wouldn't know that. You wouldn't even know me. Why should the world fall down to prove I am what I am? There's nothing wrong with what I am.

Now that the problem has come out in the open, Ralph prefers not to talk about it again. Their friendship is mended, but only partially. Once again, Ralph condemns the society they used to live in, but refuses to move forward himself to start a new world. He has planned an elaborate birthday party for Sarah, but everything he does is subservient: opens her car door, provides a recorded song (which expresses his desire for her indirectly; the film uses Belafonte's singing skills to introduce several songs), and serves her meal. But when she asks him to eat with her, he retorts, "Mr. Burton isn't permitted to sit with the customers." He later refuses her request to dance. And yet, the viewers have been shown that his birthday present to her is an enormous solitaire diamond that resembles an engagement ring.

What makes Ralph hesitate to act on his desire for Sarah becomes clear as he announces the news "You and I are not alone in the world anymore—civilization's back." In another effort to reach out to potential survivors, Ralph has been broadcasting from a radio station, WKYL, every day at noon, a trope also found in *LMoE* and the 2007 film of *IAL*. That day, his efforts have been rewarded: he has received an answer in French, probably from Europe. This sign of others will be confirmed even more clearly a few days later as a third survivor joins them in New York.

Sexual tensions between survivors is a recurrent theme in texts involving a small group, as seen in *Five*, in which the two fittest men clash over Roseanne, as they would a possession. In *WFD*, Ralph and Sarah's still platonic biracial idyll is disrupted by the arrival of Benson Thacker. Thacker's characterization is significant, since he is played by Mel Ferrer, himself a potential cypher for American race categories. As the son of a Cuban father of Spanish descent and an Irish mother, how would he identify himself with the former category of "white non–Hispanic"? This problematic label reveals clearly the fiction behind racial typing in the U.S.; if we divide whites into Hispanic and non–Hispanic categories, then why not divide black into subgroups? Although not as aggressive as Eric in *Five*, and actually explicitly denying that racism plays a role in his antagonism toward Ralph, he presents a somewhat cynical face and openly expresses his desire for Sarah. The white aggressor appears to be repeatedly foiled by the black pacifist. Given the film's open engagement of the race question, the casting of Harry Belafonte, a gentle, highly cultivated man was essential to allowing the film to even broach such a controversial topic as interracial sex. While on the one hand, his past roles categorized him as a "safe" black man, on the other, his medium brown skin and handsome features make him a "believable" object of desire for Sarah. Donald Bogle describes his career portraying the "Good Colored Boy" in *Carmen Jones* (1954), his breakout film role, but also his immense attractiveness to women, black and white (190–91).

Although it might be presumed that his West Indian origins distance him from American politics, Kimberly Fain describes Belafonte as "a close friend and confidante of Martin Luther King Jr." (88) and outlines his participation in the March on Washington (alongside Charlton Heston). Just how controversial the question of interracial romance was at the time should be pointed out: in 1959, the nation was still experiencing the southern white backlash against the *Brown v. Board of Education* decision on school segregation, which had carefully avoided ruling laws against interracial sex and marriage as unconstitutional (Patterson, *Brown* xxiii). When this film premiered in 1959 at least nineteen states still had "laws prohibiting and punishing interracial marriage" (Pascoe 270); and in the states of Alabama and South Carolina, constitutional amendments completely lifting penalties for interracial marriage were not passed until 1999 and 2000 (Pascoe 307–10).

Just as the two characters had sparred and danced around their situation for a good third of the film, the introduction of Ben simply adds another variable. The final third of the film allows tension to build between the trio as Ralph increasingly allows himself to be shut out, and Ben makes his desire for Sarah ever clearer. Sarah, however, doesn't know what she wants; and in the end, she is partially allowed to decide. Or rather, she refuses to choose at the film's closure. Ben forces a showdown, chasing Ralph around the city with a rifle, but cornered, the weapon pointed directly at him, Ralph refuses to fight, throwing his own weapon down. Ben screams "Fight, damn you. Why won't you fight?" Ben replies, "I've got work to do. Gotta save things." Sarah arrives and takes Ben's hand—a close-up on the black and the white hand coming together appears highly significant—and, yet since Ben has proven unable to shoot Ralph either, Sarah takes his hand, too. The film's final frame shows the three of them walking peacefully down the street hand in hand with the title "The Beginning" superimposed over the image. As its peaceful outcome suggests, Nama notes that *WFD* "ideologically endorsed the nonviolent integration philosophy of the civil rights movement" (51). But while it was courageous enough to overtly address the issue of racial prejudice in America, Ben's presence ultimately forecloses the constitution of the interracial couple as the new Adam and Eve.

Although it involves no element of race—apart from all the Latin Americans implicitly killed around our three survivors—one more film merits brief comment here because of its more lurid conclusion when two men compete for the affections of *The Last Woman on Earth (LWoE)*. Written by Robert Towne and directed by Roger Corman for American International Pictures, which also distributed *LMoE*, *LWoE* might be termed a postapocalyptic exploitation film,[11] using the lure of sex (*viz* the film's publicity poster) and contemporary fears of nuclear holocaust to entice audiences to theaters and drive-ins. On vacation in Puerto Rico, the tellingly named *Evelyn Gern*[12] (Betsy Jones-Moreland) and her husband, Harold Gern (Antony Carbone), survive a cataclysmic but temporary loss of oxygen because they are scuba diving, thus protected under the water and provided with oxygen above ground by their diving gear. Once again, a third wheel arrives in the form of Martin Joyce (writer Robert Towne, billed as Edward Wain), a young attorney. While the issue of race is set aside, class and masculinity enter the picture, ostensibly pitting the macho corporate gangster (Gern has been indicted for a second time in a multi-million dollar housing scandal) against the educated white-collar man. The film—written on the go, the script still being completed as location shooting began (Corman 71)—bizarrely complicates the characterization of these rivals for the affections of the last woman, however, perhaps to appeal to the teenage and young adult audiences it targeted (Whitehead 7).

A self-made-man who proves to be an authoritarian, patriarchal, representative of capitalism, Harold treats Evelyn like a possession and is ultimately interested in rebuilding civilization as it was. In contrast, the younger, more gentlemanly Martin ultimately betrays the stereotype of the man in the gray flannel suit suggested by his profession. As soon as they realize the full extent of civilization's breakdown, he opposes Harold's attempts to restore order and a work ethic. Happy to seize the day, he convinces Evelyn to join him. The film ambivalently explores how Evelyn will decide which of the two men will be her Adam, largely placing audience sympathies with Martin, but allowing Harold a final victory. As Alain Silver and James Ursini conclude, in its Darwinian parable "[t]he fittest male has survived and won the female, thereby guaranteeing the renewal of the human race" (138). Thus, while the film appeared daringly to raise the issue of female desire and choice, as Gary Morris observes (33), the last woman is forced to return to her husband through his aggression. In this respect, its pessimistic conclusion—in which the new society will simply perpetuate the violence of the old—matches those of *I Am Legend* and *The Last Man on Earth*.

The underappreciated independent film, Geoff Murphy's *The Quiet Earth* (1985), reprises this narrative dynamic of a last trio involving a white man, a white girl, and a Māori man, but with far more stunning conclusions. Based on an original novel by New Zealand SF writer Craig Harrison, this

Three. The Last White Man on Earth 143

non–Hollywood product filmed in a peripheral settler colony clearly adapts its racial dynamics to its specific cultural and geographical setting. Not only does the last white man, Zac Hobson (Bruno Lawrence), partially admit his complicity in the end of the world, he ultimately sacrifices himself leaving his red-headed companion, Joanne (Alison Routledge), to play Eve with a Māori Adam, Api (Pete Smith). Erroneously referred to as a remake of *WFD* (Shapiro 79), it nonetheless involves numerous tropes from both the Ranald MacDougall film and *TOM*, such as the use of the radio to reach other survivors, mannequin companions and "shopping" sequences, and the collection of works of art. Its conceptualization of humanity's demise is original, however, involving neither nuclear apocalypse nor pandemic, but rather an experimental energy source, known as Operation Flashlight.

Released in 1983, two years after Ronald Reagan announced his Strategic Defense Initiative, alternately known as "Star Wars," the film expresses a small nation's fear of manipulation by world powers,[13] thus somewhat exonerating its hero, Zac Hobson. A scientist on the project, Zac survives the "effect," an unexpected outcome of the initiative, which has destabilized the fabric of the universe, because he had died at the very moment the life-destroying pulse was emitted. When he meets Joanne, she asks point blank if he and his "cronies up the road there had something to do with all this?" He fudges somewhat, shifting blame away:

> Dunno. It was an American idea. They were experimenting with an energy exchange grid all around the earth. Aircraft drawing directly from that grid so they wouldn't have to refuel [...]. We were just one small unit on a whole network of stations around the world acting simultaneously. Besides, we might not have been responsible. God may have just blinked.

When Joanne breaks down in tears, however, he admits that he believes they are responsible, and that perhaps he can fix the problem.

Having developed a daily routine and become lovers, Zac and Joanne unexpectedly encounter Api, a leather-clad Māori who threatens them with an automatic weapon. At first playing upon racial stereotypes, the menacing native—descended from a people known for its ferocity in battle, a trait fetishized today in the New Zealand All-Blacks' rugby club's ritual use of the *haka* chant prior to matches—refuses to trust the "white boss." Indeed, at one point, when Joanne cries out in frustration over their antagonism, "I wouldn't ride with you if you were the last man on earth!" Api retorts, "I'm workin' on it." The men's antagonism derives not only from an ineradicable colonial history, but also because of the clear sexual attraction building between Joanne and Api. Surprisingly, Zac appears to have accepted their union, telling Joanne: "Whatever happens, I can handle it." But then he sacrifices himself, driving a semi named the "Lady Di" loaded with explosives into the grid's satellite in order to reverse the effect, which has destabilized the universe. As Joanne and Api, naked after making love on a fur coat, realize what he has done, the film concludes with Zac regaining consciousness and watching a Saturn-like planet rise on the horizon. The film thus allows for the constitution of the interracial couple and punishes the white man for participating in "an exclusive all-male club playing God with the universe." The New Zealand film thus makes much clearer and more radical statements condemning Western civilization and techno-science's implication in imperialist capitalism. Yet its final image is that of an astonished Zac who, having been absolved of his crimes through his heroic act, appears to have arrived on another plane of existence.

While they share a number of visual features and plot elements, above all their postapocalyptic setting and their focus on a tiny group of survivors, the adaptations of *I Am Legend* depart from these films' model through two central plot features. First, the films discussed above focus on and presume the continued survival of the "human race" as we know it because of the presence of a Last Woman. Second, these films posit no enemy to threaten human kind; there is no monstrous, competitor race that the Last Man must fight off. Instead, they reduce to a single opponent, the trope of other, malevolent humans that David Skal observes in what he calls "bomb shelter narratives" (11), also seen in *Panic in the Year Zero!* and most of today's zombie apocalypse treatments. Although they offer realistic extrapolations of the possibility of an apocalyptic event that threatens to erase humanity from the face of the earth, in their failure to imagine the posthuman, *WFD* and *LWoE*, are clearly less science-fictional than *LMoE*, although they are speculative. Furthermore, in their refusal to engage a monstrous Other, they cannot really be called horror films; not even skeletonized corpses can be found in the empty streets. *Five* does slightly fit this category with its sprinkling of skeletonized corpses across the postapocalyptic landscape, but *The World, the Flesh and the Devil* is completely sanitized of any abject images. Indeed, its realism is undermined by the absolute absence of human corpses; in a way, though, how all of the dead simply vanished suggests in some ways the biblical rapture, leaving a world swept clean for a new start. In contrast, the Last Man filmic narratives that adapt Richard Matheson's *I Am Legend* to the big screen maintain both the science-fictional and horror genre classifications of Matheson's novel. They nonetheless draw upon the tropes of apocalypse offered both by their literary model and those visual tropes found in these and other postapocalyptic films of their day.

Jerome F. Shapiro's *Atomic Bomb Cinema* makes clear that the 1950s and 1960s represented a peak period for the representation of the apocalypse due to the Cold War. Significantly, the final two adaptations of Matheson's *I Am Legend* were also produced during a peak production in a new kind of apocalypse film. Both Francis Lawrence's *I Am Legend* (2007), starring Will Smith, and Griff Furst's *I Am Omega* (2007), starring Mark Dacascos, transform Matheson's vampires into zombies *and* they feature a non-white actor in the role of the last man on earth. The next chapter examines, then, how Matheson's core myth has been appropriated and transformed in the context of post–9/11 America.

Four

The Color of the New Hero
Will Smith in *I Am Legend*

"*I can still fix this. Ground zero. This is my site*" (Lt. Col. Robert Neville, *I Am Legend*).

"*He believed you could cure racism ... by literally injecting music and love into people's lives.*"

"*And if she does make it to Antioch, or they get her anywhere they can make a cure—well, we go back to the way it used to be—taking care of the sick and the idiots and the slackers, and make this world the piss hole that it was. And right now we got ourselves a perfect utopia. Darwinism. Survival of the fittest*" (Vince).

On the cover of the DVD release of Francis Lawrence's eponymously titled film adaptation, *I Am Legend*, Will Smith strides determinedly toward the viewer, the ruins of the Brooklyn Bridge looming darkly behind him. Its neo-Gothic arches recall nothing so much as Caspar David Friedrich's Romantic-era paintings, *Monastery Graveyard in the Snow* (1817) or *The Abbey in the Oakwood* (1810). This first impression of confident masculinity in the face of catastrophe quickly erodes on closer inspection; the hero's brow is furrowed with worry as his compassionate gaze meets the spectator's. His accompanying canine avatar looks not at the camera, but off-frame; the German shepherd's emotive eyes and perked ears signal a lurking danger. Although its sepia tones reduce the impact, perhaps the most significant feature of this image appears in the color of Robert Neville's skin and, insofar as the story's plot is concerned, it most certainly lies in his blood. Not only does this recent adaptation of Richard Matheson's 1954 fable of the post–World War II white male under siege underscore the issue of race by casting a black man in a role previously played by Vincent Price in *The Last Man on Earth (LMoE)* and by Charlton Heston in *The Omega Man (TOM)*, it also interrogates past and present paradigms of masculinity and the dual questions of white right/white might. Above all, it does this in the context of post–9/11 America.

This chapter focuses on the changing color of the hero and what it means for the last man on earth to be black and to be the savior of humanity's future. Because of the film's success, but also because of changes in the academic world, *I Am Legend* (2007) (henceforth *IAL07)* has garnered more academic interest than any of the other films and has increased interest in Matheson's eponymous novel. But critics disagree as to its racial messages as signaling a progressive turn toward full acceptance of black Americans in the twenty-first century or as yet another erasure of blackness from the face of the nation. Not just the fact that the hero is black, but that he is a black *man,* is also of significance, given the sexual subtext beneath the racism endemic in the Americas since the introduction of slavery in the fifteenth-, sixteenth-, and seventeenth-centuries. Once again, critics disagree as to whether Will Smith is allowed to serve as a positive model of masculinity and authority—black or white—or if he has been "neutered" so as to appear unthreatening to majority white audiences in such a role of leadership. This chapter will also ask, on the level of genre, what kind of slayer is Will Smith's Neville, and how are Matheson's original vampires transformed, yet again, in this version of the story?

Significantly, *IAL07* was not the only screen adaptation of Matheson's novel to be produced in this period; partly desiring to profit from its success with a copycat product, director Griff Furst and writer Geoff Meade added a martial arts spin to the legend with *I Am Omega* (2007), a straight-to-DVD production that later aired on television's Syfy network before the first decade of the new millennium was over. They also chose to feature a hero-of-color, casting multiracial Hawaiian actor Mark Dacascos in the role of "Renchard." Like *I Am Legend,* this film invokes the zombie apocalypse, but embraces it much more fully. Although perhaps not a work of art, clearly the most esthetically inferior of the film adaptations discussed here, as a popular culture text it is worth considering what *I Am Omega* (henceforth *IAO*) brings to the dialogue between Matheson's novel and American society today. The chapter concludes on a discussion of what both of these films, with their overt messages of a multicultural America via racialized heroes, interject in the ongoing analysis of the changing image of the United States as an arbiter of right. What does the presence of a racialized hero mean in the new twenty-first century context of the War on Terror? Does it restore America's ethical position, indicating that we have a right to intervene now that we have assumed the role of righteous victim? Or does it question even further the direction a neoliberal, increasingly interventionist America is taking through its interrogation of white right?

Why Another Legend? Why Now?

Francis Lawrence's *I Am Legend* fits neatly into the growing corpus of post-9/11 disaster films that have appeared over the last decade and a half. As Steffen Hantke observes (172–73), its New York city setting allows for a visual and emotional replaying of the collective trauma the nation felt when Al-Qaeda terrorists flew planes into the twin towers of the World Trade Center, triggering a series of attacks on strategic locations on September 11, 2001, resulting in the sudden, highly public deaths of 2753 Americans and others[1] living and working on our soil. As editors Aviva Briefel and Sam J. Miller argue in the introduction to *Horror after 9/11: World of Fear, Cinema of Terror* (2011), "the horror genre has experienced a dramatic resurgence over the last decade" (1). The essays in their volume "analyze metaphorical representations of concrete events like the destruction of the World Trade Center, the Iraq War, and the tortures perpetrated at Abu Ghraib" (1). Briefel and Miller remind us that, in addition to our exposure to media saturated with images of violent tragedy, the Patriot Act also led to a certain silencing of dissent and included new assaults on individual civil rights. They underscore the significant cultural role that these horror films play in terms of "working through" such collective traumas and violations:

> In a context where we could not openly process the horror we were experiencing, the horror genre emerged as a rare protected space in which to critique the tone and content of public discourse. Because they take place in universes where the fundamental rules of our reality no longer apply [...] these productions of popular culture allow us to examine the consequences not only of specific oppressive acts funded by our tax dollars, but also of the entire Western way of life [3].

The present chapter participates in such a project, building on a perceptive piece by Steffen Hantke published in *Horror after 9/11* and responding to other recent analyses of the film.

Answering the question in the intertitle of this section seems relatively clear: the time was ripe for a new iteration of the *I Am Legend* myth in the first decade of the new millennium. But it is worth asking why a project in discussion since the late 1980s or early 1990s did not materialize until 2007, particularly given that racial tensions were at an all-time high again in the early 1990s. After the 1960s movements for major social change, both from within the system as proposed by Lyndon Johnson's Great Society social programs and from without via various civil rights, student activist, and peace movements, it seemed that the revolution had calmed down in the 1970s. Certainly, the Watergate scandal and the Energy Crisis, linked to violence in the Middle East, left a shadow on the decade, but Jimmy Carter's leadership style as a promoter of reconciliation and moral rectitude restored the nation

Four. The Color of the New Hero 149

to a sense of normalcy. John Case and Rosemary C. R. Taylor, in an introduction to a study of *Co-ops, Communes and Collectives: Experiments in Social Change in the 1960s and 1970s* (1979), describe the decade after *The Omega Man* as follows:

> Now in the late 1970s, the hot topics are the rise of the black middle class, the new conservatism on campuses, the successful integration of feminist and environmentalists into conventional politics. So the seventies are deplored as the era of apathy and collective narcissism [4].

That trend toward a more generalized affluence, social and economic conservatism, coupled with personal narcissism continued on into the 1980s.

The election of a popular conservative, Ronald Reagan, supported by voters, both young and old (Rossinow 1), presented the face of a nation united, rather than divided. In *The Reagan Years: A History of the 1980s* (2015), Doug Rossinow describes the prevailing ideology:

> Reaganism consisted of a few core components: an insistence that unfettered capitalism is both socially and beneficially good; a fierce patriotism that waves the flag, demands global military supremacy, and brooks no criticism of the United States; and a vision of society as an arena where individuals win or lose because of their own talents and efforts [1–2].

A strong leader with like-minded allies in the UK and Canada fostered the growth of the neoliberal economy, but also of the "Moral Majority" and the "Pro-Life" movements, a backlash against the achievements made by feminist, gay rights, and Civil Rights activists. This was the decade marked by Wall Street day traders, polo shirts and pleated khakis, and ultra-muscular action heroes like Arnold Schwarzenegger, Sylvester Stallone, and Jean-Claude van Damme. By the end of that decade, the Cold War appeared to be over, with Glasnost followed by the fall of the Berlin Wall in 1989 and the subsequent dissolution of the Soviet Union. "Reagan's goal of securing U.S. primacy was achieved—and the related hope of reviving U.S. national pride and self-confidence, widely perceived to have faltered following the Vietnam War, was also realized" (Rossinow 4). This description suggests that mainstream America—if we take Hollywood production designed to appeal to a mass audience as a reflection of it—perceived no compelling need to explore the collective and individual psyches in relation to anxieties about white right or paranoia about losing the position of privilege. Not only was the nation triumphant abroad, "Reaganism was also [...] the politics of the white 'backlash' against the advance of racial equality" (Rossinow 7). Robert Neville's story would certainly be a buzzkill to the climate of triumphant capitalist individualism.

The 1990s started with the promise to continue business as usual, with Reagan's vice-president, George Herbert Walker Bush, now in office as president.

And although the U.S. became engaged in a military conflict, this one seemed to exorcise the ghost of Vietnam's traumatic defeat (Chong 1–2). Operation Desert Shield, the codename for the First Persian Gulf War from August 1990 to February 1991, ended in forty-two days with a victory, the liberation of Kuwait. "But," according to Michael S. Kimmel in *Manhood in America: A Cultural History* (2006),

> the manhood regained under Presidents Reagan and Bush was the compulsive masculinity of the schoolyard bully, defeating weaker foes such as Grenada and Panama, a defensive and restive manhood, of men who needed to demonstrate their masculinity at every opportunity [192].

In spite of the general perception (among whites) that African Americans had finally achieved the equality demanded since the 1950s, black expectations had not been fulfilled as James T. Patterson documents in detail in *Freedom Is Not Enough* (2010). Spike Lee's *Do the Right Thing* (1989) had fictionalized the interracial tensions mounting again in urban areas, which exploded into real violence in the 1992 Los Angeles race riots, with more hostility expressed during and after the highly-publicized trial of former football hero O. J. Simpson for the murder of his wife Nicole Brown Simpson. The interracial couple clearly remained an untreated sore spot on the national psyche.

America demanded a change in leadership, and Democratic candidate Bill Clinton completed that decade in office, surviving a sexual scandal and military interventions in Bosnia and Kosovo. The 1990s seem to be as self-absorbed as any decade, with the .com boom replacing the day trading boom of the decade prior. Writer Haynes Johnson calls this period *The Best of Times: America in the Clinton Years* (2001) with only slight irony, referring to it as "an era characterized by accumulation of wealth and self-indulgence" (ix). Although Clinton had also considerably cleared the national debt, voters opted again for an image of assertive masculinity, electing George W. Bush, the son of the man who won the First Gulf War, as president. Little did he know that he would soon lead the nation through its most significant surprise attack since Pearl Harbor and would be embroiled not only in the Second Gulf War but also in the War on Terror. He remained in office for nearly the entire first decade of the new millennium, and his is the era of the last two adaptations of *I Am Legend* we will consider.

Although there seem to have been plenty of tension points in the later 1970s, 1980s, and 1990s, particularly regarding crises in race and masculinity (Kimmel 192–253), the period most similar to that of the original composition of Matheson's twentieth-century myth is precisely the period in which the next film adaptations of his novel occurred. In fact, the early decades of the twenty-first century actually resemble rather clearly the decade or so after

World War II, allowing us to establish a parallel in conditions between the Cold War/ Civil Rights–era publication of Matheson's novel and today. Steffen Hantke's political analysis of the 2007 film discusses at length the similarity between Cold War popular culture and the several remakes of films from that era in the early twenty-first century, asking: "What better reason to remake Cold War horror films could there be than the realization that the United States after 9/11 is eerily reminiscent of the Cold War and its foreign policies and domestic social and political climate?" (182).[2] In both periods, the nation had suffered an unexpected trauma (Pearl Harbor/ Al-Qaeda attacks), lived under constant threat of a vague and ominous enemy (Communism/ Islamic terrorists), and repressed individual civil rights in its effort to defeat the enemy (McCarthyism/ Patriot Act).

As equally clear that *IAL07* forms part of a larger context of disaster films in the post–9/11 era, it is also obvious that it participates in the evolving imagery of the zombie apocalypse that filmmakers have indefatigably explored in recent years. The "Zombie Renaissance," as Kyle Bishop terms it, began with Danny Boyle's *28 Days Later* (2002), in which Cillian Murphy plays a brilliant last man on earth, until he begins to gather a small group of survivors. Although *IAL07* refers to its monsters, clearly labeled as vampires in Matheson's novel and its first film adaptation, as "darkseekers," their physical appearance draws upon both the whitened-skinned zombie-like plague victims in *The Omega Man* and other manifestations of the "speedy zombie" found in twenty-first century zombie apocalypse films (Dendle, "And the Dead").

Will Smith as SF Hero

Talk of a projected remake of *I Am Legend/The Omega Man* had already begun in the mid–1990s (Arnett 60; Berger 57; Bradley 265), with such big names bandied about as those of director Ridley Scott—coming off the SF and SF-horror successes of *Blade Runner* (1982) and *Alien* (1979)—and Arnold Schwarzenegger, action hero par excellence with several SF films to his credit, like *The Terminator* franchise, *The Running Man* (1987), and *Total Recall* (1990). For whatever reason, these projects stalled, and Mark Protosevich's screenplay, completed in 2000, was shelved until after the turn of the millennium. Perhaps sensing a new parable for the post–9/11 era, producer/writer Akiva Goldsman, who also co-wrote the earlier Will Smith SF vehicle *I, Robot* (2004), took the project under his wing. Ostensibly, he brought in Smith and the latter's production company, Overbrook, but Warner Bros. by necessity stayed involved as they refused to give up film rights acquired for *The Omega Man* (Bradley 265). Although Smith did not officially sign onto the role of

Robert Neville until 2006, he is cited as attempting to recruit Guillermo del Toro to direct; since del Toro was busy, Francis Lawrence was hired in 2005.[3] Lawrence had cut his teeth on *Constantine* (2005), with Keanu Reeves as the title's supernatural detective, and *Legend*'s success played a significant role in his hire for the blockbuster *Hunger Games* trilogy (2013–2015). It is Smith, however, who retains our attention here.

Born in Philadelphia in 1968, Will Smith was raised in a middle-class home with two working parents, nurtured by the Baptist Church. Nonetheless, he was attracted to the nascent genre of rap music in the mid-1980s, performing as The Fresh Prince with D. J. Jazzy Jeff (Jeffrey Townes, a childhood friend). Their popularity and Smith's progressive, counter-stereotype image of the clean-cut rapper earned him a regular television series, *The Fresh Prince of Bel-Air* (1990–1996). This fish-out-of-water situation comedy mocked its protagonist's bourgeois relatives and posited this character, also named "Will Smith," as a more "authentic" (read: racially profiled) African American cultural model, coming from a single-parent home in Philly, sent to suburban California by his mother to keep him out of gang trouble. His hip, but moral, heart-of-gold image helped establish Smith as *the* rising young black actor to follow in the footsteps of Denzel Washington, with his similar medium brown skin, good looks, and clean-cut appearance. In contrast with, for example, the dark-skinned Wesley Snipes frequently cast in anti-authoritarian roles, Smith offered Hollywood a non-threatening black role model. He began to add starring role upon starring role in drama, action, and comedy features like *Six Degrees of Separation* (1993), *Bad Boys* (1995), and later *Ali* (2001), *The Pursuit of Happyness* (2006), and *Seven Pounds* (2008). Founding his own production company, Smith not only gained more control over his roles, "he is a cultural producer and image maker" (Fain 163).

The horde of hyperwhite zombie hybrids and their Alpha Male (Dash Mihok, center) attack Neville's lab. *I Am Legend*, Warner Bros. DVD.

At the time of *I Am Legend*, Smith was the highest paid actor in Hollywood (Hantke 166), and many of his breakout roles were in SF-related films. In his pioneering book *Black Space: Imagining Race in Science Fiction Film* (2008), completed prior to the release of the *IAL07*, Adilifu Nama argues that "Will Smith reinvigorated the status of blackness in SF cinema" (39). While SF films had been slow to cast actors of color in major roles until around 2000, according to Nama,

> Will Smith is a seminal figure in American SF cinema. His blend of the racially nonthreatening posture of Sidney Poitier with the charismatic bravado of Eddie Murphy [...] proved quite a successful formula. As a result, Will Smith became part film trailblazer, part comic relief, and pure pop sci-fi cool. He laid the groundwork in the 1990s for a more central, defiant, and charismatic version of black cool [39].

In addition to *I, Robot* and *Hancock* (2008), the *Men in Black* franchise released its third installment in 2012. Although the ambitious *After Earth* (2013), based on a story idea of Smith himself and co-written and directed by M. Night Shyamalan, showcasing Smith's son Jaden failed to meet expectations for U.S. audiences, it was a commercial success in Europe (Fain 166). Interestingly, it reproduces some aspects of *IAL07*, including the core scenario of a lone man attempting to survive on a postapocalyptic Earth. In this case, though, Kitai Raige (Jaden Smith) and his father Commander Cypher Raige (Will Smith)—that name choice alone raises questions about the film's aesthetic merits—have crash-landed on a hostile home planet long abandoned by a human race that has colonized space. With the more conceptually interesting *Seven Pounds* and *Hancock*, *IAL07* remains one of Smith's strongest, most dramatic performances, for as Robert Neville, he—and his dog—must carry almost the entire film on their own.

The Last Man on Earth is Black: I Am Legend

With credit retained for the Corringtons' earlier adaptation for Warner Bros., co-scenarists Protosevich and Goldsman (who also produced the film), clearly acknowledge *IAL07*'s status as a hybrid work. Indeed, Glenn Jellenik describes the Smith vehicle "more as a remake of *The Omega Man* than an adaptation of Matheson's novel" (68). As with earlier film adaptations of the 1954 novel, *I Am Legend*, critics sought a certain fidelity to the original. Before Linda Hutcheon, film theorist Robert Stam argued staunchly for other criteria for assessing adaptations in "Beyond Fidelity: The Dialogics of Adaptation" (2000). Stam raises a number of points pertinent to the 2007 film adaptation of Matheson's novel, which despite its restoration of his title seemed to stray even farther from "the fundamental narrative, thematic, and aesthetic features of its literary source" (Stam, "Beyond" 54). Stam notes that, typically, for adaptations "[t]he greater the lapse of time, the less reverence toward the source text and the more likely the reinterpretation through the values of the present" ("Beyond" 57). With half a century intervening between the novel and its eponymous film adaptation, it is thus not surprising that *IAL07* appears to have operated the greatest transformation of Matheson's core story and its various details. Furthermore, it also transforms aspects of its other acknowledged intertext, *The Omega Man*, produced well over thirty years prior to the Will Smith vehicle. And, of course, the most visible change operated by this film is the casting of a black man in the role of its hero. Stam includes casting choices among the aspects of the adaptation process from novel to film that render exact fidelity impossible. If we substitute Matheson's protagonist for his example of Gustave Flaubert's *Madame Bovary* (1857) and its film adaptations, we see clearly that

> a film, by contrast, must choose a specific performer. Instead of a virtual, verbally constructed [Robert Neville] open to our imaginative reconstruction, we are faced with a specific [actor], encumbered with nationality and accent, a [Vincent Price] or [a Charlton Heston] ["Beyond" 55].

Going beyond the marked differences between these two actors, *IAL07* changed the very race of the novel's protagonist in its film adaptations; the impact of this choice upon viewers' reception and interpretation of the story, then, is central to this chapter's analysis.

From *TOM*, the film nonetheless retains many aspects of Lt. Col. Robert Neville's characterization, with the exception, of course, of the stunning race reversal by casting Smith in the lead role. The film opens with overhead shots of the devastated city and an exciting chase scene featuring a 2007 red Mustang Shelby GT500 with white racing stripes, quoting almost verbatim the Heston film. Two significant alterations, however, make for a kinder gentler Robert Neville: at this point, he is not hunting monsters in the overgrown urban jungle, but rather deer, and he does so in the company of his very emotive German shepherd, Sam. The star's glamor exceeds that of Heston (at least for today's viewer) whose hairy torso simply cannot compete with Smith's six-pack, visibly maintained on-screen in Neville's exercise routine. Like all of the Robert Nevilles so far, he must find survival strategies to while away the time alone, including regular visits to the video store where he flirts with a mannequin, scavenging for food and fuel, and systematically hunting and killing the threatening beings, here referred to as "darkseekers," that humanity has become after an epidemic caused by a medical accident.

Each film updates the etiology of the pandemic to fit contemporary circumstances. Here, a preface sequence presents Dr. Alice Krippin (Emma Thompson) blithely announcing the discovery of a vaccine for cancer. We soon learn, via flashback as in Matheson's novel and *LMoE*, that this ostensibly beneficial discovery has resulted in a major epidemic, transforming humanity into mindless, bloodthirsty, excessively pale, and (with the help of CGI) supernaturally speedy and streamlined monsters. This film restores to Neville many of the domestic aspects of the pre–*Omega Man* texts, an aspect that Steffen Hantke suggests was also related to this version's ultimate casting choice; in contrast with Charlton Heston's biblical hero image or that of Arnold Schwarzenegger, proposed earlier, "the final decision to go with Will Smith shifts the character from exceptional action hero to American everyman" (169). Thus, like the original Neville and even Morgan, he has lost a wife and daughter to the epidemic; now, he must observe a rigidly disciplined routine, maintaining his (albeit glamorous) Washington Square townhouse bunker to stay safe. Eating is a pleasure-less chore, and really only one thing keeps him going: the family dog. Even more integral to his survival and identity since Sam represents the only other living tie to Neville's past life (in contrast with the strays found by the character's earlier avatars), he feeds and bathes the dog, almost maternally. Somehow, when we learn that he is a she, her name shortened from "Samantha," Neville's care for the animal is even more moving. As is the case with other Smith SF roles, as Sharon DeGraw argues, the sexual tensions found in Matheson's novel and *TOM* are absent from *IAL07*. Even after he meets survivors Anna (Alice Braga) and Ethan (Charlie Tahan), who have heard his daily broadcasts via radio and come to New York to find him, paternalistic friendship is all he has on his mind.

Like *TOM*, the theatrical release version of *IAL07* concludes with the heroic self-sacrifice of its hero. While he has successfully kept himself safe, he has lost Sam; hope returns when Anna and Ethan answer his radio calls signaling the existence of other survivors, but the darkseekers find his bunker and launch a massive attack. This attack is motivated by the fact that Neville is holding a particular female specimen in his basement lab. Following *TOM*, his military background has also provided him with scientific training, allowing him to conduct what appears to be rigorous experimentation to find a cure. He realizes that he has succeeded in reversing the virus' effects precisely at the moment of the attack; unable to hold off the zombie hordes—for this film clearly images its monstrous Others in resonance with the contemporary zombie apocalypse film—Neville confronts their apparent leader, sacrificing himself so that Anna and Ethan can escape with the serum that holds a cure. An alternate ending, however, was released with the DVD version of the film, in which Neville survives, accompanying Anna and Ethan to the walled enclave of uninfected human survivors in Vermont. Whether or not Neville survives, both versions of the 2007 film radically revise Matheson's original ending, which had ultimately positioned the sole-survivor Neville as the monster, taking the novel's final assertion, "I am legend," out of context. As Anna and Ethan (with or without Neville) drive through scenic New England and arrive at their destination, a voice-over narration even more completely revises Matheson's ending, by transforming Neville's legendary status from that of monstrous leftover from the past to heroic savior of humanity's future. As Steffen Hantke argues, Lawrence's film thus reverses Matheson's oppositional conclusion which called into question Neville's moral imperative. Will Smith's Neville, instead, is clearly celebrated as a culture hero who has saved a civilization, the entire human race even, implicitly worth saving, diametrically opposed to Matheson's and even *The Last Man on Earth*'s ultimately hopeless endings for humanity as we know it.

Vampires into Zombies: What's New?

A number of developments in American society and in film technology appear reflected in the various changes and updates that *IAL07* brings to Matheson's novel and its other avowed intertext, *TOM*. Let's begin with the film's setting; the move from Los Angeles (the southern California location of Matheson's novel) to New York City allows the film's visual designers to invoke the very location of the 9/11 tragedy. Advances in the technology of visual special effects (Venkatasawmy), including the digitization of the film process allowing for the near seamless integration of Computer Generated Imagery facilitated this move. Partially freed from actual location shoots, they could transform the city as they wished through the magic of virtual reality. The overall aesthetic of the postapocalyptic city is nonetheless retained from the earlier film adaptations of Matheson's novel but also invokes more recent films in the genre's post-millennium revival. For example, the protagonist's solitude is underscored by featuring him dwarfed by the towering skyscrapers, but alone in streets that should be bustling with people. CGI, however, allows the team of *IAL07* to literalize the metaphor of the urban jungle—a visual device actually present in much earlier literary models such as Mary Shelley's *The Last Man*—by depicting how nature has reclaimed the city. Grass grows tall between the sidewalk cracks, beginning to erode larger sections of cement, and deer run wild through the city streets, hunted by lions—ostensibly escaped from the Bronx Zoo.

Like all of his homologues, literary and filmic, this Neville must scavenge supplies, visiting various city locations, some directly borrowed from *TOM* (and thus indirectly derived from *The World, the Flesh and the Devil*). Just as Heston's character went "shopping" and encountered mannequins, so does Smith's; instead of viewing *Woodstock* in a movie theater, Smith's Neville watches *Shrek* (2001) on a home DVD system. Although he must perform regular "zombie" maintenance, as did his literary model, Will Smith's Neville enjoys luxury digs in a Washington Square townhome, images of which closely resemble Heston's fortress-like dwelling, complete with high-powered spotlights, in *TOM*. Like Ralph Burton in *WFD*, Smith's Neville collects art masterpieces attempting to preserve the accomplishments of Western civilization.

Janina Subramanian, in her perceptive comparison of *IAL07* with John Sayles' *Brother From Another Planet* (1984) notes "[t]he gentrification of poor and working-class neighbourhoods" (39) occurring in the 1980s and largely complete by the turn of the century. In a reversal of the white flight associated by some critics with Matheson's original novel,[4] we see the re-bourgeoisification of urban neighborhoods that has occurred in this affluent section of New York, one that in the twenty-first century now includes African Americans.

As in *TOM*, we see our hero ambivalently coded, open to multiple interpretations. Unlike Matheson's working-class anti-hero, *IAL07* the film constructs its protagonist solidly within the bourgeois elite (a class frequently passed off in popular-genre film as the American norm), as his gentrified home suggests. Like the other film Nevilles, Will Smith's character is a military officer with scientific training; his middle-class status works to distance him from potentially negative images of African Americans. In great contrast with Lisa's urban black discourse in *TOM*, his English accent and grammatical usage is standard. Whereas Heston's Neville was "the man, but he's cool," the message about Smith's Neville to a majority white, middle-class audience is "yes, he's black, but he's like us." And yet, unlike any other iteration of Robert Neville, however, as an African American, Will Smith's character bears an ancestral burden shared by neither Price's nor Heston's white-skinned characters: the history of slavery, segregation, injustice, and oppression. In spite of Janina Subramanian's argument that his affluent dwelling divorces Smith's Neville from "any kind of historical connection to the black community" (50), the color of the new hero's skin inevitably changes everything. But just what does this change of race bring to the character and to the film's ultimate message?

Besides the most obvious feature—the differences in age and skin color of the protagonist—there are some significant differences in this new film, some of which restore aspects of Matheson's original. Above all, *IAL07* restores to Robert Neville the wife and family that *TOM* robbed him of. Structurally, the effective use of flashback—present in the novel and all of its screen adaptations—explains the catastrophe that led up to the current situation, but it also fills in the backstory of Neville's pre-holocaust life, building further sympathy for his current plight. Not only does he appear in these as a loving husband and father, his inability to save his family haunts him still. The only remnant of his former domestic contentedness that remains is the puppy he had given his daughter for Christmas, and that she lovingly left with him to keep him company when his military duties required that he stay in the city as everyone else was evacuated. That puppy has now grown into a dog, and the film's writers fully exploit the melodramatic potential of man's best friend as a companion for the last man on earth. Building on the brief sequences with the stray found in Matheson's novel and *LMoE*, by transforming Sam into a family pet, the last surviving remnant of meaningful human relationships for Neville, they masterfully multiply the sense of tragedy the viewer will feel when the animal, attacked and infected, must be euthanized by Neville himself.

Furthermore, Neville's interactions with Sam reveal that the current situation has *not* hardened him. Although like previous slayers, he consults a map and his watch, and systematically checks apartments both for supplies and darkseekers, he does not appear to have become a monster himself. Not only does his careful bathing and feeding of Sam humanize Neville, it actually maternalizes him; the good father before the breakdown of society, he is the good mother in its aftermath. He speaks to the animal lovingly and patiently, clearly teaching it how to respond and survive in the current situation. Unfortunately, a situation he has not expected—a glimmer of intelligence in a single darkseeker, the analog of Ben Cortman referred to only as the "Alpha Male" in the film's cast list—results in the animal's loss. At this point, the viewer realizes, as well, that the social interaction with the dog was a major element in his ability to maintain a grip on his sanity, to maintain hope for the future in a seemingly hopeless situation as the last man on earth. And, like his forerunners, this Neville is going to learn the hard way that what he refers to as the "hive," is not comprised solely of drones.

The physical construction of Neville's nemeses, the "darkseekers," also owes some debt to *TOM*, although Gretchen Bakke situates it within a trend in twenty-first century horror films of whitening the monstrous Others. But whereas the early 1970s had not yet solidified the iconography of the zombie, rendering the plague victims as somewhat ambiguous monsters, mutants rather than outright zombies or undead, by 2007 the zombie renaissance was in full swing. Whereas Matheson's novel sought to supply a rational, "scientific" explanation for a supernatural monster from the Gothic tradition, namely, the vampire, it did not fully disavow the supernatural, allowing the efficacy of religious symbols as a deterrent. Paradoxically, although *IAL07* offers a nominally secular account of its monsters, invoking religion only tangentially and in relation to Neville's role as humanity's savior, it restores a sort of numinous mystery to the darkseekers' construction. Although a prologue indicates clearly that these transformed beings are the formerly human victims of a virus, their depiction—again, the result of CGI technology—in the film lends them a supernatural air. Their lithe build, eerie hive-like behavior, preternatural speed, and demonic screams all make them ghost-like; in this sense they also diverge from the excessively corporeal zombies of contemporary hits like Robert Kirkman's *The Walking Dead* franchise, *Zombieland* (2009), and other recent iterations of this theme.

With their excessively pale skin and lithe forms, the darkseekers do, perhaps, resemble one filmic vampire, an early adaptation of Stoker's *Dracula*: F. W. Murnau's *Nosferatu* (1922) and its reprise by Werner Herzog in 1979. As suggested in the introduction to this chapter, foregrounding the significance of the neo-Gothic architecture of the Brooklyn Bridge, the twenty-first century *I Am Legend* rediscovers a Gothic heritage seemingly lost in the ultra-hip, ultra-contemporary *The Omega Man*, restoring to its monsters a preternatural eeriness absent from the Family. Our first real good look of the darkseekers occurs not in an action sequence, but rather in a scene fraught with the fear and suspense associated with the Gothic and horror genres. Neville follows a trail of blood—possibly that of his emotive canine companion—into a dark building; struggling with his fear, he slowly searches for Sam in the maze of corridors. He then sees a group of apparently human figures, huddled in a circle, their backs turned, bizarrely vibrating in a synchronized wave of motion. They are bald and pale, shirtless, but wear pants; the audience is never quite able to grasp what they are doing, as the suspense is ruptured by Sam's whine, Neville's gaze landing on an individual darkseeker feeding on a deer. Gunfire explodes and the monster shrieks and writhes preternaturally. Both dog and human run. As a slayer, this Neville is *not* the relentless, systematic killer found in Matheson's novel, but rather a fearful interloper on territory he knows no longer belongs to him.

Whereas in that sequence the darkseekers are clearly portrayed by human actors, in another sequence their posthuman evolution is portrayed as even more spectral in nature with the use of CGI technology. Lured into a trap by his enemies and having had to put down his beloved companion Sam after she is attacked and infected by their demonic dogs, a disheartened and clearly suicidal Neville drives out at night, parking at the docks. Although one might think he is safe in his large black SUV (yet another symbol of his upper-middle class status), he is not; for the horde of darkseekers, phantom-like with their lithe, streamlined bodies eventually attacks. Following *TOM*, just as Rosalind Cash saved Charlton Heston from the Family, on cue, Brazilian actress Alice Braga as Anna, drives in to save Will Smith from the horde.

The overt evacuation of the darkseekers' connection to supernatural monsters coupled with the film's scientific logic of the virus to explain the apocalypse cannot completely cover a religious subtext that carries through all of the film adaptations from Matheson's novel. References both to organized, Judeo-Christian religion as well as a more nebulous metaphysics of synchronicity recur throughout the film. At the very beginning, the remnants of civilization in the urban jungle include a glimpse of a wall bearing the image of a butterfly and a poster declaring "God still loves us." The butterfly motif recurs each time we see Neville's daughter in the flashback sequences, as she makes the shape of a lepidopterid with her fingers, suggesting a sign that binds her to her father. Furthermore, Neville, his wife Zoe (Salli Richardson), and daughter Marley (Willow Smith) pray together before taking their leave during New York's evacuation, perhaps in an effort to acknowledge the significant role played by Christianity in providing enslaved Africans in America with hope and offering strength and guidance to them through the additional difficulties during the later battle for civil rights (Harvey). As a scientist, however, Neville expresses skepticism when Anna attempts to convince him to find the survivors' colony, referred to as Bethel, with her and Ethan. Not only is Bethel a location of biblical significance (in Hebrew it means "the House of God" and the Old Testament includes numerous references to such a city), when pressed, she admits "God told me. He had a plan." It is only in the film's concluding moments, as Neville glimpses a butterfly tattooed onto Anna's back that a divine plan appears validated, connecting the poster image to Marley's sign-language to Anna's mission to find Neville. In this manner, Smith's Neville is connected back to Heston's as the divinely ordained savior of humanity.

When Is a Black Man "Safe"? Race in I Am Legend *(2007)*

In his 1996 landmark study of race in *The Planet of the Apes* franchise, Eric Greene posits about the original 1970s films that at that time "[w]hite stood as the unquestioned standard for and embodiment of human" (49). He goes on to wonder: "We must ask if U.S. audiences then—or now—would have accepted, for instance, an African or Asian man or woman as the symbol of humanity?" (49) He implies that the mid-1990s were perhaps still not ready for a dream that had become a reality a decade later, for the third film adaptation of Matheson's 1954 novel does just that. Does Smith's casting as Robert Neville and his characterization in the film mark a milestone in race relations, signifying that American audiences are ready to embrace a black hero? Subramanian concludes not only of Will Smith's success, but also that of political leaders like Colin Powell, Condoleezza Rice, and Barack Obama, that

> [s]uch contemporary African American icons represent a patriotically multicultural future in which blackness can be divorced from its historical associations with violent injustice. *I Am Legend* exemplifies and complicates this "colourless" American nationalism (37).

But Subramanian also critiques this assimilation as a form of racial erasure. Engaging her and other analyses of race and masculinity in *IAL07*, this section teases out the complexities of what it means when the last man on earth is black.

Nama observes the increasing presence of black characters in SF films in the twenty-first century arguing that "[i]n the wake of September 11, black representations in the SF films of today may function to assuage an acute case of domestic paranoia" (40). Published in 2008, Nama's study of race in SF film, *Black Space*, addressed Smith's career as SF action hero without considering *IAL07*. In an unpublished conference paper, Sharon DeGraw provides us with an even more extensive account of Smith's SF film career from his first blockbuster hit, *Independence Day* (1996), through the relative failure, *After Earth* (2013). She traces Smith's rise out of the proverbial ghetto of sidekick and comic relief status typically allowed black actors to become one of Hollywood's top-paid leading men (Subramanian 44–45) and an influential producer (Fain 149). DeGraw attributes part of that success to a process of a gradual acclimatization of mainstream white audiences to Smith's presence, a process allowed by an initial "neutering" or rendering "safe" of the black male on screen. Over time, Smith's talent and charisma have allowed him to take on increasingly central, powerful roles, says DeGraw. Much of her argument engages the problem of masculinity, as well, demonstrating that race and gender are categories that are inextricably linked in the American imagination. DeGraw argues that because SF is a genre frequently seen as "an asexual cinematic niche" (4), "Smith was able to launch relatively quickly and successfully from a secondary role to protagonist as a result" (4).

Citing both Nama and black SF author Steven Barnes, DeGraw discusses how in Hollywood film, "fears of black male sexuality, particularly in connection to white women, prompt indirect narrative strategies which prevent or lessen sexual behavior" (5). And while she attributes Smith's later, more sexualized leading roles to a contemporary trend through which "'white apprehension' about black male sexuality is slowly waning" (7), she acknowledges that early in his career "Smith combined his signature comedy with a new action hero role, charming the audience and disarming the seriousness of the situation and any controversy the racial revision entailed" (8). Both DeGraw (22–23) and Subramanian (48) note that whereas in *The Omega Man*, Charlton Heston was allowed to engage in an interracial sexual relationship, Will Smith's Robert Neville remains chaste. Even in Smith's next SF film *Hancock*, in which he has an overtly sexualized relationship with a white woman (Charlize Theron), DeGraw notes that the potentially threatening sexual charge is neutralized for audiences since the film forecloses the constitution of the interracial couple by situating their actual sexual union in the Jim Crow past and invoking the specter of lynching (27).

Ultimately, DeGraw concludes that when cast as Robert Neville in *IAL07*, "Smith's literal replacement of an iconic white male actor heralds a new age for SF" (18), but Bakke and Subramanian remain more skeptical of the progress made in terms of Hollywood's representations of race in this film.

Subramanian, like DeGraw, underscores Will Smith's construction as a "safe" black male, arguing that "[h]is star image combines contradictory qualities that simultaneously mark his blackness while foreclosing its narrative significance and, more precisely, the potential political significance of blackness after 9/11" (45). Because one of the major filmic strategies used by Hollywood to make the black man "safe" for white audiences is to desexualize him (the other is to use him as comic relief), addressing how the black Neville's masculinity is constructed by the film proves necessary here.

As already mentioned, *IAL07* restores to Robert Neville the family that was taken away from him in *TOM*; flashbacks clearly characterize him as a loving father and husband. Although she is lighter in skin tone and has straightened hair, his wife is nonetheless African American, so controversy from either community (black or white) about interracial relationships is foreclosed. (Besides the history of anti-miscegenation laws designed to "protect" white women from black males, black activists have also criticized interracial relationships, particularly during the Black Power era reflected in *TOM* [Kennedy 109–23].) Since *The Cosby Show* (1984–1992), the present black father has become a positive counter-stereotype to the negative image of the single black mother; paternal actors like Morgan Freeman have had enormous success in the white-dominated Hollywood film industry. Thus, portraying the black Neville as a good father and husband makes him "safe," in that his sexual energies have been appropriately channeled into building a racially homogenous family and being a responsible community member, even a leader, as seen in flashback interactions depicting his command over other soldiers in the evacuation situation. Smith's mentoring of his own children's acting careers (his daughter Willow plays Marley Neville, for example) further reinforces the association of fatherhood with the actor. It also allows him to conform to a "safe" form of heterosexual, patriarchal masculinity. There appear to be no "queer" nuances attached to our Neville or to Will Smith's career; he is not known to have performed comedy in drag like Martin Lawrence or Tyler Perry. Indeed, Smith specifically avoided roles that might undermine his heteronormative star persona (Fain 164), with the exception of his portrayal of a gay hustler in *Six Degrees of Separation* (1993).

Like Charlton Heston, Smith's *body* is iconic and plays a central role in his construction as a male lead; from a tall but scrawny adolescent in *Fresh Prince* he grew into a powerful physical form, maintained on screen in *IAL07* during workout sequences. The potential for disruption that Critical Race Theorists attribute to the black male body must be reined in for the Hollywood film. Indeed, as the bodybuilding sequences show, this is a highly trained and disciplined black body. Any potentially negative valence is further neutralized by counterbalancing the reassuring images of physical strength needed in a savior figure with moments of fear and doubt. Of all the Robert

Nevilles—including Price's Robert Morgan—Will Smith's appears to be the most vulnerable on screen, vulnerable to both physical attack and to mental breakdown. For example, the aggression released during the exciting car chase and deer-hunting sequence at the film's opening is immediately countered with the image of Neville cowering in his bath-tub at night, desperately hugging Sam for mutual comfort—like a child with his teddy bear—as we hear the horrible sounds of the horde lurking outside (a trope repeated in every version of the myth). Furthermore by balancing his masculinity with the "feminine" activities of mothering Sam, the film also helps keep in check any perceived dangerous potential from an unruly black body.

Beyond the work performed in the film itself, the choice of Will Smith to play the black action hero is significant, as well. Rather than embodying the contestatory black male, Smith's artistic and financial success position him "as a figure of neoliberalism" (Subramanian 45); "his star image affirms the multicultural values of the US" (*ibid*). Indeed, Smith resembles the images of successful "post-black" African Americans interviewed and described in Ytasha L. Womack's *Post Black: How a New Generation is Redefining African American Identity* (2010) and Touré's *Who's Afraid of Post-Blackness? What It Means to Be Black Now* (2011). If we look briefly at some of Smith's mainstream work, we can see this pattern quite clearly. Smith's career began to take off precisely when Denzel Washington—Hollywood's previously "safe" black star—began to take riskier roles, for example, portraying the title role in Spike Lee's biopic *Malcolm X* (1992). In contrast, Smith starred in Michael Mann's (a mainstream white director) biopic, *Ali* (2001). Granted, Muhammad Ali embraced an oppositional politics early in his career; notably changing his name from Cassius Clay after his conversion to Islam, he controversially rejected serving in the Vietnam War. The ultimate image, however, that the American public has of Ali is that of a sports hero, a figure who typically represents a political "neutral" and, of course, of the courageous man fighting serious physical illness (significantly an illness that took his power away). Ali's codification as an "American hero" appears in the ubiquitous title cover images and stories on grocery store magazines just after his passing in summer 2016. Like Smith, Ali entered the mainstream and represents a conformist model of black success: handsome, medium-brown skinned, articulate, and eventually paternal. Similarly, the neoliberal ideology of *The Pursuit of Happyness*, could not be more clearly stated in its stereotype-defying narrative of a black single-father's struggle for success in the 1980s stock market boom. That film holds out the (for some troubling) message that the route to success for a black man in a white man's world is to embrace its work ethic and capitalist values to find happiness in professional success and financial security, i.e., to be like the majority white audience.

Following critiques of the post-black movement by Houston A. Baker and Merinda K. Simmons in *The Trouble with Post-Blackness* (2015), Subramanian exposes a certain hypocrisy behind *IAL07*'s overt messages. She argues that the film reflects an ideology that celebrates a multicultural America in which black men can rise to become successful leaders (Neville's status as a military official) and thinkers (his scientific knowledge) only when their blackness is effectively erased. But her acknowledgment that Smith's "blackness generates connotations that the film ultimately cannot manage" (46) opens the film up to oppositional readings about that erasure. In spite of the film's efforts to neutralize Smith's blackness, to render him "safe" (Subramanian 53), it also flags him as black in a number of ways beyond the obvious marker of the actor's skin color. For beginners, the hunt sequence at the film's opening transports Neville from the streets of New York back to humanity's origins in Africa as he leaves the car to stalk the deer through tall grass, only to have his prey stolen from him by a pride of lions. This sequence also reveals that man is no longer the earth's top predator. These images work to decenter Eurocentric white hegemony as the human universal.

Once again, the popular genre film reveals its ambivalence in terms of the social messages it conveys. In his analysis of blackface minstrelsy, Eric Lott insists we must "see the popular as a sphere characterized by forms of social and political conflict" (6); he continues:

> Since the popular emerges at the intersection of received symbolic forms, audiences' experiences of authority and subordination in the workplace, home, and social ritual, and new articulations by various producers of symbolic forms [...] it is itself a crucial place of contestation, with moments of resistance to the dominant culture as well as moments of supersession [6].

By its very nature, then, popular culture needs to reach a wide audience; to reach the widest possible audience, it cannot make clear cut, potentially controversial statements about hot topics like race, religion, and politics. The Hollywood blockbuster is often considered an "ideological" text, viewed as largely conveying mainstream beliefs and attitudes, feeding the public what it wants to eat. But it is also a text produced by a large group, a group which includes individuals who might themselves want to convey counter messages. Those messages may be overt or covert, and sometimes the covert messages contradict the overt ones. Above all, *IAL07* conveys the mixed and conflicting attitudes toward race currently held in the United States, but it also offers a modicum of hope if we situate it within a larger trend toward the acceptance of a black hero. It also reminds viewers of white guilt and of the ethical bankruptcy of a purportedly egalitarian democracy founded upon the inequalities of slavery in the tradition of Western Enlightenment values of mastery and conquest, just as it condemns the hubris of the techno-science used to enact Euro-American world dominance.

Without a doubt, as Sharon DeGraw observes, in *IAL07*, "the future of the world rests on the death of the black character" (19). But, as she also notes, it is the blood of a black man that saves the world (20), and "Smith's Neville offers a black Messiah figure" (20). Such imagery has come a long way from Charlton Heston's 1950s and 1960s religious blockbusters which depicted Israelites, including Jesus, as white. With Lt. Col. Robert Neville played by Will Smith, a black man is "taking on the most elevated position of knowledge and authority in the movie" (DeGraw 18). Although Smith's character has been given a slight demotion in military rank from Heston's,[5] his development of a cure for the virus at the film's conclusion trumps the apocalyptic cock-up of white, British scientist Dr. Alice Krippin[6] (Emma Thompson in an uncredited role) who engineered the virus in the first place.[7] The film's prologue—unique to this adaptation as all other versions begin like the novel with sequences involving Neville's postapocalyptic daily routine—offers an oblique but significant glimpse at the film's race-reversal politics. Krippin explains her breakthrough discovery, the cure for cancer in a pre-apocalyptic interview, using the following simplistic analogy: "you picture a virus as a car being driven by a very bad man ... then you replace that driver with a cop." Given that racial profiling and police violence have been a frequent source of urban riots (Abu-Lughod), a mainstream white audience here may envision a black man being chased by a white man in this scenario, following the binary thinking of Western civilization, black equals bad and white equals good. In *IAL07*, however, we will see a good black man being chased by a horde of bad whites. Furthermore, Krippin's breakthrough cure, as we soon discover, has actually caused the film's zombie apocalypse, turning humanity into the darkseekers. Thus, we must mentally reverse her imagery: the cop in the car turns out to be a bad cop. The bad white cop is not a new image in American popular culture, but the passing image is significant to the film's anti-racism message: "don't be fooled by appearances, don't use racial profiling; in this film, the hero is black."

This overt message of anti-racism is explicitly iterated late in the film by the hero himself. Throughout the film, Bob Marley and his music have been running motifs. "Three Little Birds," with its iconic line "Every little thing's gonna be all right," punctuates the film's soundtrack as Neville listens to this updated music (in contrast with Matheson's Neville's classical; *LMoE*'s and *TOM*'s jazz), which also serves to code this hero's blackness. At the same time, Bob Marley is an appropriate choice because of the musician's huge appeal to white audiences, his personal history with racism from both groups growing up biracial in Jamaica, and his reinterpretation of Rastafarianism as an inclusive, syncretic religion (Stephens 148–50). As Subramanian observes, this track appeared on Marley's 1984 album, *Legend*, a title with obvious resonance for this film. Furthermore, it "associates Smith with Marley—a sole revolutionary who survives against the odds" (52), but who will also become a martyr for the cause. Although Marley died of a brain tumor, he had been the victim of an assassination attempt in 1976. Gregory Stephens considers Marley with Frederick Douglass and Ralph Ellison as contributing to a "new culture" of "radical equality" (182), based in a "transracial philosophy" (167) involving both black liberation and multiracial redemption (218). He describes Marley's "moral authority" (219) and his "quasi-messianic qualities" (150). Neville offers a much more straightforward account of Marley in *IAL07*. Underscoring the generation gap between Neville and his fellow survivor Anna (further distancing the possibility of sex between these two characters), Neville must explain who Bob Marley is, and why he named his daughter after this musician: "He believed you could cure racism ... by literally injecting music and love in people's lives." This key dialogue further connects Smith's Neville to Marley, as the former will inject his blood-serum into the Alpha Female (Joanna Numata) darkseeker in an attempt to cure her. Ultimately, Neville's self-sacrifice renders him a messianic savior-figure like Marley has become.

Just as the film's musical choices code its Neville as black, its choice of visual entertainment further allows it to make overt anti-racist messages. With Anna and Ethan's arrival, Neville at first has difficulty adjusting to the presence of other humans in his home; he is clearly likened to Shrek (Mike Myers), the ogre, who refuses to open himself up to the friendship offered by Donkey (Eddie Murphy). Ethan watches the DreamWorks animated blockbuster, *Shrek*, which thematizes racism and segregation through the trope of Lord Farquaad's (John Lithgow) apartheid-like project to round up all of the "fairytale creatures" and park them in reserves away from mainstream society.

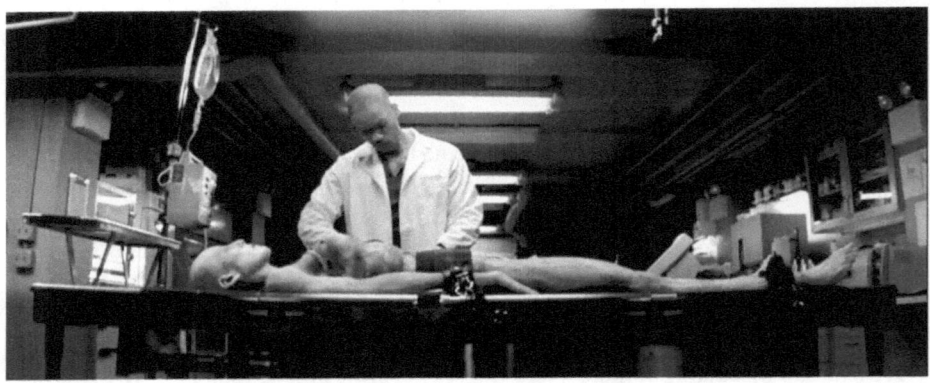

"I can fix this!" Neville's (Will Smith) "dominating medical gaze" (Stephanou 25) rests upon his test subject, the Alpha Female (Joanna Numata). *I Am Legend*, Warner Bros. DVD.

As Shrek and Donkey argue about dividing up the latter's domain to make room for the former (a scene whose dialogue Smith—like Heston viewing *Woodstock*—recites from memory), *IAL07* underscores the role of space and territory in racial conflict (Abu-Lughod), arguing for the sharing of resources. *Shrek* also emits a message about appearances and acceptance through Princess Fiona's (Cameron Diaz) curse; if you recall, the beautiful princess by day becomes an ogre at night, and she finds happiness and true love only when she embraces her inner ogre and marries Shrek.

When Is White the Threat? Hyperwhite Monsters in I Am Legend

In addition to the blackness of the film's protagonist, critics have also not failed to notice the extreme whiteness of the darkseekers' skin. As Subramanian observes, "[t]he racial connotations of *I Am Legend* are highlighted by its use of zombie film conventions" (46):

> Just as such connotations in *Night of the Living Dead* (Romero US 1968), are made meaningful by its 1968 context, so contemporary zombie films' post-apocalyptic settings are particularly significant in relation to contemporary disasters and to anxieties about disease, chemical warfare, contamination and other forms of technology and science gone awry (see Bishop 23). As the unfortunate by-product of a virus designed to cure cancer, *I Am Legend*'s zombies—"darkseekers"—ghoulishly embody twenty-first century fears of modern medicine and genetic engineering, while its deserted New York setting recalls the scenes of destruction following both 9/11 and Hurricane Katrina [46].

Subramanian only briefly notes the whiteness of *IAL07*'s darkseekers, but Gretchen Bakke spends much more time deconstructing the significance of black heroes and white villains in her on-line essay, "How the Black Guys Got to Kill All the White Guys and Still Be Good: An Essay on the Changing Dynamics of Race in American Action Cinema" (2008).

Just as DeGraw sees a progression from sidekick to hero across Will Smith's career, Bakke observes a similar development for black actors across a wider swathe of what she refers to as "action" films, although a good bit of her corpus—like DeGraw's analysis of Smith's SF films—may also be considered SF-horror films (1–2). Above all, Bakke is interested in the apparent license to kill only recently granted black characters in Hollywood film, a license premised on the increasing identification of whiteness with villainy through the creation of what she terms "hyperwhites—that is whites over-endowed with traditionally white characteristics (cultural as well as racial)" (10). Citing such franchises as *Blade* (1998), starring the ebony-skinned Wesley Snipes who justifiably kills a predatory race of white vampires (3), and *Underworld* (2003), in which racialized werewolves rise up against elite vampires, Bakke argues that such films are "premised upon the perpetration of genocide" (4). In her discussion of *IAL07*, Bakke recognizes that this notion is slightly nuanced, in that Neville seeks a cure rather than the darkseekers' destruction, and that the darkseekers represent the true forces of destruction:

> White men and their dogs, in this film, kill everything they gain access to. They infect everything they do not eat. A black man puts an end to this, and in making him into the civilizing agent *the filmmakers turn an old story about colonization, savagery, and skin color on its head*. More than this, though, I am Legend, is remarkable, though not alone, in positing that the solution to the troubles of white men is *a multiracial hybrid in which [...] [a] black man's immunity mixed with a white woman's biology* provides the serum to save the world [5–6; emphasis added].

This film, then, falls into a pattern of "a narrative unseen even 15-years ago in which black men kill white men, usually in large numbers, in order to save civilization as we know it *from the whites*" (9). And while Bakke sees this as a progressive trend overall, she also notes that this elevation of the black character to the role of savior of the human race actually perpetuates the stereotype of a sacrificial, "magic" black character present in film since after World War II (12–13).

DeGraw notes the brief thematization of lynching in another Will Smith SF vehicle, *Hancock*; similarly, Subramanian offers a fleeting glimpse of the specter of lynching in *IAL07*, only to dismiss it: "His portrayal of a vulnerable yet cool Neville tends to diffuse the racial implications of white hordes (and white zombie-dogs) chasing a lone black man" (49). But the latent power of such imagery supports this reading of the film's racial ambivalence, which quavers between conservative reaffirmations of the dominant American ideology of neoliberalism and color-blind multiculturalism versus oppositional messages about the racially motivated forms of violence that subtend our nation, both past and present.

One possible reading of the black hero's vulnerability to the threat of attack by a horde of white villains is precisely that of lynching. In the historical lynching, a white mob "avenged" itself on the black man for his (most often imagined) sexual assault of a white woman. One interpretation of the lynching motif in *IAL07* actually follows this path: the Alpha Male darkseeker (Dash Mihok) attacks Neville precisely in order to liberate his female mate, held against her will and experimented on by Neville in his quest to find a cure. Bakke specifically likens Neville's injection of the female darkseeker with a phallic needle to a form of rape, an accomplishment of the sexual intercourse that both Subramanian and DeGraw deny in their interpretations of Neville as a "safe" black character. If we note that the legendarily large penis of the black man is substituted with a needle—a metaphor for a small penis—in

IAL07 we see that he remains "safely" deflated. But there is another interpretation as well, if we return to discussions of urban territory and privilege. In this reading, the white hordes represent the American white underclass who feel disenfranchised by the success of the middle-class black.

A detailed analysis of the representation of the darkseekers supports this interpretation. These exceptionally thin, excessively pale-skinned, predominantly male beings come out at night to hunt, accompanied by their dogs; they might hunt deer or they might hunt a "coon," a Southern pejorative for an African American, but also, of course, the diminutive of the stereotypical prey of hillbillies, the raccoon. Whereas Bakke links the hyperwhite vampires in the *Underworld* and *Blade* franchises to decadent white elites, the darkseekers in *IAL07* represent the white underclass that threatens to destabilize the tenuous truce in American race relations through its violent, hate-motivated actions. Rather than more highly evolved creatures, the darkseekers resemble the inbred, devolved creatures in Wes Craven's *The Hills Have Eyes* (1977) and Alexandre Aja's 2006 remake, or the cave people in Neill Marshall's *The Descent* (2005): Gothic figures of pre-urban humanity threatening modern humans (Phillips 113–16).

In terms of the film's literal coding, as Neville tries to cure the disease first in lab rats, he notes that the eventually successful "compound 6" involves "partial pigmentation return" in the test subject. Thus, when given to humans, their color will return. A factoid of human genetics should be noted here; obviously, it is widely accepted that humanity first evolved in Africa. In that case, black skin is actually the human default; white skin developed as a mutation, evolving in northern climates where the sun shone less often. Humans with *less* skin pigmentation (melanin) were favored because they could absorb vital vitamin D from the sun more effectively; in contrast, the original humans who evolved in Africa needed lots of melanin to protect them from the harmful effects of the sun's rays. These films reverse the established norm in American society of white as default, underscoring humanity's black origins.

Neville's Moral Imperatives and the War on Terror

This adaptation, like Matheson's novel, concludes with a reference to the title and its link to the hero: his status as legend. But whereas Matheson's Neville admits his questionable moral status, accepting the new society's designation of him as a monstrous legend like the vampires he believed himself to be slaying, Lawrence's film uses these words to codify its Neville's heroic status. Thus, it is Anna who asserts in voice-over as she and Ethan drive up to Antioch's gates that:

> In 2009, a deadly virus burned through our civilization, pushing humankind to the edge of extinction. Dr. Robert Neville dedicated his life to the discovery of a cure and the restoration of humanity. On September 9, 2012, at approximately 8:49 p.m., he discovered the cure. And at 8:52, he gave his life to defend it. We are his legacy. This is his legend.

Thus, as Jeffrey A. Weinstock notes,

> the most significant deviation from Matheson's novel—and the infection vampire subgenre in general—the diseased human beings in *I Am Legend* are represented as non-human or sub-human monsters [....] In this way, *I Am Legend* carefully avoids anything that might call into question the ethical stance of its hero, Neville, as he fends off these monsters and works to cure or kill them [65].

Without taking into consideration the color of this Neville's skin, as Weinstock rightfully observes, the film's overt message ensures that doubt cannot be cast upon the ethical imperative of its hero. But what does casting a black actor in the role of humanity's savior change in *I Am Legend* in terms of the original novel's interrogation of the ethical position of Western civilization, which has used its techno-science as a tool for conquest? Is Will Smith's Robert Neville any different than his predecessors? This ethical position is made even stronger by casting a black man in the role.

At a most basic level, if racism is at the core of the white man's burden of guilt, then how can we charge a black man with those sins? Let us recall that the original Neville's ultimate sin, the reason that he accepts his own death and his status as legend, is his indiscriminate slaying of vampires, his killing both mindless predators and sentient beings alike. The root of the problem is his misapprehension of the Other, his failure to distinguish between individuals, that is, his overgeneralization, his stereotyping, his *racism*. As the former victim of racism who has overcome all obstacles on his way to reach his position of knowledge, leadership, and material wealth, the black Neville escapes this trap. Or does he?

The black man is the new figure of post–9/11 America, because, all Americans can now assume the position of victim of a phenomenon akin to the race terrorism of the Jim Crow era. Jihadist Muslims have issued a *fatwa* against all Americans, indiscriminately generalizing that we are all decadent materialists without respect for the one true God. Conversely, as Anne Canavan observes about representations of post–9/11 fears in Colson Whitehead's literary zombie novel, *Zone One* (2011), terrorists resemble Neville's monstrous Others, "people who looked like us but were secretly monsters" (42). Therefore, as the Department of Homeland Security and various other military and intelligence services would have it, as well as the conservative news media, we *are now fully justified in pursuing the war on terror*. Will Smith is the new face of America, a face determined to survive and to find a cure to reconvert all those suffering from fundamentalist Islamic terrorist beliefs back to embrace the wonders of Western techno-science. Or so we might interpret the film's covert messages. And yet, just as GIs in Vietnam faced the problem of distinguishing between Vietcong and non-combatant locals, leading to the deaths of many innocent bystanders, so the War on Terror pushes the limits of identifying real from imagined threats, fostering a globalized anti–Islamic sentiment, placing agents and civilians in the morally ambiguous situation in which Neville ultimately finds himself in every version of this American myth since its origin in Matheson's novel.

Thus, even the 2007 Neville must be seen in the end as guilty of racism; his misapprehension of the darkseekers has led him to kill indiscriminately, to perform medical experiments upon, and otherwise oppress and abuse a group of racialized Others. Indeed, Bakke notes how—in spite of the film's efforts to the contrary—Smith's Neville actually has much in common with his literary prototype. She observes that whereas for the most part, the viewer will share Neville's perception that

> [t]hese whites are [...] entirely devoid of human culture, [...] they have no language, no moral values, no sense of economy, no plans. Of course, Robert Neville,[8] is wrong at least in part, about these hive-whites; they do have individual attachments and a strong, if not nuanced, sense of retribution. Like him they also keep dogs and like him they also set traps [4].

Thus, for all the film's efforts to construct Smith's Neville as a "safe" black man, fully justified in his slaying activities, undertaking such activities normally in self-defense, he finds himself stuck in the same pattern that led to the ethical and literal demise of Matheson's original "hero who is not one," to invoke Ryan Baker's seminal study of the problematic ethics at work in this post–World War II legend. Not only has he misapprehended the nature of his enemy, preferring to see them as "all the same" and thus being unprepared for the strategic trap laid for him by the Alpha Male who has defied his presumptions both in terms of intelligence (the ability to lay the trap, to train dogs) and social capacities (the ability to lead other darkseekers in an attack and his attachment to his mate, the female Neville has kidnapped), he has also committed all of the same sins of *hubris* in the name of science that his white forerunners have done. He is thus guilty of genocide in his rampage against the darkseekers, and so we return to the ultimate racism of the Nazis as he uses science as a justification for what amounts to kidnapping and torture.

Indeed, although his skin color would appear to exonerate Smith's Neville of many of the sins of his literary and filmic forefathers, his implication with institutional science maintains a link to the abuses that have been undertaken by Western civilization in its name. Several sequences underscore

Neville's deep engagement with experimental research upon animal and human subjects. A subtle link to the mad scientist of SF-horror films past appears in the descent to his underground laboratory, a forbidden zone where Sam the dog cannot accompany him. His rows of caged rats reveal the monstrous effects of the virus on animals, but the viewer cannot help thinking about the cruelties of any animal research lab. An outsider's perspective further reveals the horrors that occur here, as Neville takes Anna on a tour, explaining his research. She sees a series of photographs whose sepia tones recall late nineteenth century images used to identify criminals and other "degenerate" types of humanity as described in Stephen Jay Gould's exposé *The Mismeasure of Man* (1981). The grim expressions on the faces of the dead darkseeker subjects that Neville had attempted to cure lend the photos an air that underscores their victimization. With their baldpates they even resemble Nazi concentration camp victims. By underscoring the violence of scientific research on animal and human subjects, the film subtly casts a shadow upon Neville's moral rectitude, as he becomes implicit in the systems of domination that prevail in Western capitalist society.

Steffen Hantke focuses more specifically on the political meanings of *IAL07* than on its racial messages, but like Subramanian, he argues that it ultimately supports a conservative ideology (166–67). Placing the film in its historical context at the end of the Bush era, Hantke stresses the conclusion of the film (as it was released in cinemas), which ends with the black man, Neville, sacrificing himself to save a white boy, Ethan (Charlie Tahan), and a Latina woman, Anna (Alice Braga). Having made contact with these other survivors, Neville learns that a conclave of normalcy exists; unfortunately, in his compulsion to find a cure, he places them all in danger because of the Alpha Male's desire to rescue his mate. He holds off the horde's attack so that Anna and Ethan can escape with the serum he has developed, sacrificing his own life in the process. Hantke interprets their destination, a walled-in New England village in Vermont, as linking

> the United States' future, as it unfolds to the survivors of the traumatic catastrophe, with its past. This future lies in small towns, in the political ideals of what Republican candidates during the 2008 presidential election incessantly referred to as "Main Street America," equating it with—an equally loaded term—"real America" [168].

Hantke's interpretation in some ways brings us full circle to Kathy Davis Patterson's reading of Matheson's novel as an allegory for white fear of black invasions of the city in the wake of *Brown v. Board of Education*. In effect, with New York City destroyed and taken over by the racialized enemy, the hyperwhite darkseekers, "good" white America (read: prosperous liberals) rejects the urban space, returning to its small-town roots. Hantke argues that even the film's alternative ending, in which Neville survives and rides north to Vermont with Anna and Ethan, "still falls squarely within the same ideological parameters" (180). The requirement that the black man must die in the cinematically released ending implicitly supports readings by DeGraw and Subramanian.

Subramanian makes a perceptive observation in her analysis of how *IAL07* deploys its representations of race relations in America. Acknowledging that "[t]he devastated city is also a poignant reminder of 9/11," she also argues that "the World Trade Center and its destruction should not be divorced from their ideological and global significance. The Twin Towers themselves represented the very worst of global capitalism, including the support of western financial interests at the expense of the poverty-stricken third world" (51). American financial and political leaders, in addition to exploiting the third world, have historically exploited racial tensions in the U.S. in order to garner support from a white (and increasingly Hispanic) American underclass and middle class for a political and economic agenda that is contrary to its own political interests. Through the metaphor of the increasing sentience of the darkseekers—the Alpha Male's emotional attachment to the female and his ability to set a trap for Neville—we might also see a subversive message about *white rage*; by casting Will Smith as the—from this perspective—villainous representative of western neoliberal capitalist imperialism, the film—once again—uses racial conflict to cover over the actual issue of class difference.

Bakke's analysis points at another problem of western global capitalism, the society and economy that whites have created. She interprets the vampires and zombies of these films as figures of unsustainability:

> There is a greed and thoughtlessness in their reproductive strategies that should now be easily recognizable as an index of their whiteness; they care not what they destroy in their quest to create, via scientific means, newer, better, stronger, and more powerful versions of themselves [31].

In contrast, through the injection of his blood, the black hero saves the world from the hyperwhites by injecting color into the humanity of the future.

Of course, we can read this simply as yet another reifying myth about the inauthenticity of white civilization being countered by the "authentic" aspects of black and other minority cultures. But Bakke concludes that the genocide perpetrated in these films is that of the whites:

> The multiracial future, the only future possible, is premised upon the removal of whites, or the stripping of their powers, the distribution and dilution of their attributes, with some life (i.e., blackness) and some flexibility (i.e., femaleness) so thoroughly mixed in that a return to the old ways is, simply put, impossible [37].

This notion, the imagining of the future of humanity without whites brings me to my concluding arguments for this chapter: the notion that such narratives are, in a sense, preparing us precisely for the post-white future. The final adaptation of Matheson's novel to be discussed here further contributes to that project.

The Worst for Last? I Am Omega

Explicitly developed by director Griff Furst and screenwriter/second male lead Geoff Meed to cash in on the success of the Will Smith blockbuster about to be released, *I Am Omega* was a straight-to-DVD production, which also debuted on the cable television Syfy channel March 21, 2009. Riffing on the titles of both *The Omega Man* and *I Am Legend*, it also credits Matheson's novel, paying clear homage in its opening sequence to the original Neville, but largely departing from it in its plot outline. Casting martial arts performer Mark Dacascos (b. 1964) in the lead role, the film develops the cross-fertilization between *The Last Man on Earth* and Romero's *Night of the Living Dead*, followed by the last decade's explosion of zombie films. It thus features its hero "Renchard" in martial arts fight sequences with the gruesome, abject zombies typical of post-millennium films like *Zombieland* or AMC's television series, *The Walking Dead*. Along with its clever title, Dacascos' intense presence are perhaps the only interesting aspects of this film. Even the spectacle of his sculpted body does not make up for the absurdity of facing the zombie apocalypse with no better weapons than a pair of *nunchaku*; furthermore, the transformation of the infected Ruth—certainly an unconventional damsel in distress who turns out to be a Mata Hari—into your standard horror film babe decreases the ambiguity of Matheson's original narrative. Although she expresses a will and wit of her own, Brianna (Jennifer Lee Wiggins) represents in some respects a throwback to the women of the 1950s SF-horror films, helpless victims waiting for a hero to save them.

Truly an ensemble production, professional stunt man Geoff Meed—who also plays one of Brianna's kidnappers, the racist villain Vincent (one of the film's frequent winks to the vampire-zombie canon, named after Price)—wrote a scenario possibly tailored for Dacascos. Meed also teamed up with Furst on *Universal Soldiers* (2007), and he has written several other horror scripts for the television and video market in addition to over sixty acting credits (IMDb.com). Furst—also a working actor with over seventy credits—has directed some fifteen films, mostly in the horror genre for television, including the rather pretentious *Wolvesbayne* (2009). This werewolf film alternates from present-day to stylized historical sequences, featuring Dacascos as a sort of King Werewolf, also including an updated Van Helsing as a monster hunter, cashing in on the trend of slayer films like Stephen Sommers' 2004 film of that name. Dacascos, now a household name in the U.S. for his role as The Chairman in *Iron Chef America* (2004–2014), made an international reputation in the French historical werewolf film, *The Brotherhood of the Wolf* (2001). Born in Hawaii, his exotic good looks and multiracial heritage have allowed him to be cast in numerous ethnic roles, from that of an eighteenth-century Native American in the French film, to unnamed "Thai Boxers" and other Asian *senseis*, to a role as the Chinese Wo Fat filmed in his home state in *Hawaii Five-O* (2010–2014). Clearly this production lacked the impact of the Will Smith film as well as the complexity of the other texts discussed here, but it nonetheless bears at least a cursory discussion.

The film's opening sequence is arguably its most interesting, as it pays evident homage not only to Matheson's novel, but also to the *LMoE*, the adaptation its budget and early claustrophobic atmosphere most nearly matches. It opens quietly with its last man "Renchard" (Dacascos) alone at home, seeking productive ways to while away the hours of his solitude and to reinforce his bunker against future zombie onslaughts. The details of the interior set pay respects to the very films that *IAO*, perhaps best read as a "mockbuster," seeks to pastiche: we see photos of Renchard's ostensibly deceased family and German shepherd dog; he talks to a bust, as did Heston's Neville; and he marks off the days on a wall calendar. Only the location of his fenced-in, rural home has changed: from Matheson's suburbs to *The Omega Man*'s downtown Los Angeles, Renchard's home, surrounded by the California desert, serves to completely isolate him from the last remnants of human society. Like Price's Morgan and Smith's Neville, he ceaselessly attends to his fenced-in desert compound and attempts to communicate with the outside world, in this case, via satellite connection. When he answers a call for help from a young woman trapped in the city, Brianna, the film takes something of a left turn away from Matheson's dark vision for the end of humanity.

Above all, the film adds another element into the generic mix of Matheson's SF-horror hybrid: martial arts/action film. To showcase Dacascos' special skill set, Renchard's mission to save Brianna includes numerous zombie slayings—sometimes laced with humor—along the way. Those slayings escalate at the film's conclusion as the bombs Renchard has placed throughout its sewer system explode, destroying Los Angeles and presumably, with it, the hordes of zombies overrunning the city. The film proposes two other twists: first, it attributes Brianna with the immunity from which a cure might be developed if she can reach "Antioch," a presumed enclave of human survivors in a town whose name invokes the cradle of Christianity. Second, Renchard's nemeses include a sort of alternate society in the form of Vince and Michael, ex-military rednecks who temporarily kidnap Brianna in order to prevent her arrival at Antioch. For them, the postapocalyptic world is better than the previous bleeding-heart liberal haven, as Vince declares, "Right now, we got ourselves a perfect utopia. Darwinism. Survival of the fittest." This film offers the happiest ending of the cycle as hero—there is absolutely no question as to the morality of Renchard's campaign of terror—and the spunky damsel ride off into the sunset. The casting of the multiracial Dacascos who will repopulate the planet with this ostensibly "white" girl, also a potential female savior with her immunity, also offers the most progressive ending of all of the films.

As the dialogue quoted in epigraph to this chapter illustrates, *IAO* does not buffer any political or social messages it wishes to emit. *IAO07* offers an overt message of post–9/11 America as one of racial integration, with the black man rising to a role of leadership and then acting as the savior of the human race; its monstrous Others are ambiguously coded, but can be read as an uncivilized white underclass that wishes to destroy the surface image of American racial harmony. In a less subtle manner than the Hollywood blockbuster, Griff Furst's independent, low-budget project overtly exposes the undercurrent of racism carried forward from the contemporary U.S. of the viewer into this near-future postapocalyptic setting. Although its casting choice of martial-arts star, Mark Dacascos, offers a somewhat lighter shade of color to the hero of the future, the actor's light brown skin and slightly Asian features clearly code him as non-white. In this film, the human villains—Vince (scenarist Geoff Meed) and Mike (Ryan Lloyd)—are definitely white, and the non-white hero gets the girl in the end; furthermore, its hyperwhite zombies are indubitably coded as irremediably lost from human reason and must be eliminated. Our hero finally appears to have recovered the position of moral right.

Although the film clearly credits Matheson's novel, after its opening sequences the film dramatically departs from its literary model, openly joining the burgeoning series of zombie films produced in the first decades of the twenty-first century. The film also makes a location change; on the one hand, it returns to Matheson's southern California, but Renchard lives in a rural, desert area outside Los Angeles. Like Neville, though, he has created something of a bunker, its windows boarded up, and his daily routine involves similar tasks, such as scrounging for supplies, burning slain zombies, and maintaining his physical edge through workouts. After a first kill sequence, in which he defends himself with a machete, a gun, and a trap, he must destroy the bodies of these hyperwhite monsters, gruesome with their hollow eyes and prominent spinal columns, with fire.

The interior of Renchard's home invokes its literary and filmic precursors in multiple ways: there is a photo of a German shepherd with votive candles placed around it; the kitchen is the center of activity; it includes a mannequin to whom Renchard quips; maps on the wall; and a photo of a wife and child. His computer screensaver bearing the image of his newborn son establishes him as a family man, accentuating the pain of his current loneliness—which the filmmakers also go to pains to express during the first third of the film—with the loss of loved ones. Instead, the discovery of a living rabbit reveals that he is still capable of human feeling, as he smiles in wonder at the sight—until he is attacked and forced to defend himself. Whereas Price's Neville managed his solitude with alcohol, and *IAO* includes a homage sequence in which a drunken Renchard transitions from hysterical laughter to tears, he also has recourse to the twenty-first century remedy of prescription drugs, presumably sleeping pills, anti-depressants, and possibly even anti-psychotics.

Once again, media broadcasts provide the backstory, although with a twist; we hear a radio announcer describing flesh eating bacteria as the cause of the epidemic, but then Renchard realizes he is having an aural hallucination, a sequence adopted almost word-for-word from *The Omega Man* as Dacascos, like Heston to the phone system, wills the hallucination to stop with a command: "There is no radio!" He also suffers from visual hallucinations, seeing zombies when there are none, an intensification of his decaying mental state, a vulnerability he shares with other Nevilles. Following the earlier films, he reaches out to find other survivors, but updating his technology; rather than radio, he uses a computer having apparently hacked into NASA's satellite system. Like Heston, he quips, "Another day, another dollar," as he heads out on his daily routine to scavenge for supplies in to restock his dwindling stores. Like Will Smith naming the mannequins at the DVD store, he drily greets a mummified body at a convenience store, "Hey, Paul."

These activities are, of course, punctuated by zombie attacks; of all the Robert Nevilles, Renchard appears to have the clearest moral imperative. His slaying activities appear to be *always* in self-defense, rather than a systematic genocide; he does, however, consult maps, checking off locations for a related purpose: he is setting a network of explosives to blow up downtown Los Angeles because "there is a huge hive" there. Furthermore this film's extremely gruesome, speedy, and aggressive zombies appear on the surface to have absolutely no redeeming social values or remnants of intelligence; they also can burst forth from the ground like the risen dead. And yet, even here, in one sequence they are glimpsed pushing a dumpster but no apparent purpose is revealed, and later Renchard admits that their increased presence precisely where Brianna is holed up seems "almost like they called in reinforcements." Significantly, in terms of discussions of race, the pandemic that has turned humanity into zombies attacks the *skin*, the visible site of a fictional category. A radio announcer specifically indicates that the disease causes a deficiency in the skin (akin to Northern Europeans' lack of pigmentation): the "dermal layer is in a constant state of atrophy," that the disease causes.

Renchard's mind-numbing routine is suddenly interrupted by a message on his computer: an attractive young woman on camera, "Hello, can you see me!" Thinking this is another hallucination, Renchard reacts violently; when she contacts him again, he still hesitates, knowing the dangers of entering the "downtown district" where she is holed up. Here, the urban stigma is maintained, linking the inner city with racial danger. Introducing herself, Brianna also offers hope, expressing her goal of reaching a settlement of thousands of uninfected survivors in the mountains called Antioch. Although this adaptation almost completely evacuates any religious subtext found in other versions of Matheson's legend, this town references an ancient biblical city referred to as the cradle of Christianity.

Echoing *TOM*, Renchard dresses for dinner—although his meal comes from stored military rations—and reads the story of Hercules accompanied to classical music. He must, however, be coerced into saving Brianna by the villains, Vincent and Mike. They drive up to his compound in a white 1983 Ford Econoline van, the serial killer vehicle par excellence, honking for him to come out. Their racism is immediately signaled as Vince addresses Renchard: "Hey compadre! [...]. What's the matter? No speakee the English?" Their presumption that he is Mexican may be a self-conscious nudge not only at the general population's generalizations but also at Hollywood's frequent practice of casting any actor with light brown skin in a wide range of "ethnic" roles, from Latinos to Native Americans to Semitic peoples from the Middle East (i.e., "Arabs"). Indeed, Dacascos' resume reveals that he has played just such a range of roles.

Vincent and Mike are ex-Marines called "Roughnecks"—a thinly veiled reference to "rednecks"—who, at first, pretend to belong to the survivors' colony in Antioch, and who want his help finding Brianna, revealing another twist in this film: a woman will save humanity. The martial-arts expert Renchard, although he does have skills as a former special-ops demolition man, is divested of his association with experimental science, perhaps another step in his moral exoneration. Instead, Brianna's natural immunity is essential to finding a cure: "She's got the antivirus. Something in her blood. She's the savior of mankind." Later, these men, clearly coded as "white trash" via Vince's southern accent and racist palaver, reveal their true colors and actual goal: ensuring that Brianna never reaches Antioch. They envision a world in which there is no place for either Brianna or Renchard, and eventually say so. Indeed, undertones of a lynching motif appear in their coercion of Renchard to get in their van, as Vince refers to his "little on-line romance" with Brianna. Once again, the white man objects to the man of color making contact with the white woman and presumes sexual intentions that may or may not be present.

The core narrative's Darwinist subtext that humanity may eventually evolve into its next phase recurs in *I Am Omega* in a number of ways, beginning with the blood that will redeem all of humanity, present in every version of the story since Matheson's novel. The theme of blood, genetics, and their link to the scourge of racism appears in relation to Brianna's immunity, but also to Vince's ignorance. He makes fun of southern white stereotypes as inbred hillbillies, in spite of his own associations with this group, joking:

"What's the slogan of the state of Alabama? 'Fifteen last names and proud of it?'" The film deflates historic concerns about miscegenation here, since endogamy is associated with inbreeding and birth defects, placing interracial relationships under the more positive umbrella of exogamy. Eventually Vince makes the speech cited in epigraph to the chapter: "Right now, we got ourselves a perfect utopia. Darwinism. Survival of the fittest." Deeming himself amongst the fittest in a kill-or-be-killed world, in which the strong prey on the weak, he admits to Renchard that he wants to prevent Brianna from reaching Antioch. His reactionary mentality further aligns with that of a white underclass encouraged by the racist ideology promulgated by white elites in the U.S. south and still today encouraged to support conservative, anti-immigrant political campaigns like that of Donald Trump because they fear that material, social, and political advances for minority Americans must mean their own regression.

Mike has died in a zombie attack en route to the inner city, and Renchard manages to lose Vince. He searches for Brianna amid the urban ruins, which becomes a pretext for additional zombie-slaying sequences both before and after he finds her. Like Lisa in *TOM*, Brianna reveals her spunk, shooting zombies, as well as choosing the newly-formed couple's cars, upgrading each time from a lime green custom 1976 Oldsmobile Omega to a mint condition 1972 Chevrolet Corvette. Vince finds them once again and nabs Brianna, leaving Renchard for dead; this allows for a gratuitous potential rape scene compounded with necrophilia, as Vince has been treating Mike's dead body as if he were still alive and places it on top of a restrained Brianna. The hero prevails, however, and Renchard finds them to save the girl. He and Brianna kiss to the backdrop of the urban apocalypse as the city explodes in the background behind them; triumphant rock and roll plays on the soundtrack as the film concludes on the happy ending, as the couple heads for the hills and the safety of the new society being built in Antioch.

Thus, in addition to removing any ethical dilemma that Renchard faces, this film also very clearly concludes on the constitution of the heterosexual, but interracial couple. Although Brianna is clearly white, her brown hair distances her from the "Aryan" stereotype of the blue-eyed, blonde white supremacist; she may be Italian in origin, a group once also a discriminated-against minority in America, viewed as "less" white than northern Europeans. Although Renchard has been shown to be psychologically vulnerable through his drug use and hallucinations, it seems clear that the hope for the future brought by Brianna, coupled with their new sexual attraction will redeem him. Instead of sacrificing himself for humanity, then, this final version of Matheson's Robert Neville, has significantly reduced the threat to humanity by blowing up the zombie hive in Los Angeles; he is not afraid to leave his bunkered home and join the new society precisely because as a multiracial man in America he has been exonerated of the burden of white guilt borne by his white predecessors in Matheson, *LMoE*, *TOM* and even—through his connection to science—by the black hero in *IAL07*. *I Am Omega* concludes on the hopeful note that a multicultural American society *can* be rebuilt in the new, post-white era.

Post-White

Steffen Hantke insists that *IAL07* has "one strong and single-minded ideological thrust" (166): a conservative message that supports the war on terror, the return to small town America, with a thin veneer of multiculturalism. But he also offers an important insight about the Hollywood blockbuster: "Surrounding this [ideological] core, however, are layers of visual details and kernels of un-, or under-, developed ideas that provide points of departure for viewers unable or unwilling to invest themselves in the film's core ideology" (166). This chapter's analysis has focused precisely on these kernels of resistance to the nation's dominant contemporary ideology in order to tease out the oppositional messages that these SF-horror films convey about humanity's future. Similarly, in spite of their generally critical analyses of representations of race and blackness in *IAL07*, Bakke, DeGraw, and Subramanian also point toward glimpses of a more progressive ideology. Indeed, Bakke cites in epigraph to her study a comment on the nature of the blockbuster film, originally made by Fred Pfeil, as "the place where collective social desire for transformation and salvage, revolution and restoration, anarchy and obedience is simultaneously fastened and split" (Pfeil qtd. Bakke 1).

Thus, although DeGraw, Bakke, and Subramanian demonstrate that whiteness remains the American norm, and that Hollywood tacitly acknowledges a continued subtext of racism in American society through its process of "neutering" or rendering "safe" its lead male characters of color, *IAL07* and to an even greater extent *IAO* nonetheless participate in an ongoing process of the "browning" of America. One of the key roles of science-fiction narrative is to extrapolate the future in order to prepare humanity for it; apocalyptic films clearly help us envision the possibility of humanity's extinction or our evolution into some form of posthuman being. Although the catalyst for that extinction or transformation evolves over time, linked more clearly to nuclear weaponry during the Cold War and to biological epidemics in the twenty-first century, the novel and films examined here present a core narrative of humanity's apparent extinction, the struggle of a lone human survivor to overcome the odds against him, and then conclude with his demise in favor of a new order of being and society. These texts also engage the problem of science, the question of race, and a subtext of military might.

And while the threat of epidemic illness appears to be a very real problem in contemporary society, the real problem being addressed in these films is the construction of race, the violence meted out by man upon man in the name of race, and the manner in which masculinity has been constructed around the ability to perform violence and the sexual desire that motivates procreation. These stories' conclusions *all* reveal the erosion of the presumption of white supremacy that has been at the core of the global expansion of European civilization, a supremacy aided and justified by Western technoscience used to develop the military might at the root of imperial power. But in addition to the way in which they reveal the "legend," the "myth," behind white superiority, they also eventually stage the disappearance of the white man, ushering in a new "post-white" era.

Just as DeGraw tracks the progress of Will Smith's path-breaking career from safe, comic roles which defuse his potential as a powerful black man to elicit fear in majority white audiences, his appearance as the last man on earth in *IAL07* contributes radically to the evolving story first published by Richard Matheson in 1954, but also to subsequent developments in Hollywood film and Western media in general. Although Smith is sacrificed in the film's theatrical release conclusion, his screen presence operates a radical shift in changing the mythology from that of fear of a black planet to fear of a planet dominated by ignorant and/or greedy whites. The fact that mass American audiences can envision a black man as its leader and hero remains significant, even if he is a highly educated and cultivated, middle-class black man. *I Am Omega* takes this evolution even further by eliminating its white villains altogether, allowing the racialized hero to have the girl, to become a new Adam. These films represent the first step in a mainstream (white) American audience accepting the fact that humanity's future is actually one, not in which we have become "colorblind" or eliminated the category of race, but rather in which the white race will become submerged in a sea of color, ushering in the post-white era.

In *The Color of the Future* (1999), Farai Chideya examines race relations and attitudes in America at the dawn of the twenty-first century, arguing the need to prepare for a major reconceptualization of whiteness as no longer the default race of the nation. She also insists that discussions of race must go beyond the black-and-white dichotomy that have dominated the discourse, finding instead ways to embrace the increasingly multiracial, brown faces of the young Americans she interviews. Armed with statistics from the U.S. Bureau of the Census, she asserts that "[a]round the year 2050, whites will become a minority" (5), also noting that in 1950—just before the publication of Matheson's novel *I Am Legend*—America was nearly 85 percent non–Hispanic white" (4). As an American myth, the story of Robert Neville engages the problem of race, evolving over time to grapple with different concerns appropriate to the period of each adaptation. In its final iterations, it posits a non-white hero, thus fully accusing the regime of the white man: Western imperialist capitalism grounded in Judeo-Christian ideologies, as having brought humanity to the brink of extinction through its *hubris* in applying science without thought to the ethical consequences and for waging war by indiscriminately killing a misunderstood enemy. It also lays the groundwork—along with a growing corpus of popular culture texts—for America to embrace its future as a non-white nation.

Building on Bakke's thesis that we have reached a point at which a number of Hollywood action films reveal that the elite hyperwhites have become the enemies of humanity, this chapter concludes with a brief survey of contemporary SF film and television series which reveals the continuing empowerment of heroes of color. All of these texts mark steps in the cultural progress being made toward conceiving the world of the future as "post-white," signaling the rejection of racism as the dominant ideology and the nation's working toward a more meaningful acceptance of American culture as multicultural, multi-colored. Adding to Bakke's examples of the *Blade* franchise starring Wesley Snipes and the Wachowski (then) brothers' vision of a truly multicultural humanity of the future in the *Matrix*, we must add Denzel Washington's lead role in *The Book of Eli* (2010) and the stunning success of Samuel L. Jackson in *Iron Man* (2008) and *The Avengers* (2012) linked franchises (Fain 167). But, the rise of British-African actor Idris Elba marks a significant moment in the acceptance of the black hero. From a secondary character in a leadership role as captain of the *Prometheus* in Ridley Scott's 2012 *Alien* follow-up film, Elba jumped to an epic lead role as Stacker Pentecost in Guillermo del Toro's *Pacific Rim* (2013). Before saving humanity from kaiju monsters in this homage to Japanese SF film, Pentecost proclaims, "Today, we are canceling the apocalypse!" Featured as Heimdall—traditionally considered the "whitest of the gods" in Norse mythology (Lindow 170)—in the *Thor* franchise (2011–), he is cast as Stephen King's last gunslinger, Roland Deschain—another literary character conceived as white—in Nikolaj Arcel's and Akiva Goldsman's film adaptation of *The Dark Tower* (2017).

In addition to these visions of black men saving the world, science fiction film and television continues to push the envelope in terms of envisioning a future that decenters the white male from his position as king of the hill in its empowerment of women, men of color, and LGBTQ characters. Joss Whedon's *Doll House* (2009–2010) focuses on a female heroine, Echo (Eliza Dushku), and replaces her white handler, Paul Ballard (Tahmoh Penikett), with a black one, Boyd Langton (Harry Lennix). J. J. Abrams, Alex Kurtzman, and Roberto Orzi feature female agent Olivia Dunham (Anna Torv) in their series, *Fringe* (2008–2013). Similarly, *Orphan Black* (2013–2016) follows Sarah Manning's (Tatiana Maslany) identity quest after she discovers she is a clone.

The 2017 reboot, *24: Legacy*, of the cult series *24* (2001–2010) features black actor Corey Hawkins as Eric Carter, Jack Bauer's (Kiefer Sutherlund) heir apparent. Above all, the former Wachowski brothers, now sisters Lana and Lily, populate their SF series, *Sense8* (2015–) with superpowered transgender and queer heroes, creating some of the most exciting and emotionally impactful episodic SF viewing in the genre's screen history.

Indeed, *Sense8* opens with a steamy sex scene between white transgender (male to female) heroine Nomi Marks (Jamie Clayton) and her black lover, Amanita (Freema Agyeman), and features another interracial couple, the South Asian Kala Dandekar (Tina Desai) and Eurotrash heist artist Wolfgang Bogdanow (Max Riemelt), as well as a Latino gay couple, film star Lito Rodriguez (Miguel Àngel Silvestre) and his lover Hernando (Alfonso Herrera). But perhaps the most significant contribution toward the mainstreaming of the interracial couple occurs in the television adaptation of Robert Kirkman's zombie apocalypse comic series, *The Walking Dead* (2010-). Set in the Deep South, the series indirectly addresses regional racial history, most particularly through the stereotypical redneck characters Merle (Michael Rooker) and Darryl Dixon (Norman Reedus). While the elder brother, Merle, cannot shake the racial attitudes with which he was indoctrinated, Darryl's developmental trajectory is centered on his transformational journey from white trash to redemptive hero, as he forms a new multiracial family which also includes at least one Lesbian member, Tara Chambler (Alanna Masterson). For several seasons viewers have followed the romance between the not-quite southern belle Maggie Greene (Lauren Cohan), who grew up on a plantation-like farm, and her Korean lover, then husband Glen Rhee (Stephen Yeun). The redheaded ultra-white Sgt. Abraham Ford (Michael Cudlitz) has been involved in two interracial romances, first with the Latina Rosita Espinosa (Christian Serratos) and then with the African American Sasha Williams (Sonequa Martin-Green). Although the group of survivors remains, admittedly, led by the southern white sheriff Rick Grimes (Andrew Lincoln), his interracial relationship with the ebony-skinned Michonne (Danai Gurira) marks a signal moment in the acceptance of interracial relationships in American popular culture. This series overall has consistently included more than the requisite single token black character, and although for a time it seemed like the black man in the group was destined to die—from T-Dog (Irone Singleton) to Tyreese (Chad L. Coleman) to Bob (Lawrence Gilliard, Jr.) to Noah (Tyler James Williams)—the increasing significance of Morgan Jones (Lennie James) and Father Gabriel Stokes (Seth Gilliam) demonstrates that black men, too, can survive the zombie apocalypse.

Science fiction is the privileged genre for humanity to envision its future. It may offer a utopian vision, anticipating the wonderful developments that technology might bring to increase our lifespan, enhance our quality of life, and allow us to travel vast distances in both space and time. But it often frequently tends toward the dystopian, expressing our anxieties about the dangers of science and technology and even those destructive forces inherent in our own natures. Clearly, the apocalyptic narratives discussed in this book feature dark visions of humanity's near extinction, caused by its own ill-considered use of technology; they also envision posthuman species that might evolve and take our place on earth. But above all, with the election of the black hero, the evolution of the particular myth at the core of *I Am Legend* culminates with an interpellation, a call to contemporary Americans to begin envisioning our future as post-white. Granted, many other films and particularly episodic series have gone much further in their post-white, post-hetero visions of human society on earth, but Will Smith's Robert Neville remains a significant figure in SF film and television's projection of a the color of the future for a still majority white America.

Conclusion: *I Am Legend* as American Myth

The Planet of the Apes franchise represents a significant intertext for *The Omega Man* not only because of Charlton Heston's starring role in both films, but also because of those films' evolving and ambiguous messages about race. Just as the 2007 film version of *I Am Legend* turned racial messages on their head by substituting a black hero for one who had been previously conceived as white, the recent *Apes* reboot supplants the white hero with an ape hero. Already in Rupert Wyatt's *Rise of the Planet of the Apes* (2011), the ape Caesar (Andy Serkis) quickly upstages his white, human handler Will Rodman (James Franco), focalizing the narrative and garnering audience sympathy as we follow the young chimp's *Bildungsroman* toward his eventual status as a revolutionary hero. Matt Reeves' *Dawn of the Planet of the Apes* (2014) further codifies that status as Caesar has created a peaceful society for the apes, and human viewers are led to identify with the racialized ape, condemning humans with anti-ape prejudices, like Carver (Kirk Acevedo), as "ass-holes." The film's overt message undoes the binary assumptions at the core of racism (white/human equals good; black/ape equals bad) by revealing good and bad individuals in both species. Lead-up media prior to the release of *War for the Planet of the Apes* (2017) suggests further codification of Caesar's heroic status in the franchise's next installment, which reprises the team of Andy Serkis in the lead role,[1] directed by Matt Reeves in a scenario by Mark Bomback. Thus, science-fiction film in the twenty-first century continues on its journey facilitating not only our ability to envision a world that is post-white, but also one that is posthuman.

Published prior even to Tim Burton's (regrettable) remake of *Planet of the Apes* (2001), Eric Greene already had identified the visual texts adapted from Pierre Boulle's novel, as "an American myth" in his landmark study, *Planet of the Apes as American Myth: Race and Politics in the Films and Television Series* (1996). Greene argues convincingly that the concepts and characters developed by American screenwriters from the 1963 French novel—a text which also ambivalently engages discourses about race and colonialism relative to France's history in Africa and Southeast Asia—have achieved the status of "myth." This analysis of Richard Matheson's 1954 novel *I Am Legend* and its several film adaptations concludes by making a similar argument. While it may simply be yet another variation on a far older literary text turned myth, that of Daniel Defoe's *Robinson Crusoe* (1719), the story of Robert Neville as the Last Man (who wasn't) has demonstrated the enduring yet mutable properties of the mythical figure.

As literary adaptations, the various screen versions of *I Am Legend* are not unusual, since SF and horror film are genres that often rely upon literary source materials for their inspiration. In their introduction to the edited volume, *Monstrous Adaptations: Generic and Thematic Mutations in Horror Film* (2007), Richard J. Hand and Jay McRoy offer insight into the analytical process undertaken here and its conclusion. Returning to the notion that faithfulness is not necessarily a criterion for assessing an adaptation's ultimate value, be it aesthetic quality or entertainment value, they raise the question of myth and its role in the horror film. Many horror films translate myths, particularly those about monsters such as vampires and werewolves, to the screen. Some of these now "mythical" monsters, like both Frankenstein (the mad scientist) and his monster, originated in literary texts. Hand and McRoy refer to Chris Baldick's classic study of Mary Shelley's *Frankenstein* (1818); in it Baldick:

> argues that in spite of the plurality of interpretation, a literary text is a fixed entity, whilst a myth, in a Lévi-Straussian sense, "is open to all kinds of adaptation and elaboration, but it will preserve at the same time a basic stability of meaning" (Baldick, 1987: 2). The word "mythos"—as used by Aristotle—means "the basic action"; hence, myth, or the "mythic" connotations of a specific work, occupies a critical ontological space, one freed from the tyranny of a specific plot or character arc. The myth of a work exists at its simplest, most memorable and irreducible pattern. Myths are more organic than concretised text: they resist reducibility. A myth lives, and the "truth" of it is not to be found in the earliest version but, as Lévi-Strauss claims, in all its versions [Hand and McRoy 2].

Pace Baldick, Audrey Fisch and Susan Tyler Hitchcock have recently made convincing arguments that, indeed, Shelley's story and its protagonists have been so widely appropriated and adapted for a range of purposes that Frankenstein has become a modern myth in spite of its literary origins. And that while details and context may change, the core symbolic valence of the Frankenstein myth—men playing at God may use what they believe to be reason to create monsters, and that instrumental reason/science is really no different than religious belief/superstition—remains the same. Similarly, the Last Man is in the process of becoming a legend or myth in his own right, as well, and our particular last man, Robert Neville, is also a particularly American myth, but one that reaches back toward the European heritage for the Enlightenment values and imperial interventions that subtend the foundation of our "democracy" and our foreign interventions beginning with World War I, but increasing since World War II.

As an American myth, *I Am Legend* addresses key concerns linked to national identity as the United States emerged from World War II as a major world power: the inextricable connections between violence, race, and masculinity. Matheson's novel, through the allegorical figure of the last white man battling for survival against a horde of Others, indirectly engages the ethical dilemmas of war, the concept of race as a key motivator for conflict (and conquest), and the patriarchal heritage of the Judeo-Christian tradition, in which the construction of masculinity is based upon images of authority and power. Furthermore, it invokes science's particular role in Western civilization's ascendancy to world dominance through the oppression of racialized Others, coupled with a brand new fear that overturned a formerly unquestioned faith in the notion of Progress: fear in the post–Hiroshima era that humanity may have engineered the means for its own demise. As we have seen, those core concerns—the morality of war, the potential for misuse of scientific developments, and insecurities about race and masculinity—remain, but evolve, in the novel's adaptation to film over the decades.

Matheson's 1954 novel allegorizes the repressed trauma and survivor's guilt of the World War II combat veteran, ultimately questioning not only the racial politics of Nazi Germany, but also those of the United States of America. In addition to its long history of slavery and then segregation, the U.S. had denied the entrance of Jewish refugees from Europe, indiscriminately killed German soldiers, and had dropped the atomic bomb on Japanese civilians. It also explores how the damaged GI's masculinity has been compromised by his combat experiences and troubled reinsertion into peacetime society. It further engages the moral ambiguities of the more recent Korean War, yet another ideologically motivated and racially complicated military intervention, in which Cold War bomb-rattling intensified the threat of nuclear apocalypse. Although it can conversely be read as an expression of white America's fears about the beginnings of racial integration, feeding paranoia about being overrun and even extinguished by black hordes, the text's anguished conclusion acknowledges the white man's guilt through Neville's acceptance of the rightness of his death in his final assertion, "I am legend."

The seminal novel's first film adaptation in 1964, *The Last Man on Earth*, remains the most faithful to its original, largely because similar socio-political circumstances prevailed. Although the casting of Vincent Price as Neville's avatar Robert Morgan further accentuates the growing sense of a crisis in masculinity across the long 1950s, Salkow's film maintains many of the Cold War anxieties present in Matheson's novel. Its Italian location and cast, as Casali observes, add an additional layer to its engagement of lingering post-war fears about fascism, but this Hollywood film ultimately undermines the critical message that concludes its model. Instead of admitting his own guilt and accepting his just demise for having ruthlessly attempted genocide, Morgan accuses the new race of human-vampire hybrids of being "freaks."

In the period between the first and second film adaptations of *I Am Legend*, American society underwent a major paradigm shift as the post-war baby boom generation participated in a wide array of social movements that precisely targeted the core values of the United States that had won World War II. The racial tensions that had been building since the publication of Matheson's novel the same year as the *Brown v. Board of Education* decision to integrate American schools, and its subsequent failure to effectuate any real change in race relations led the non-violent Civil Rights movement to turn radical. No longer willing to accept the imperatives of Cold War rhetoric, the nation's youth protested intervention in Vietnam and questioned an increasingly morally compromised authority. These conditions and the violent images of urban rioting, police brutality, and war in Southeast Asia all informed how Matheson's novel was updated for contemporary concerns as *The Omega Man* by screenwriters John Corrington and Joyce Hooper Corrington, released in 1971. Although fully reinvested with an authoritative, patriarchal masculinity, Charlton Heston's Robert Neville represents an ambivalent figure, emblematic of a society in transition from a conformist, patriarchal, predominantly white America to an individualistic, more egalitarian and youth-centered society, a society attempting to come to grips with its complex racial history. Indirectly invoking the war in Vietnam, the film ambiguously addresses the contemporary crisis in race relations, offering a positive image of black Americans in the heroic figures of Lisa and Richie, allowing its white protagonist to engage in an interracial sexual relationship but also playing perhaps on white fears about urban violence through its depiction of the Family. The film kills off its great white hero in the end, offering a glimmer of hope for humanity's survival through a predominantly white group of survivors which nonetheless allows for some future diversity in its inclusion of at least one Asian, one Latin American, and one African American survivors.

While ongoing discussions about a third adaptation of Matheson's novel began as early as the late 1980s, it took an American tragedy as significant as the attack on Pearl Harbor in 1941 and a substitute for the Cold War to trigger the realization of the eponymously named film, *I Am Legend* to be made in 2007. The apocalyptic mode of post–9/11 America and the moral ambiguities of the subsequent War on Terror rendered the soil fertile for the seeds for a new version of this American myth. With African American blockbuster star, Will Smith, cast as Robert Neville, this film's producers radically changed the nature of the myth, but also overtly addressed the question of racism in America. Although the film's politics clearly reinforce the American status quo, accepting neoliberal capitalism and embracing a conservative move away from urban centers toward the idyllic village, its overtly anti-racist messages cannot be denied. In spite of some critics' desire to see the film as simply painting a colored veneer over an essentially white hero, *I Am Legend* participates in a larger Hollywood trend toward the acceptance of non-white heroes. Gretchen Bakke's identification of its darkseekers as a new species of hyperwhite monsters, allegorical figures for the destructive and unsustainable practices of Western civilization legitimates oppositional readings of the film. The straight-to-DVD adaptation of Matheson's novel, *I Am Omega*, also released in 2007 goes even farther in its accusation of white racism for endangering America's future. Its hero-of-color, Renchard, played by multiracial Hawaiian actor Mark Dacascos—in contrast with his literary and filmic models—defeats his racist foes, survives the zombie apocalypse, and drives off into the sunset with the new Eve.

American myth or not, the complexity of Matheson's novel and its enduring core story confirm *I Am Legend*'s status as a classic text of American science fiction and horror literatures. Although the films it has inspired vary in their aesthetic quality, their polyvalent messages reflect how the popular culture text engages the issues at the heart of the nation.

Chapter Notes

Introduction

1. A Spanish short, *Soy leyenda* (1967) directed by Mario Goméz Martín, is listed in IMDb.com, and Vincent Chenille cites an unproduced French screenplay written by Claude Chabrol and Paul Gégauff in the early 1970s (92).

2. Linnie Blake provides a compelling account of 1980s horror in *The Wounds of Nations* (101–22).

3. One of McFarland's external reviewers—to whom I am extremely grateful for very frank comments that greatly improved the manuscript during the final editing stage—observes that for Matheson himself, Neville never was a monster, citing an interview. I wish to clarify here that, in spite of Matheson's own interpretations of his text or assertions of his intent, the vast majority of academic critics reading this text agree that the stunning reversal of Neville's character from hero to monster is one of the author's major contributions to the genre (see, for example, Pulliam and Fonseca 69–70).

Chapter One

1. For convenience's sake, parenthetical citations from Matheson's *I Am Legend* (the movie tie-in edition cited in the list of Works Cited that follows) will provide the page number only, rather than the cumbersome full MLA format for a work by an author for whom several publications are cited (Matheson, *Legend* 170).

2. For a more detailed bio-bibliography of Matheson's life and works, see Pulliam and Fonseca (1–22). Much of this information is generally available, and the Wikipedia entry on Matheson is quite thorough (http://en.wikipedia.org/wiki/Richard_Matheson); I have also consulted biographical information found in Berger, Bloom, and interviews by Arnett and Winter. In addition, Bradley provides a thorough account of his screenwriting career.

3. Dual dates indicate initial publication of the short story and airdate for the television adaptation.

4. Unless otherwise indicated ("emphasis added"), italics used in citations are found in the original text.

5. J.P. Telotte offers a thorough review of the literature on SF film in his handbook, *Science Fiction Film* (2001). Sobchack complicates the account presented here, identifying an additional approach to the development of SF film, a group which "sees the 'ideal' SF film as being opposite to and totally separate from the horror film; it eschews those so-called SF films which overtly or surreptitiously present elements that are not empirically based, elements of superstition, mysticism, or religion (the magical and miraculous) most often associated with the horror film. The SF purist sees science fiction as a kind of "prophetic 'neo-realism,'" which reality corroborates after the fact" (55).

6. This coyness represents just one of a number of aspects of Matheson's text and its adaptations that has been appropriated by the contemporary zombie apocalypse narrative.

7. Leskosky's analysis of these films reveals that they, too, participate in the Cold War-era anxieties about invasion and human annihilation that the Last Man and other apocalyptic

narratives express and exploit. Furthermore, he observes a resurgence of these films since the year 2000; he links them not to 9/11, but rather to fears about genetic engineering, a theme in common with the 2007 *I Am Legend* (331).

8. A future book project of mine involves extended analyses of the Last Man in literary precursor texts to *I Am Legend*, including Shelley's *The Last Man* and M.P. Shiel's *The Purple Cloud*.

9. Charles Hoge constructs an interesting argument by tracing Matheson's vampires back to the vampires of the Middle Ages, as contrasted with the Victorian Vampires.

10. In an essay published as I finished this chapter, Adryan Glasgow also applies Waller to the novel, observing that "Neville is by turns resigned to the drudgery of extermination and highly self-critical of his own tendency toward violence. Extermination in *I Am Legend* is far from wild work" (33). Glasgow thus appears to distinguish between the "morally righteous" "wild work" of Van Helsing and the outright "tedium of extermination," but then a paragraphs later he admits that "[w]ild work continues to be performed, despite having lost its redemptive capacity" (33).

11. Referred to as "one of the most disastrous generals of this century" (Clayton 52), Nivelle had been considered a hero and risen to the rank of commander-in-chief on the Western Front in 1916. His overconfidence prior to a subsequently disastrous offensive at the Chemin des Dames bridge over the Aisne River, however, triggered a mutiny among French troops. My thanks to Travis Johnson for bringing this figure to my attention.

12. The matter of his discharge remains unclear as some sources assert that he was "[w]ounded in combat" (Bloom 171) or released for a "combat-related injury" (Winter 26); Matheson tells interviewers that his medical release was not from a battle wound but because of a bad case of trench foot (McGilligan 236; O'Connell and Sallis 200–201).

13. Matheson also wrote a screen adaptation of this novel, filmed in 1967 as *The Young Warriors*, directed by John Peyser for Universal Studios. It has not been released on DVD and even a VHS copy has proven unobtainable.

14. The American Psychiatric Association's *Diagnostic and Statistical Manual of Mental Disorders*, fifth edition (DSM-5), describes the diagnostic criteria for PTSD as follows, most of which apply quite clearly to Robert Neville.

- Criterion A: "Exposure to actual or threatening death, serious injury, or sexual violence" (271);
- Criterion B: "Presence of [...] intrusion symptoms associated with the traumatic event(s)," including:
  o 1. "Recurrent, involuntary, and intrusive distressing memories of the traumatic event(s)"
  o 2. "Recurrent distressing dreams in which the content and/or affect of the dream are related to the traumatic event(s)";
  o 3. "Dissociative reactions (e.g., flashbacks) in which the individual feels or acts as if the traumatic event(s) were recurring" (271).
- Criterion C: "Persistent avoidance of stimuli associated with the traumatic event(s)" evidenced by:
  o 1. "Avoidance or efforts to avoid distressing memories, thoughts, or feelings about or closely associated with the traumatic event(s)";
  o 2. "Avoidance of or efforts to avoid external reminders [...] that arouse distressing memories" (271);
- Criterion D: "Negative alterations in cognitions and mood associated with the traumatic event(s)" including:
  o 1. "Inability to remember an important aspect of the traumatic event(s)" (271);
  o 2. "Persistent and exaggerated negative beliefs or expectations about oneself, others, or the world (e.g., 'I am bad,' 'No one can be trusted,' 'The world is completely dangerous' [...])" (272);
- Criterion E: "Marked alterations in arousal and reactivity" including:
  o 1. "Irritable behavior and angry outbursts";
  o 2. "Reckless or self-destructive behavior";
  o 3. "Hypervigilance";
  o 4. "Exaggerated startle response";
  o 5. "Problems with concentration";
  o 6. "Sleep disturbances"; (272)
- Criterion F: "Duration of the disturbance [...] is more than 1 month" (272);

- Criterion G: "The disturbance causes clinically significant distress or impairment in social, occupational, or other important areas of functioning" (272).

15. In his reexamination of trauma in Bram Stoker's *Dracula*, Jamil Y. Khader offers interesting insight to Neville's situation and Matheson's blurring of the relationship of hunter and hunted, as well. In his reading, Stoker's novel makes it "possible for the victims and survivors to come to terms with their traumatic experiences and relegate them to the past" ("Un/Speakability" 83). He also identifies the moral ambiguities of Van Helsing's team in their treatment of Lucy, but also questions "the ethical imperative to bear witness to trauma's victims that may in itself end up repeating the horrors of originary trauma. Lucy's narrative of vampiric transformation and destruction [...] shows the limits and impossibility of witnessing" (Khader, "Un/ Speakability" 78).

16. This and other translations from French-language studies of Matheson are my own.

17. This term applies to racist stories and novels, mostly from the turn of the nineteenth to the twentieth century, but continuing long into our era, which describe Asian invasions of the Western world (see Ransom, "Yellow Perils").

18. The inclusion of even a single woman in the postapocalyptic narrative radically changes its tone and outcome as seen particularly in the films *Five* (1951), *The World, the Flesh and the Devil* (1957), and *The Last Woman on Earth* (1960); see the discussion of these films at the end of chapter three.

19. Whereas Patterson links Neville's rejection of the female vampires' sexual advances to fears of miscegenation (23), Jamil Khader's reading of *Dracula* through the lens of trauma theory and psychoanalysis links this sexualization of the vampire-victim relationship precisely to the complex "intersubjective psychosexual entanglements between persecutors and victims" ("Un/Speakability" 88). Much of his reading of Stoker's novel applies to *I Am Legend*, but even more clearly given the latter novel's post–World War II context.

20. The polyvalence of Matheson's novel is one of the main reasons of its ability to sustain extended academic criticism; grief theory offers another path this study could have taken, as suggested by Pamela Boker's study of *The Grief Taboo in American Literature: Loss and Prolonged Adolescence in Twain, Melville, and Hemingway* (1996). Her analyses of these canonical American writers apply quite readily to Matheson.

21. Fabien Boully rightly posits that "in effect, *Duel* is about only one thing: the problematic status of David Mann's masculinity, the source of his manifest personality crisis" (118). And Fernando Gabriel Pagnoni Berns also identifies some two dozen Matheson short stories preoccupied by their protagonists' crisis in masculinity. As the finishing touches were being completed on this manuscript, Pulliam and Fonseca published their study of Matheson's entire *oeuvre*, seeing the crisis in masculinity as one of its overarching themes.

22. This biographical note suggests the inspiration for another of Matheson's iconic short stories adapted by Rod Serling as a *Twilight Zone* episode, "Third Rock from the Sun."

23. Since writing this, Adryan Glasgow's discussion of *Legend*'s status as a "pedagogy of whiteness" linked to American colonial expansion in the post–World War II context was published.

24. Tiffany A. Bryant constructs an argument in favor of Matheson's progressive treatment of a racial Other in her fine analysis of "From Shadowed Places" (1960), a potentially controversial story because it features a black female academic performing a juju ritual to effectively exorcize a demon from a privileged white man. Bryant argues that by positioning Dr. Lurice Howell as a figure of authority and undermining the certainties of his rationalist white characters, Matheson constructs a narrative that "portrays racist and sexist issues while expressing progressive antiracist and antisexist sentiments" (143). The present reading of *I Am Legend* aligns with Bryant's interpretation of this 1960 story.

25. In addition to the 1950s Bible blockbusters which would cement Charlton Heston's stardom, many of the postapocalyptic films already mentioned begin with explicit citations from the Bible or implied references to it; for example, in *Five* African American survivor Charles cites the creation story, and Roger Corman prefaced a number of his postapocalyptic films with Biblical passages.

26. I am not fully convinced by Wenk's arguments here, for which he recruits Julia Kristeva's *Strangers to Ourselves*; Ruth is the name of Matheson's real-life wife (Sharp 239), which he borrowed for a recurring character name in various works, including "Shipshape Home" (1952), analyzed by Oakes (65), and the well-known *Twilight Zone* episode, "Little Girl Lost." In the latter, the mother of the little girl lost in the fourth dimension is called "Ruth," while her father is "Chris." Just as he used his real-life wife's name for characters, Matheson also used his sons,' *Christian* and Richard *Christian* Matheson, names, not only here, but also in *What Dreams May Come* (1978).

27. Whereas Charles Hoge links this interpellation to the medieval tradition of "real" vampire accounts (9), Jamil Khader invokes this chant in his reading of the two men's relationship through the lens of queer theory, work that I will build on in chapter two.

Chapter Two

1. The phrase is derived from a 1955 bestselling novel by Sloan Wilson, *The Man in the Gray Flannel Suit*. Its protagonist, Tom Rath, epitomizes post-reinsertion GI angst, as he tries to reconcile the "four completely unrelated worlds" in which he lives: "the crazy, ghost-ridden world of his grandmother and dead parents"; "the isolated, best-not-remembered world in which he had been a paratrooper"; "the matter-of-fact, opaque-glass-brick-partitioned world" of the while-collar office, and home, with his wife and kids, "the only one of the four worlds worth a damn" (26). Rath ultimately resists the temptation to become a cynical but elegant phony, ready to be a yes-man to get ahead in this world, the type of man that he refers to disparagingly as "the man in the gray flannel suit. "Published a year after Matheson's *I Am Legend*, its realistic treatment of post-war male anxieties resonates heavily with the SF-horror novel, but concludes happily, as Tom is rewarded for his honesty and all of the stressors in his life magically resolve themselves.

2. Much of this information is generally available; this portrait draws upon the biography of her father by Victoria Price, as well as film studies by Clark and Meikle.

3. Harry Benshoff cites the following anecdote: "Vincent Price, and Peter Lorre filmed a television pilot entitled 'Collector's Item,' in which they played a pair of crime-fighting antique dealers. Perhaps their monstrously fey personas came too close to denoting homosexuality, for the pilot was never sold" (251).

4. Written by playwright John Gay, there appears to be no published version of the stage production, whose complete title is "Vincent Price as Oscar Wilde: an evening of diversions and delights: being an evening spent with Sebastian Melmouth (Oscar Wilde) on the 29th of November, 1899, Paris, France." Wilde (1954–1900) was an Anglo-Irish writer whose affair with Lord Alfred Douglas led to his highly-publicized trial for sodomy in 1895.

5. Although I draw heavily on Benshoff's work because it is the most extensive articulation of this concept, a number of other film critics, historians and scholars make similar assertions or cite them from contemporary reviews (see Heffernan 97, for example). Even Price's daughter cites Paul Mayersberg's characterization of Price's roles as always being "a nonvirile aesthete" (qtd. Price 216); she acknowledges her father's implementation of camp as theorized by Susan Sontag, as well (218).

6. The character of Phibes also drew on Price's reputation as an art expert; Price, whose talents were honed on the London stage, was on the intellectual side; thus, in spite of his on-stage persona of a villain "during the 1950s this began to be offset by his growing identity as an art expert," says his daughter Victoria Price in her biography of him (190). Such was his status that President Eisenhower appointed him to the Indian Arts & Crafts Board (222). He also became well-known for his interest in antiques. Once again, Benshoff ties these activities to associations with the queer: "[t]he association of gay men with antiques and nostalgia is complex and again related to the discourse of camp" (209). Kevin Heffernan also attributes "Price's well-publicized expertise in gourmet cooking" to his developing "over the top" persona (214).

7. I have an extended project in the works to examine this corpus in detail.

8. This and other car identifications I owe to the Internet Car Movie Database (imcdb.org).

9. All SF buffs know the original *Star Trek* television series' catchphrase for the medical officer of the *U.S.S. Enterprise*, Dr. Bones McCoy (DeForest Kelley): "I'm a doctor, Jim, not a [...]." Interestingly, precursors to that phrase appear in these SF-horror films. In this case, however, Price's Morgan reverses the lines of a character in an earlier such film. In Corman's *Attack of the Crab Monsters* (1957), technician Hank Chapman stresses to two sailors, "I'm no scientist, I'm a technician and a handyman," thus distancing himself from the scientists sent to study the effects of nuclear testing on a Pacific island. Played by Russell Johnson, later cast as The Professor on *Gilligan's Island* (1964–1967), the latter day viewer can enjoy the irony. Also noteworthy in this context, a romantic triangle forms between Hank and the two scientists, Martha Hunter (Pamela Duncan) and Dale Drewer (Richard Garland); although he is the most competent, useful, and possibly intelligent character in the film, Hank sacrifices himself to save humanity by killing the crab monster. Thus, the working-class, everyman figure is shut out of the Darwinian equation, leaving the bourgeois couple (Martha and Dale were already an item, but she grows attracted to Hank because of his positive qualities) intact. Finally, this film also includes some queer comic relief with the casting of a rather effeminate actor as one of the two Seamen (in bell-bottoms and all) to whom Hank initially clarifies his position.

10. IMDb offers an intriguing reference to a 1925 thriller titled, "The Last Man," directed by Bertram Bracken, for which I am attempting to find more information.

11. Invoking Foucault and Hardt and Negri instead of Agamben, Aspasia Stephanou rightly discusses how, in Matheson's novel, the mindless vampires represent "*zoë*"; she associates Neville with the sentient vampires, arguing that both "insist on life as the zoë/bios distinction, excluding the swarms of vampires a bare life" in order to justify their slaughter (19). I would argue that the text remains more ambiguous, blurring this distinction as Neville (and Morgan in the first film adaptation) struggles to maintain *bios*, by listening to classical/jazz music, for example, but repeatedly slips back into *zoë*, a state not much different than that of the horde.

12. *The Zombie Movie Encyclopedia* (2001), in fact, includes an entry on *LMoE*; its author, Peter Dendle, asserts that despite "the Hollywood trimmings of a vampire" found in the film, "I know a zombie when I see one" (100). In contrast, he does not include an entry on *The Omega Man*, but does mention it in relation to *I Am Legend* in the *LMoE* entry (99).

13. Incidentally, while this nickname occurs in the novel (147–49; 162) as well, and was probably inspired by Matheson's friendship with detective-fiction writer William Campbell Gault and "his charming wife Virge" (Matheson to O'Connell and Sallis 201), to me, it invokes the male name "Virgil," rather than the woman's name Virginia. The connection to Virgil, however, becomes significant if we realize that his dead wife becomes Neville's guide into the Dantesque world of death and fire of the novel's mass graves.

Chapter Three

1. Again, as for Matheson and Price, much of this information is generally available on-line; however, my reading of Heston's biography is largely influenced by Emilie Raymond's study *From My Cold Dead Hands* (2006), as frequent citations indicate.

2. Bradley informs us that the crew shot on Sundays and holidays to benefit from the actually empty streets (152)—as opposed to the CGI necessary for such images in the more recent *I Am Legend* film. Bradley also cites the dubious honor of the film being spoofed during a Halloween episode of *The Simpsons*: "The Homega Man" in "Treehouse of Horror VIII" aired October 26, 1997 (155).

3. I have published in French and delivered an as yet unpublished paper in English on contemporary Haitian-Canadian writers' use of the zombie as a trope for Haiti and Haitians under the Duvalier régime; they repeatedly depict ashen, white or pale skin as a sign of a person having become a zombie (see Ransom, "Ce zombi" and "Black Zombie"). Gary D. Rhodes' compelling study of the classic 1930s horror film *White Zombie* (1932)—a work whose methodology partially inspired my work here—discusses the bases in Haitian folklore for this figure, as does botanical anthropologist Wade Davis.

4. Grier also had a role in the iconic Blax-

ploitation vampire sequel, *Scream Blacula Scream* (1973).

5. A convention of 1950s and 1960s apocalyptic films was to cite Bible passages in epigraph or to have characters recite Bible verses, such as in *Five* (1951) and several of Roger Corman's films.

6. Hudson's highly-publicized death of AIDS in 1985 and the subsequent lawsuit by his male partner revealed that hindsight is 20/20 for those who perceived the crisis, buying into the notion that masculinity and heterosexuality are inextricably linked.

7. This film's opening sequence (after the Nativity Scene prologue), in which Judah Ben-Hur, the Israelite noble, is reunited with his childhood friend, now Roman governor Quintus Arrius (Jack Hawkins), is fraught with homosocial tension when watched through the lens of queer theory.

8. This invokes for me the burlesque treatment of the interracial couple Tom and Helen Willis on the television sitcom *The Jeffersons* (1975–1985).

9. Given the high standards of movie make-up art today, the make-up jobs on *The Omega Man* appear almost amateurish; it is unclear if the obviousness of the disguise is the result of a desired statement (as seen, for example, in the recent BBC zombie-themed series, *In the Flesh* [2013–2104], in which the returned dead are partially reintegrated into society but forced to wear thick foundation make-up and contact lenses in order to "pass" as living).

10. Only a few critics have addressed the potential meanings of this activity (see, for example, Hantke 169; Khader, "Will the Real" 553), which recurs in *The Omega Man* and so will be addressed in chapter three.

11. Roger Corman, king of the exploitation flick, explains the premise: "'Exploitation' films were so named because you made a film about something wild with a great deal of action, a little sex, and possibly some sort of strange gimmick; they often came out of the day's headlines" (34).

12. This is such an unusual name and the only other text to my knowledge that uses it are the early French crime novels and silent *feuilleton* short-film series, *Fantomas*. It makes me wonder if the name was used in reference to the French series.

13. This is also a subtext in Harrison's earlier novel, *Broken October: New Zealand, 1985* (1976), which imagines an armed uprising by Māori activists linked in part to the discovery of key minerals on indigenous peoples' lands and various powers' desire to obtain them.

Chapter Four

1. There were 466 fatalities of non-U.S. citizens from 64 countries: https://en.wikipedia.org/wiki/Casualties_of_the_September_11_attacks

2. Perhaps significantly, the second decade of the twenty-first century has seen a number of biblical epics and other "toga films" also popular in the 1950s, as well, such as *Exodus: Gods and Kings* (2014), *Noah* (2014), and *Ben-Hur* (2016) with muscular white actors like Russell Crowe and Christian Bale filling roles like those formerly performed by Charlton Heston.

3. The Wikipedia article for the film offers a detailed, footnoted account of this process: http://en.wikipedia.org/wiki/I_Am_Legend_%28film%29.

4. Subramanian addresses Kathy Davis Patterson's discussion of Matheson's novel as an expression of "the growing anxiety of white citizens toward integration" (Subramanian 49), but she says that Patterson "overlooks the novel's setting in Compton, an area of Los that was beginning to diversify racially in the 1950s" (49). To be precise, the literary Robert Neville lived in the neighboring suburb of Gardena, near Compton Boulevard (Matheson, *Legend* 25)

5. Flashback dialogue addresses him once as "Colonel" but this is appropriate verbal address for officers in the ranks of lieutenant colonel, as well as full colonel.

6. Steffen Hantke identifies this choice of surname with the filmmakers' desire to further villainize her character, echoing a turn of the twentieth century homeopath and wife murderer Dr. Hawley Harvey Crippen (171). See also: https://en.wikipedia.org/wiki/Hawley_Harvey_Crippen

7. Once again, America can envision a black man as its leader before it will choose a white woman, if we continue the parallels between Will Smith and Barack Obama made by Subramanian (53), adding that of Dr. Krippin as a stand-in for Hilary Clinton.

8. Erroneous comma in the original; unfortunately, this otherwise perceptive, well-argued and well-documented essay is plagued by errors of spelling and punctuation, most notably the random application of "'s" (or not) for the possessive or (erroneously) the plural.

Conclusion

1. A quick look at the relatively unknown British actor, Andy Serkis, is of interest here. A serious dramatic actor in various British television series, his rise to Hollywood stardom occurred in SF-horror-fantasy roles; the voice of Gollum in Peter Jackson's *The Lord of the Rings* trilogy (2001–2003), he then was Kong in Jackson's *King Kong* (2005). Through the magic of contemporary film technology's blurring of make-up, live action, blue-screen, and CGI as the ape Caesar, Serkis has become a major star figure whose face few Americans would recognize. Although identifiably "white," his ethnic heritage makes him an appropriate choice for the role of an oppressed minority figure: his original family name is Serkissian, and his grandparents most probably lost family members during the Armenian genocide at the hands of the Ottoman Empire in 1915.

Filmography and Bibliography

Films and Television Series

The Abominable Dr. Phibes. Dir. Robert Fuest. Perf. Vincent Price. MGM, 1971.
The Addams Family. Creator David Levy. Perf. John Astin, Carolyn Jones. Filmways, 1964–1966.
After Earth. Dir. M. Knight Shyamalan. Perf. Will Smith, Jaden Smith. Columbia Pictures, 2013.
The Alfred Hitchcock Hour. Perf. Alfred Hitchcock. Shambley, 1962–1965.
Alfred Hitchcock Presents. Perf. Alfred Hitchcock. Alfred Hitchcock Productions/Shamley, 1955–1962.
Ali. Dir. Michael Mann. Perf. Will Smith. Columbia Pictures, 2001.
Alien. Dir. Ridley Scott. Perf. Sigourney Weaver. Twentieth Century–Fox, 1979.
Apocalypse Now. Dir. Francis Ford Coppola. Perf. Martin Sheen. Zoetrope Studios, 1979.
Attack of the Crab Monsters. Dir. Roger Corman. Perf. Richard Garland. American International Pictures, 1957.
Attack of the Giant Leeches. Dir. Bernard L. Kowalski. Perf. Ken Clark. American International Pictures, 1959.
The Avengers. Dir. Joss Whedon. Perf. Robert Downey, Jr. Paramount Pictures, 2012.
Bad Boys. Dir. Michael Bay. Perf. Will Smith, Martin Lawrence. Don Smith/Jerry Bruckheimer Pictures, 1995.
Batman. Creators Bill Finger, Lorenzo Semple, Jr., William Dozier. Perf. Adam West. Twentieth Century–Fox Television, 1966–1967.
Battle for the Planet of the Apes. Dir. J. Lee Thompson. Perf. Roddy McDowell. Twentieth Century Fox, 1973.
Beneath the Planet of the Apes. Dir. Ted Post. Perf. James Franciscus. Twentieth Century–Fox, 1970.
Ben-Hur. Dir. William Wyler. Perf. Charlton Heston, Jack Hawkins. MGM Studios, 1959.
Ben-Hur. Dir. Timov Bekmambetov. Perf. Jack Huston. MGM Studios, 2016.
Blade. Dir. Stephen Norrington. Perf. Wesley Snipes. New Line Cinema, 1998.
Blade Runner. Dir. Ridley Scott. Perf. Harrison Ford. Warner Bros., 1982.
The Book of Eli. Dir. The Hughes Brothers. Perf. Denzel Washington. Alcon Entertainment, 2010.
The Boys in Company C. Dir. Sidney J. Furie. Perf. Stan Shaw. Golden Harvest Company, 1978.
The Box. Dir. Richard Kelly. Perf. Cameron Diaz, Frank Langella. Warner Bros., 2009.
Bride of Frankenstein. Dir. James Whale. Perf. Boris Karloff, Elsa Lanchester. Universal Studios, 1935.

Brother from Another Planet. Dir. John Sayles. Perf. Joe Morton. Anarchist's Convention Films, 1984.
The Brotherhood of the Wolf. Dir. Christophe Gans. Perf. Samuel LeBihan, Mark Dacascos. Canal+, 2001.
A Bucket of Blood. Dir. Roger Corman. Perf. Dick Miller. Alta Vista Productions, 1959.
Buckskin. Creator Harold Swanton. Perf. Tom Nolan, Betford Productions, 1959.
Butch Cassidy and the Sundance Kid. Dir. George Roy Hill. Perf. Robert Redford, Paul Newman. Twentieth Century–Fox, 1969.
Coffy. Dir. Jack Hill. Perf. Pam Grier. American International Pictures, 1973.
The Comedy of Terrors. Dir. Jacques Tourneur. Perf. Vincent Price, Peter Lorre, Boris Karloff. American International Pictures, 1964.
Coming Home. Dir. John Ashby. Perf. Jon Voigt, Jane Fonda. Jerome Hellman Productions, 1978.
Constantine. Dir. Francis Lawrence. Perf. Keanu Reeves. Warner Bros., 2005.
The Cosby Show. Perf. Bill Cosby. Carsey-Werner Productions, 1984–1992.
Dark City. Dir. William Diterie. Perf. Charlton Heston. Paramount Pictures, 1950.
The Dark Tower. Dir. Nikolaj Arcel. Perf. Idris Elba, Matthew McConaughey. Sony Pictures Entertainment, 2017.
Dawn of the Planet of the Apes. Dir. Matt Reeves. Perf. Gary Oldman, Andy Serkis. Twentieth Century Fox, 2014.
The Day the World Ended. Dir. Roger Corman. Perf. Richard Denning. Golden State Productions, 1955.
De Sade. Dir. Cy Endfield. Perf. Keir Dullea. American International Pictures, 1969.
The Deer Hunter. Dir. Michael Cimino. Perf. Robert DeNiro. EMI/Universal Studios, 1978.
The Descent. Dir. Neill Marshall. Perf. Shauna MacDonald. Lion's Gate Films, 2005.
The Devil Rides Out. Dir. Terence Fisher. Perf. Christopher Lee. Seven Arts/Hammer Films, 1968.
Dollhouse. Creator Joss Whedon. Perf. Eliza Dushku. Twentieth Century Fox, 2009–2010.
Do the Right Thing. Dir. Spike Lee. Perf. Spike Lee, John Turturro. 40 Acres and a Mule Productions, 1989.
Dr. Phibes Rises Again. Dir. Robert Fuest. Perf. Vincent Price. MGM, 1972.
Dracula. Dir. Dan Curtis. Perf. Jack Palance. Latglen Ltd., 1974.
Dracula. Dir. Tod Browning. Perf. Bela Lugosi. Universial Pictures, 1931.
Dracula's Daughter. Dir. Lambert Hillyer. Perf. Gloria Holden. Universal Studios, 1936.
Dragonwyck. Dir. Joseph L. Mankiewickz. Perf. Vincent Price, Gene Tierney. Twentieth Century–Fox, 1947.
Duel. Dir. Steven Spielberg. Perf. Dennis Weaver. Universal Television, 1971.
Edward Scissorhands. Dir. Tim Burton. Perf. Johnny Depp, Vincent Price. Twentieth Century Fox, 1990.
Elysium. Dir. Neill Blomkamp. Perf. Matt Damon, Jodie Foster. Tristar, 2013.
Exodus: Gods and Kings. Dir. Ridley Scott. Perf. Christan Bale. Twentieth Century Fox, 2014.
Family Affair. Creator Don Fedderson, Edmund L. Hartmann. Perf. Brian Keith, Sebastian Cabot. Don Fedderson Productions, 1966–1971.
Fanatic (aka *Die! Die! My Darling*). Dir. Silvio Narazzino. Perf. Tallulah Bankhead, Stefanie Powers, Peter Vaughan. Columbia Pictures/ Hammer Films, 1965.
Five. Dir. Arch Oboler. Perf. William Phipps, Susan Douglas Rubes. Arch Oboler Productions, 1951.
The Fly. Dir. Kurt Neumann. Perf. David Hedison, Vincent Price. Twentieth Century–Fox, 1958.

Foxy Brown. Dir. Jack Hill. Perf. Pam Grier. American International Pictures, 1974.
The Fresh Prince of Bel-Air. Creator Andy and Susan Borowitz. Perf. Will Smith, James Avery. NBC/Quincy Jones Productions, 1990–1996.
Friday the 13th. Dir. Sean S. Cunningham. Perf. Betsy Palmer. Paramount/Warner Bros., 1980.
Fringe. Creators J. J. Abrams, Alex Kurtzman, and Roberto Orzi. Perf. Anna Torv, Joshua Jackson. Warner Bros., 2008–2013.
Full Metal Jacket. Dir. Stanley Kubrick. Perf. Matthew Modine, Adam Baldwin. Warner Bros., 1987.
Gilligan's Island. Creator Sherwood Schwartz. Perf. Bob Denver, Alan Hale. United Artists/CBS, 1964–1992.
The Great Mouse Detective. Dir. Ron Clements, Buddy Matinson. Perf. Vincent Price. Walt Disney Studios, 1986.
The Greatest Story Ever Told. Dir. George Stevens. Perf. Max von Sydow, Charlton Heston. MGM, 1965.
Hancock. Dir. Peter Berg. Perf. Will Smith, Charlize Theron, Jason Bateman. Columbia, 2008.
Have Gun—Will Travel. Creator Herb Meadow, Sam Rolfe. Perf. Richard Boone. Columbia Broadcasting System, 1960.
Hawaii Five-O. Creator Leonard Freeman, Alex Kurtzman. Perf. Alex O'Laughlin, Scott Caan. Kurtzman Orci/CBS Productions, 2010–.
The Hills Have Eyes. Dir. Alexandre Aja. Aaron Stanford, Kathleen Quinlan. Twentieth Century Fox, 2006.
The Hills Have Eyes. Dir. Wes Craven. Perf. John Steadman. Blood Relations Productions, 1977.
House of Usher. Dir. Roger Corman. Perf. Vincent Price. American International Pictures, 1960.
House of Wax. Dir. Andre de Toth. Perf. Vincent Price. Warner Bros., 1953.
The House on Haunted Hill. Dir. William Castle. Perf. Vincent Price. Allied Artists, 1959.
Hunchback of Notre Dame. Dir. William Dieterle. Perf. Charles Laughton. RKO Radio Pictures, 1939.
The Hunger Games. Dir. Gary Ross. Perf. Jennifer Lawrence. Lion's Gate, 2012.
I Am Legend. Dir. Francis Lawrence. Perf. Will Smith. Warner Bros., 2007.
I Am Omega. Dir. Griff Furst. Perf. Mark Dacascos. The Asylum/Echo Bridge Home Entertainment, 2007.
I Robot. Dir. Alex Proyas. Perf. Will Smith, Bridget Moynahan. Twentieth Century Fox, 2004.
I Spy. Perf. Bill Cosby, Robert Culp. NBC, 1965–1968.
The Incredible Shrinking Man. Dir. Jack Arnold. Perf. Grant Williams. Universal Studios, 1957.
Independence Day. Dir. Roland Emmerich. Perf. Will Smith, Bill Pullman. Twentieth Century Fox, 1996.
Iron Chef America. Perf. Alton Brown, Mark Dacascos. Triage Entertainment/Food Network, 2004–2014.
Iron Man. Dir. John Favreau. Perf. Robert Downey, Jr., Gwyneth Paltrow. Paramount/Marvel, 2008.
It Came from Outer Space. Dir. Jack Arnold. Perf. Richard Carlson. Universal Studios, 1953.
Jaws 3-D. Dir. Joe Alves. Perf. Dennis Quaid. Universal Studios, 1983.
Jeremiah Johnson. Dir. Sidney Pollack. Perf. Robert Redford. Warner Bros., 1972.

Julia. Creator Hal Kanter. Perf. Diahann Carroll. Twentieth Century Fox, 1968–1971.
The King and I. Dir. Walter Lang. Perf. Deborah Kerr, Yul Brynner. Twentieth Century-Fox, 1956.
King Kong. Dir. Peter Jackson. Perf. Jack Black. Universal Pictures, 2005.
The Last Man on Earth. Dir. Sidney Salkow, Uberto Ragona. Perf. Vincent Price. American International Pictures, 1964.
The Last Woman on Earth. Dir. Roger Corman. Perf. Betsy Jones-Moreland. American International Pictures, 1960.
Laura. Dir. Otto Preminger. Perf. Gene Tierney, Vincent Price. Twentieth Century–Fox, 1944.
Little Big Man. Dir. Arthur Penn. Perf. Dustin Hoffman. National General Pictures, 1970.
Little Shop of Horrors. Dir. Roger Corman. Perf. Jack Nicholson. American International
Lord of the Rings trilogy. Dir. Peter Jackson. Perf. Elijah Wood, Ian McKellen. New Line Cinema, 2001–2003.Pictures, 1960.
Loose Cannons. Dir. Bob Clark. Perf. Dan Aykroyd. TriStar, 1990.
Mad Men. Creator Matthew Weiner. Perf. Jon Hamm, Elizabeth Moss. Lionsgate Television, 2007–2015.
Malcolm X. Dir. Spike Lee. Perf. Denzel Washington, Angela Bassett. Forty Acres and a Mule, 1992.
The Man Who Knew Too Much. Dir. Alfred Hitchcock. Perf. James Stewart, Doris Day. Paramount, 1956.
The Mask of Fu Manchu. Dir. Charles Brabin. Perf. Boris Karloff. MGM, 1932.
Matrix. Dir. Wachowski Brothers. Perf. Keanu Reeves, Laurence Fishburn. Warner Bros., 1999.
McCabe and Mrs. Miller. Dir. Robert Altman. Perf. Warren Beatty, Julie Christie. Warner Bros., 1971.
Men in Black. Dir. Barry Sonenfield. Perf. Will Smith, Tommy Lee Jones. Columbia Pictures, 1997.
The Monster Club. Dir. Roy Ward Baker. Perf. Vincent Price, Donald Pleasance. Thriller Video, 1981.
The Munsters. Creator Ed Haas, Norm Liebmann. Perf. Fred Gwynne, Yvonne DeCarlo. CBS Television/Universal, 1964–1966.
Mystery. Perf. Vincent Price. Public Broadcasting Service, 1981–1989.
Night and Fog. Dir. Alain Resnais. Perf. Michel Bouquet. Argos Films, 1955.
Night Gallery. Creator Rod Serling. Universal Television, 1969–1973.
Night of the Eagle (aka *Burn, Witch, Burn*). Dir. Sidney Hayes. Perf. Peter Wyngard, Janet Blair. Independent Artists, 1962.
Night of the Living Dead. Dir. George A. Romero. Perf. Duane Jones. New Line Cinema, 1968.
The Night Stalker. Dir. John Llewelyn Moxey. Perf. Darrin McGavin. ABC Television, 1972.
Nosferatu. Dir. F. W. Murnau. Perf. Max Schreck. Prana-Film, 1922.
Nosferatu. Dir. Werner Hertzog. Perf. Klaus Kinski, Isabelle Adjani. Gaumont, 1979.
The Omega Man. Dir. Sidney Salkow. Perf. Charlton Heston, Rosalind Cash. Warner Bros., 1971.
Orphan Black. Creators Kim Coghill, Andrew De Angelis, Jeff Dettsky. Perf. Tatiana Maslany. BBC, 2013–2017.
The Outer Limits. Creator Leslie Stevens. United Artists Television, 1995–2002.
Pacific Rim. Dir. Guillermo del Toro. Perf. Idris Elba. Warner Bros., 2013.
Panic in the Year Zero! Dir. Ray Milland. Perf. Ray Milland, Frankie Avalon. American International Pictures, 1962.

Patton. Dir. Franklin J. Schaffner. Perf. George C. Scott. Twentieth Century-Fox, 1970.
The Pit and the Pendulum. Dir. Roger Corman. Perf. Vincent Price. American International Pictures, 1961.
Planet of the Apes. Dir. Franklin J. Schaffner. Perf. Charlton Heston. Twentieth Century-Fox, 1968.
Planet of the Apes. Dir. Tim Burton, Perf. Mark Wahlberg, Helena Bonham Carter. Twentieth Century Fox, 2001.
Platoon. Dir. Oliver Stone. Perf. Charlie Sheen, Tom Berenger. Orion Pictures, 1986.
Prometheus. Dir. Ridley Scott. Perf. Noomi Rapace, Idris Elba. Twentieth Century Fox, 2012.
The Pursuit of Happyness. Dir. Gabriele Muccino. Perf. Will Smith, Thandie Newton. Columbia Pictures/Overbrook, 2006.
The Quiet Earth. Dir. Geoff Murphy. Perf. Bruno Lawrence, Alison Routledge, Pete Smith. Cinepro, 1985.
The Raven. Dir. Lew Landers. Perf. Bela Lugosi, Boris Karloff. Universal Studios, 1935.
The Raven. Dir. Roger Corman. Perf. Vincent Price. American International Pictures, 1963.
Rear Window. Dir. Alfred Hitchcock. Perf. James Stewart, Grace Kelly. Paramount, 1954.
Rise of the Planet of the Apes. Dir. Rupert Wyatt. Perf. James Franco, Andy Serkis. Twentieth Century Fox, 2011.
Rocketship X-M. Dir. Kurt Neumann. Perf. Lloyd Bridges. Lippert Productions, 1950.
Room 222. Creator James L. Brooks. Perf. Michael Constantine, Lloyd Haynes. Twentieth Century-Fox, 1970-1973.
The Running Man. Dir. Paul Michael Glaser. Perf. Arnold Schwarzenegger. TriStar, 1987.
Scream of the Wolf. Dir. Dan Curtis. Perf. Peter Graves. Metromedia, 1974.
Sense8. Creators J. Michael Straczynski, Lana Wachowski, Lilly Wachowski. Perf. Doona Bae, Jamie Clayton. Netflix, 2015-2018.
Seven Pounds. Dir. Gabriele Muccino. Perf. Will Smith, Rosario Dawson. Columbia Pictures, 2008.
Shrek. Dir. Andrew Adamson, Vicky Jones. Perf. Mike Myers, Eddie Murphy. DreamWorks, 2001.
The Simpsons. Creator James L. Brooks, Matt Groening, Sam Simon. Perf. Dan Castallaneta. Gracie Films/ Twentieth Century Fox Television, 1989-.
Six Degrees of Separation. Dir. Fred Schepisi. Perf. Will Smith, Stockard Channing. MGM, 1993.
Somewhere in Time. Dir. Jeannot Szwarc. Perf. Christopher Reeve, Jane Seymour. Universal Studios, 1980.
Soylent Green. Dir. Richard Fleischer. Perf. Charlton Heston. MGM, 1973.
Star Trek. Creator Gene Rodenberry. Perf. William Shatner. Desilu/Paramount, 1966-1969.
Star Wars. Dir. George Lucas. Perf. Mark Harmon, Carrie Fisher, Harrison Ford. Lucasfilms, 1977.
Tales of Terror. Dir. Roger Corman. Perf. Vincent Price, Peter Lorre. American International Pictures, 1962.
Teenage Caveman. Dir. Roger Corman. Perf. Robert Vaughan. American International Pictures, 1957.
The Ten Commandments. Dir. Cecil B. DeMille. Perf. Charlton Heston, Yul Brynner. Paramount Pictures, 1956.
The Terminator. Dir. James Cameron. Perf. Arnold Schwarzenegger. Orion Pictures, 1984.
Terminator 2: Judgement Day. Dir. James Cameron. Perf. Arnold Schwarzenegger. Orion Pictures, 1991.
Them! Dir. Gordon Douglas. Perf. James Whitmore. Warner Bros., 1954.
The Thing from Another World. Dir. Charles Nyby. Perf. Kenneth Tobey. RKO Radio Pictures, 1951.

The 13 Ghosts of Scooby Doo. Perf. Casey Kasem. Hanna-Barbera, 1985.
Thor. Dir. Kenneth Branagh. Perf. Chris Hemsworth, Anthony Hopkins. Paramount Pictures/Marvel Studios, 2011.
Thriller. Dir. John Landis. Perf. Michael Jackson, Vincent Price. Optimum Productions, 1982.
The Tingler. Dir. William Castle. Perf. Vincent Price. Columbia Pictures, 1959.
The Tomb of Ligeia. Dir. Roger Corman. Perf. Vincent Price. American International Pictures, 1964.
Total Recall. Dir. Paul Verhoeven. Perf. Arnold Schwarzenegger. TriStar, 1990.
Transformers. Dir. Michael Bay. Perf. Shia Laboeuf. DreamWorks/Paramount, 2007.
28 Days Later. Dir. Danny Boyle. Perf. Cillian Murphy. DNA Films, 2002.
24. Creators Robert Cochran and Joel Surnow. Perf. Kiefer Sutherland. Twentieth Century Fox, 2001–2010.
24 Legacy. Creators Robert Cochran, Manny Coto, Evan Katz. Perf. Corey Hawkins. Twentieth Century Fox, 2016–.
The Twilight Zone. Creator Rod Serling. CBS, 1959–1964.
Underworld. Dir. Len Wiseman. Perf. Kate Beckinsale, Scott Speedman. Screen Gems, 2003.
Universal Soldiers. Dir. Griff Furst. Perf. Kristin Quintrall. Asylum, 2007.
Vertigo. Dir. Alfred Hitchcock. Perf. James Stewart, Kim Novak. Paramount, 1958.
The Walking Dead. Creator Frank Darabont. Perf. Andrew Lincoln, Norman Reedus. American Movie Classics, 2010–.
Wanted: Dead or Alive. Perf. Steve McQueen. CBS, 1959.
The War of the Worlds. Dir. Byron Haskin. Perf. Gene Barry. Paramount, 1953.
War for the Planet of the Apes. Dir. Matt Reeves. Perf. Andy Serkis, Woody Harrelson. Twentieth Century Fox, 2017.
What Dreams May Come. Dir. Vincent Ward. Perf. Robin Williams. Polygram, 1998.
White Zombie. Dir. Victor Halperin. Perf. Bela Lugosi. Universal, 1932.
Will Penny. Dir. Tom Gries. Perf. Charlton Heston. Paramount, 1968.
Wolvesbayne. Dir. Griff Furst. Perf. Mark Dacascos. Asylum, 2009.
The World, the Flesh and the Devil. Dir. Ranald MacDougall. Perf. Harry Belafonte, Inger Stevens, Mel Ferrer. MGM, 1959.
Woodstock. Dir. Michael Wadleigh. Perf. Jimmy Hendrix, Janis Joplin, Crosby, Stills & Nash. MGM, 1970.
The Young Warriors. Dir. John Peyser. Perf. James Drury, Steve Carlson. Universal Studios, 1967.
Zombieland. Dir. Ruben Fleischer. Perf. Woody Harrelson. Jesse Eisenberg. Columbia Pictures, 2009.

Books and Articles

"About the Authors." *Books by John William Corrington and Joyce H. Corrington.* 2017. http://www.jcorrington.com/authors/. Accessed January 3, 2017.
Abrams, Fredrick R. M.D. Foreword to Spitz xxiii–xxxv.
Abu-Lughod, Janet L. *Race, Space, and Riots in Chicago, New York, and Los Angeles.* Oxford: Oxford University Press, 2007.
Agamben, Giorgio. *Homo Sacer: Sovereign Power and the Bare Life.* Trans. Daniel Heller-Roazen. Stanford: Stanford University Press, 1998.
American Psychiatric Association. *Diagnostic and Statistical Manual of Mental Disorders.* 5th edition. Washington, D.C.: American Psychiatric Association, 2013.

Arnett, Robert. "The Macabre Cinema of Richard Matheson: Interview." *Creative Screenwriting* 5.5 (1998): 57–63.

Arnold, David. *Colonizing the Body: State Medicine and Epidemic Disease in Nineteenth-Century India*. Berkeley: University of California Press, 1993.

Astic, Guy. "Richard Matheson et le cinéma de la hammer." Chenille, Dollé, Mellier 155–64.

Auerbach, Nina. *Our Vampires, Ourselves*. Chicago: University of Chicago Press, 1995.

Bacon, Simon. "Locked in Time: Trauma, Memory, and the Barthesian *Punctum* in Richard Matheson's Fiction." Mathews and Haedicke 211–24.

Baker, Houston A., and K. Merinda Simmons, eds. *The Trouble with Post-Blackness*. New York: Columbia University Press, 2015.

Baker, Ryan. "'Conclusion of All Our Yesterdays': The Jungian Text of *The Omega Man*." *Science Fiction America: Essays on SF Cinema*. Ed. David J. Hogan. Jefferson, NC: McFarland, 2006. 196–206.

Bakke, Gretchen. "How the Black Guys Got to Kill All the White Guys and Still Be Good: An Essay on the Changing Dynamics of Race in American Action Cinema." *Social Science Research Network*. October 8, 2008. http://papers.ssrn.com/sol3/papers.cfm?abstract_id=1374994.

Barnes, Steven. "Can a Brother Get Some Love? Sociobiology in Images of African-American Sensuality in Contemporary Cinema." *Afro-Future Females: Black Writers Chart Science Fiction's Newest New-Wave Trajectory*. Ed. Marleen S. Barr. Columbus: Ohio State University Press, 2008. 182–90.

Bean, Annemarie, James V. Hatch, and Brooks McNamara. *Inside the Minstrel Mask: Readings in Nineteenth-Century Blackface Minstrelsy*. Hanover: Wesleyan University Press, 1996.

Benshoff, Harry M. *Monsters in the Closet: Homosexuality in the Horror Film*. Manchester, UK: Manchester University Press, 1997.

Benshoff, Harry M., and Sean Griffin. *Queer Images: A History of Gay and Lesbian Film in America*. Lanham, MD: Rowman & Littlefield, 2006.

Berger, Christian K. "The Macabre Cinema of Richard Matheson: Bibliographical Essay." *Creative Screenwriting* 5.5 (1998): 56–57.

Bishop, Kyle. "Dead Man *Still* Walking: Pondering the Zombie Renaissance." *Journal of Popular Film and Television* 37.1 (2009): 16–25.

Biskind, Peter. *Seeing Is Believing: How Hollywood Taught Us to Stop Worrying and Love the Fifties*. London: Pluto, 1983.

Blaisdell, Anne. *Nightmare*. New York: Harper, 1961.

Blake, Linnie. *The Wounds of Nations: Horror Cinema, Historical Trauma and National Identity*. Manchester, UK: Manchester University Press, 2008.

Bloom, Harold, Ed. "Richard Matheson." *Modern Horror Writers*. New York: Chelsea House, 1995. 171–85.

Boal, Iain, Janferie Stone, Michael Watts, and Cal Winslow, eds. *West of Eden: Communes and Utopia in Northern California*. Oakland, CA: PM Press, 2012.

Bogle, Donald. *Toms, Coons, Mulattoes, Mammies, and Bucks: An Interpretive History of Blacks in American Films*. 3rd edition. New York: Continuum, 1994.

Boker, Pamela A. *The Grief Taboo in American Literature: Loss and Prolonged Adolescence in Twain, Melville, and Hemingway*. New York: New York University Press, 1996.

Booker, M. Keith. *Monsters, Mushroom Clouds, and the Cold War: American Science Fiction and the Roots of Postmodernism, 1946–1964*. Westport, CT: Greenwood, 2001.

Bould, Mark, Andrew M. Butler, Adam Roberts, and Sherryl Vint, eds. *The Routledge Companion to Science Fiction*. New York: Routledge, 2009.

Boulle, Pierre. *Planet of the Apes*. 1963. Trans. Xan Fielding. New York: Gramercy, 2000.
Boully, Fabien. "'Presque un Film de Camion Hanté': Masculinité en Crise et Contrechamp Fantastique dans *Duel* (1971) de Steven Spielberg." Chenille, Dollé, Mellier 113–27.
Bradbury, Ray. "Praise for Richard Matheson." Matheson. *Legend* n.p.
Bradley, Matthew R. *Richard Matheson on Screen: A History of the Filmed Works*. Foreword by Richard Matheson. Jefferson, NC: McFarland, 2010.
Briefel, Aviva, and Sam J. Miller. Introduction. *Horror After 9/11: World of Fear, Cinema of Terror*. Austin: University of Texas Press, 2011. 1–10.
Broderick, Mick, ed. *Hibakusha Cinema: Hiroshima, Nagasaki, and the Nuclear Image in Japanese Film*. London/New York: Kegan Paul, 1996.
Brooks, Christopher. "When Is a Hero Not So? America, Robert Neville, and *I Am Legend*." *The Image of the Hero in Literature, Media and Society*. Pueblo: Colorado State University Press, 2004. 477–81.
Bryant, Tiffany A. "Reading Progressive Race and Gender Identity Markers in 'From Shadowed Places.'" Mathews and Haedicke 143–56.
Bugliosi, Vincent, with Curt Gentry. *Helter Skelter: The True Story of the Manson Family*. 1974. New York: Bantam, 1995.
Butler, Judith. *Gender Trouble: Feminism and the Subversion of Identity*. 1990. New York: Routledge, 1999.
Canavan, Anne. "Which Came First, Zombies or the Plague? Colson Whitehead's *Zone One* as Post-9/11 Allegory." *Representing 9/11: Trauma Ideology, and Nationalism in Literature, Film, and Television*. Ed. Paul Petrovic. Lanham, MD: Rowman & Littlefield, 2015. 41–52.
Carlin, Bob. *The Birth of the Banjo: Joel Walker Sweeney and Early Minstrelsy*. Jefferson, NC: McFarland, 2007.
Carney, Raymond. "Richard Matheson." *Dictionary of Literary Biography. Vol. 8. Twentieth-Century American Science Fiction Writers Part II: M-Z*. Detroit, MI: Gale, 1981. 12–14.
Carroll, Noël, and Lester H. Hunt, eds. *Philosophy in the Twilight Zone*. Malden, MA: Wiley-Blackwell, 2009.
Casali, Arianna. "*I Am Legend* by Richard Matheson: The Post-Apocalyptic Setting of Human Nature from the USA to Italy and Back." *Translating America: Importing, Translating, Misrepresenting, Mythicizing, Communicating America. Proceedings of the 20th AISNA Biennial Conference Torino, September 24–26, 2009*. Ed. Marina Camboni, Andrea Carosso, and Sonia Di Loreto. Torino: Otto, 2010. 431–39.
Case, John, and Rosemary C. R. Taylor, eds. *Co-Ops, Communes and Collectives: Experiments in Social Change in the 1960s and 1970s*. New York: Pantheon, 1979.
Castellana, Cristina. "Holding on to Self: The Masculine Drive in 'Investigating Jericho' and *I Am Legend*." *The Journal of Dracula Studies* 10 (2008): 26–30.
Chafe, William H. *The Unfinished Journey: America Since World War II*. 3rd ed. New York: Oxford University Press, 1995.
Chenille, Vincent. "Les Adaptations de *Je Suis Une Légende*." Chenille, Dollé, and Mellier 91–102.
Chenille, Vincent, and Marie Dollé. Introduction. Chenille, Dollé, and Mellier 7–10.
Chenille, Vincent, Marie Dollé, and Denis Mellier, eds. *Richard Matheson. Il est une légende: Actes du Colloque de l'Université de Picardie Jules Verne et de la Bibliothèque Nationale de France*. Amiens: Encrage, 2011.
Chideya, Farai. *The Color of Our Future*. New York: William Morrow, 1999.
Childs, Erica Chito. "The Prime-Time Color Line: Interracial Couples and Television."

Fade to Black and White: Interracial Images in Popular Culture. Lanham, MD: Rowman & Littlefield, 2009. 33–67.

Chong, Sylvia Shin Huey. *The Oriental Obscene: Violence and Racial Fantasies in the Vietnam Era.* Durham: Duke University Press, 2012.

Christie, Deborah. "A Dead New World: Richard Matheson and the Modern Zombie." Christie and Lauro 67–80.

Christie, Deborah, and Sarah Juliet Lauro, eds. *Better Off Dead: The Evolution of the Zombie as Posthuman.* New York: Fordham University Press, 2011.

_____. "Introduction." Christie and Lauro 1–4.

Clark, Mark. "Vincent Price." *Smirk, Sneer and Scream: Great Acting in Horror Cinema.* Jefferson, NC: McFarland, 2004. 90–104.

Clasen, Mathias. "Vampire Apocalypse: A Biocultural Critique of Richard Matheson's *I Am Legend.*" *Philosophy and Literature* 34.2 (Oct. 2010): 313–28.

Clayton, Anthony. "Robert Nivelle and the French Spring Offensive, 1917." *Fallen Stars: Eleven Studies of Twentieth Century Military Disasters.* Ed. Brian Bond. London: Brassey's, 1991. 52–64.

Cohan, Steven. *Masked Men: Masculinity and the Movies in the Fifties.* Bloomington: Indiana University Press, 1997.

Comer, Joshua. "Another Time: Novelizing History After the Canon in Matheson." Mathews and Haedicke 225–38.

Connell, R. W. *Masculinities.* Oxford: Polity, 1995.

Corman, Roger, with Jim Jerome. *How I Made a Hundred Movies in Hollywood and Never Lost a Dime.* 1990. New York: Da Capo, 1998.

Corrington, Joyce Hooper. Interview. Special Features. *The Omega Man.* Warner Bros. 2003. 2007. DVD.

Cumings, Bruce. *The Korean War: A History.* New York: Modern Library, 2010.

Davis, Wade. *Passage of Darkness: The Ethnobiology of the Haitian Zombie.* Chapel Hill: University of North Carolina Press, 1988.

_____. *The Serpent and the Rainbow.* 1985. New York: Touchstone, 1997.

Dawidziak, Mark. "Richard Matheson's 'I Am Legend': The Censored Screenplay." Richard Matheson. *Visions Deferred.* Colorado Springs, CO: Gauntlet, 2009. 11–29.

Defoe, Daniel. *Robinson Crusoe.* 1719. Ed. Thomas Keymer. New York: Oxford University Press, 2007.

DeGraw, Sharon. "Will Smith: Black Masculinity in Science Fiction Film." Unpublished Manuscript.

Dendle, Peter. "And the Dead Shall Inherit the Earth." Christie and Lauro 159–62.

_____. *The Zombie Movie Encyclopedia.* Jefferson, NC: McFarland, 2001.

Dumbrell, John. *Rethinking the Vietnam War.* New York: Palgrave Macmillan, 2012.

Dyer, Richard. *Stars.* 1979. New edition. London: BFI, 1998.

_____. *White.* London: Routledge, 1997.

_____. "White." *The Matter of Images: Essays on Representations.* London: Routledge, 1993. 141–63.

Dziemanowicz, Stefan. "Horror Begins at Home: Richard Matheson's Fear of the Familiar." *Studies in Weird Fiction* 14 (1994): 29–36.

Ellison, Ralph. *The Invisible Man.* New York: Random House, 1952.

Ethridge, Benjamin Cane. "Causes of Unease: Horror Rhetoric in Fiction and Film." MA Thesis. California State University, San Bernardino, 2004.

Fain, Kimberley. *Black Hollywood: From Butlers to Superheroes, the Changing Role of African American Men in the Movies.* Santa Barbara, CA: Prager, 2015.

Fisch, Audrey. *Frankenstein.* Westfield, CT: Helm Info, 2009.

Foster, Gwendolyn Audrey. "Monstrosity and the Bad-White-Body Film." *Bad: Infamy, Darkness, Evil, and Slime on Screen*. Ed. Murray Pomerance. Albany: State University of New York Press, 2004. 38–53.

_____. *Performing Whiteness: Postmodern Re/Constructions in the Cinema*. Albany: State University of New York Press, 2003.

Gates, Jaym, and Erika Holt, eds. *Rigor Amortis*. Calgary: Edge SF & F, 2011.

Giles, James R. *The Spaces of Violence*. Tuscaloosa: University of Alabama Press, 2006.

Gladchuk, John Joseph. *Hollywood and Anticommunism: HUAC and the Evolution of the Red Menace, 1935–1950*. New York: Routledge, 2007.

Glasgow, Adryan. "'Wild Work': The Monstrosity of Whiteness in *I Am Legend*." Mathews and Haedicke 31–43.

Gould, Stephen Jay. *The Mismeasure of Man*. New York: Norton, 1981.

Greene, Eric. *The Planet of the Apes as American Myth: Race and Politics in the Films and Television Series*. Jefferson, NC: McFarland, 1996.

Hagood, Amanda. "Giant Bugs and Shrinking Men: Domesticating Technology in the *Incredible Shrinking Man*." Mathews and Haedicke 89–101.

Hall, Donald E. *Queer Theories*. London: Palgrave/Macmillan, 2003.

Hand, Richard J., and Jay McRoy, eds. *Monstrous Adaptations: Generic and Thematic Mutations in Horror Film*. Manchester, UK: Manchester University Press, 2007.

Hantke, Steffen. "Historicizing the Bush Years: Politics, Horror Film, and Francis Lawrence's *I Am Legend*." Briefel and Miller 165–185.

Haring, Kristen. *Ham Radio's Technical Culture*. Cambridge, MA: MIT Press, 2007.

Harvey, Paul. *Through the Storm, Through the Night: A History of African American Christianity*. Lanham, MD: Rowman & Littlefield, 2011.

Hautecloque, Isabelle. *Fantômes et fantasmes des maisons hantées dans le roman anglo-saxon du 20ème siècle de J.Herbert, S.Jackson et R.Matheson*. Ph.D. Dissertation. University of Aix-en-provence, 1994.

Heffernan, Kevin. "'A Sissified Bela Lugosi': Vincent Price, William Castle, and AIP'S Poe Adaptations." *Ghouls, Gimmicks, and Gold: Horror Films and the American Movie Business, 1953–1968*. Durham: Duke University Press, 90–111.

Heineman, Kenneth J. *Campus Wars: The Peace Movement at American State Universities in the Vietnam Era*. New York: New York University Press, 1993.

Hendershot, Cyndy. *I Was a Cold War Monster: Horror Films, Eroticism and the Cold War Imagination*. Bowling Green, OH: Bowling Green State University Press, 2001.

Henry, Patrick. *We Only Know Men: The Rescue of the Jews in France During the Holocaust*. Washington, D. C.: Catholic University Press, 2007.

Herzberg, Bob. *Hang 'Em High: Law and Disorder in Western Films and Literature*. Jefferson, NC: McFarland, 2013.

Heston, Charlton. *The Actor's Life: Journals 1956–1976*. Ed. Hollis Alpert. New York: Dutton, 1978.

_____. *In the Arena: An Autobiography*. New York: Simon & Schuster, 1995.

Hitchcock, Susan Tyler. *Frankenstein: A Cultural History*. New York: Norton, 2007.

Hoge, Charles. "'Crawling Out of the Middle Ages': The Deep Literary Roots of the Vampires in *I Am Legend*." Mathews and Haedicke 3–15.

Hudson, Janice Hagwood. "Is Gothic Dead?: The Evolution of the Vampire Novel." MA Thesis. California State University-San Bernardino, 2010.

Hunt, Lester H. Introduction. Carroll and Hunt 1–4.

Hutcheon, Linda. *A Theory of Adaptation*. New York: Routledge, 2006.

Ingold, Charles. "Hegemony and Patriarchy in Portrayals of the Protagonist and Antagonists in Film Versions of *I Am Legend*." *The Image of the Hero II*. Pueblo, CO: Society for the Interdisciplinary Study of Social Imagery, Colorado State University-Pueblo, 2010. 217–23.

Jancovich, Mark. "'Charlton Heston Is an Axiom': Spectacle and Performance in the Development of the Blockbuster." *Film Stars: Hollywood and Beyond*. Ed. Andy Willis. Manchester: Manchester University Press, 2004. 51–70.

_____. "The Dilemmas of Masculinity: The Fiction of Richard Matheson." *Rational Fears: American Horror in the 1950s*. Manchester, UK: Manchester University Press, 1996. 129–65.

Janicker, Rebecca. "Gender, Sexuality, and Marriage in a *Stir of Echoes* and *Earthbound*." Mathews and Haedicke 117–27.

Jellenik, Glenn. "Last-Person Narration: Cultural Imagination at the End of the World as We Know It." Mathews and Haedicke 59–71.

Johnson, Haynes. *The Best of Times: America in the Clinton Years*. New York: Harcourt, 2001.

Kamen, Henry. *The Spanish Inquisition: A Historical Revision*. New Haven: Yale University Press, 1998.

Kennedy, Randall. *Interracial Intimacies: Sex, Marriage, Identity, and Adoption*. Princeton, NJ: Pantheon, 2003.

Khader, Jamil. "Un/Speakability, Impossible Witnessing, and Radical Otherness: Reconsidering Trauma in Bram Stoker's *Dracula*." *College Literature* 39.2 (2012): 73–97.

_____. "Will the Real Robert Neville Please, Come Out? Vampirism, the Ethics of Queer Monstrosity, and Capitalism in Richard Matheson's *I Am Legend*" *Journal of Homosexuality* 60.4 (2013): 532–57.

Kim, Hun Joon. *The Massacres at Mt. Halla: Sixty Years of Truth Seeking in South Korea*. Ithaca: Cornell University Press, 2014.

Kimmel, Michael S. *Manhood in America: A Cultural History*. 2nd edition. New York: Oxford University Press. 2006.

King, Stephen. *Danse Macabre*. New York: Everest House, 1981.

Krulik, Ted. "Reaching for Immortality: Two Novels of Richard Matheson." *Critical Encounters II: Writers and Themes in Science Fiction*. Ed. Tom Staicar. New York: Fred Ungar, 1982. 1–14.

LaCapra, Dominick. *Writing History, Writing Trauma*. Baltimore: Johns Hopkins University Press, 2001.

Lampley, Jonathan Malcolm. *Women in the Horror Films of Vincent Price*. Jefferson, NC: McFarland, 2011.

Langer, Lawrence L. *Holocaust Testimonies: The Ruins of Memory*. New Haven: Yale University Press, 1991.

Lavender, Isiah, III. "Critical Race Theory." Bould, et al. 185–93.

____. *Race in American Science Fiction*. Bloomington: Indiana University Press, 2011.

Leiber, Fritz. *The Conjure Wife*. 1943. New York: Orb, 2009.

Leskosky, Richard J. "Size Matters: Big Bugs on Screen." *Insect Poetics*. Ed. Eric C. Brown. Minneapolis: University of Minneapolis Press, 2006. 319–41.

Lindow, John. *Norse Mythology: A Guide to the Gods, Heroes, Rituals, and Beliefs*. Oxford: Oxford University Press, 2002.

Lott, Eric. "Blackface and Blackness: The Minstrel Show in American Culture." Bean, Hatch, and McNamara 3–32.

Lovecraft, H. P. *Supernatural Horror in Literature*. 1927, New York: Dover, 1973.

Lunde, Giuliana. "A Plague of Silence: Social Hygiene and the Purification of the Nation in Camus's *La Peste*." *Symposium* 65.2 (2011): 134–57.

Matheson, Richard. *Abu and the 7 Marvels*. Springfield, PA: Gauntlet, 2002.

_____. *Beardless Warriors*. 1960. New York: Tor, 2008.
_____. *Bid Time Return*. New York: Viking, 1975.
_____. *Collected Stories. Volumes 1–3*. Ed. Stanley Wiater. Colorado Springs, CO: Gauntlet, 2003–2005.
_____. *Earthbound*. 1989. New York: Tor, 2004.
_____. Foreword. Meikle 7–9.
_____. *Generations*. Colorado Springs, CO: Gauntlet, 2012.
_____. *The Gun Fight*. New York: M. Evans. 1993.
_____. *Hell House*. 1971. New York: Tor, 1999.
_____. *I Am Legend*. 1954. New York: Tor, 1995. 2007.
_____. *Journal of the Gun Years*. New York: M. Evans. 1991.
_____. *The Memoirs of Wild Bill Hickock*. 1996. New York: Tor, 2009.
_____. "The Night Creatures." *Visions Deferred*. Colorado Springs, CO: Gauntlet, 2009. 31–176.
_____. *Now You See It*. New York: Tor, 1995.
_____. *Other Kingdoms*. New York: Tor, 2011.
_____. *The Path: A New Look at Reality*. New York: Tor, 1999.
_____. *Shock!* New York: Dell, 1961.
_____. *Shock II*. New York: Dell, 1964.
_____. *Shock III*. New York: Dell, 1966.
_____. *Shock Waves*. New York: Dell, 1970.
_____. *The Shrinking Man*. 1956. New York: Tor, 1994. 2001.
_____. *Somewhere in Time*. 1975. New York: Ballantine, 1980.
_____. *Someone Is Bleeding*. New York: Lion, 1953.
_____. *The Twilight Zone Scripts, Vols. 1 and 2*. Ed. Stanley Wiater. Springfield, PA: Edge Books, 2001–2002.
_____. *What Dreams May Come*. New York: Putnam, 1978.
Mathews, Cheyenne. "A 'Private and Particular Hell': Mathesonian Noir in the *Twilight Zone*." Mathews and Haedicke 183–95.
_____. "Lightening 'The White Man's Burden': Evolution of the Vampire from the Victorian Racialism of *Dracula* to the New World Order of *I Am Legend*." *Images of the Modern Vampire: The Hip and the Atavistic*. Ed. Barbara Brodman and James E. Doan. Madison, NJ: Fairleigh Dickinson University Press, 2013. 85–98.
_____. "Introduction: Richard Matheson: Wisdom Writer." Mathews and Haedicke xi–xviii.
Mathews, Cheyenne, and Janet V. Haedicke, eds. *Reading Richard Matheson: A Critical Survey*. Lanham, MD: Rowman & Littlefield, 2014.
McClelland, Bruce A. *Slayers and Their Vampires: A Cultural History of Killing the Dead*. Ann Arbor: University of Michigan Press, 2006.
McFarlane, Brian. *Novel to Film: An Introduction to the Theory of Adaptation*. Oxford: Clarendon, 1996.
McGilligan, Pat. "Richard Matheson: Storyteller." *Backstory 3: Interviews with Screenwriters of the 1960s*. Berkeley: University of California Press, 1997. 229–56.
Meikle, Denis. *Vincent Price: The Art of Fear*. Foreword Richard Matheson. Afterword Roger Corman. London: Reynolds & Hearn, 2003.
Mellor, Anne K. *Mary Shelley: Her Life, Her Fiction, Her Monsters*. New York: Methuen, 1988.
Merril, Judith. *Shadow on the Hearth*. New York: Doubleday, 1950.
Meyer, Stephenie. *Breaking Dawn*. New York: Little, Brown, 2008.
_____. *Eclipse*. New York: Little, Brown, 2007.

_____. *New Moon*. New York: Little, Brown, 2006.
_____. *Twilight*. New York: Little, Brown, 2005.
Mitchell, Charles P. "*The Last Man on Earth* (1964)." *A Guide to Apocalyptic Cinema*. Westport, CT: Greenwood, 2001. 93–97.
Modleski, Tania. *The Women Who Knew Too Much*. New York: Methuen, 1988.
Montalbano, Margaret. "From Bram Stoker's *Dracula* to Bram Stoker's '*Dracula*.'" Stam and Raengo. *Companion* 385–98.
Moreland, Sean. "Shambling Towards Mount Improbable to Be Born: American Evolutionary Anxiety and the Hopeful Monsters of Matheson's *I Am Legend* and Romero's Dead Films." *Generation Zombie: Essays on the Living Dead in Modern Culture*. Ed. Stephanie Boluk and Wylie Lenz Jefferson, NC: McFarland, 2011. 77–89.
Moreman, Christopher M. "Let This Hell Be Our Heaven: Richard Matheson's Spirituality and Its Hollywood Distortions." *Journal of Religion and Popular Culture* 24.1 (Spring 2012): 130–47.
Morey, Anne. Introduction to *Genre, Reception, and Adaptation in the 'Twilight' Series*. Ed. Anne Morey. Burlington, VT: Ashgate, 2012. 1–14.
Morrell, David. *First Blood*. New York: M. Evans, 1972.
Morrison, Toni. *Playing in the Dark: Whiteness and the Literary Imagination*. Cambridge: Harvard University Press, 1992.
Nama, Adilifu. *Black Space: Imagining Race in Science Fiction Film*. Austin: University of Texas Press, 2008.
Neilson, Keith. "Richard Matheson." *Dictionary of Literary Biography. Vol. 8. Supernatural Fiction Writers: Fantasy and Horror, 2: A. E. Coppard to Roger Zelazny*. New York: Scribner's, 1985. 1073–80.
Oakes, David A. "Richard Matheson." *Science and Destabilization in the Modern American Gothic: Lovecraft, Matheson, and King*. Westport, CT: Greenwood Press, 2000. 63–90.
O'Connell, Jack, and James Sallis. "Paradoxa Interview w/Richard Matheson." *Paradoxa: Studies in World Literary Genres* 18 (2003): 195–210.
Pagnoni Berns, Fernando Gabriel. "(Male) Matter and Its Dissolution: Crisis of Masculinities as Horror in Richard Matheson's Short Stories." Mathews and Haedicke 103–15.
Pascoe, Peggy. *What Comes Naturally: Miscegenation Law and the Making of Race in America*. Oxford: Oxford University Press, 2009.
Patterson, James T. *Brown v. Board of Education: A Civil Rights Milestone and Its Troubled Legacy*. Oxford: Oxford University Press, 2001.
_____. *The Eve of Destruction: How 1965 Transformed America*. New York: Basic Books, 2012.
_____. *Freedom Is Not Enough: The Moynihan Report and America's Struggle Over Black Family Life from LBJ to Obama*. New York: Basic Books, 2010.
_____. *Grand Expectations: The United States, 1945–1974*. New York: Oxford University Press, 1996.
Patterson, Kathy Davis. "Echoes of *Dracula*: Racial Politics and the Failure of Segregated Spaces in Richard Matheson's *I Am Legend*." *Journal of Dracula Studies* 7 (2005): 19–27.
Pearson, Wendy Gay. "Queer Theory." Bould et al. 298–307.
Pfeil, Fred. "Revolting Yet Conserved: Family Noir in *Blue Velvet* and *Terminator 2*." *Postmodern Culture* 2.3 (1992): sec 19.
Pharr, Mary. "Vampire Appetite in *I Am Legend*, '*Salem's Lot*, and *The Hunger*." *The Blood Is the Life: Vampires in Literature*. Eds. Leonard G. Heldreth and Mary Pharr. Bowling Green, OH: Bowling Green State University Press, 1999. 93–103.

Phillips, Kendall R. *Dark Directions: Romero, Craven, Carpenter, and the Modern Horror Film.* Carbondale: Southern Illinois University Press, 2012.
Plantinga, Carl. "Frame Shifters: Surprise Endings and Spectator Imagination in the *Twilight Zone*." Carroll and Hunt 39–57.
Presnell, Don, and Marty McGee. *A Critical History of Television's* The Twilight Zone. *1959–1964*. Jefferson, NC: McFarland, 1998.
Price, Victoria. *Vincent Price: A Daughter's Biography.* New York: St. Martin's, 1999.
Pulliam, June, and Anthony J. Fonseca. *Richard Matheson's Monsters: Gender in the Stories, Scripts, Novels, and* Twilight Zone *Episodes.* Lanham, MD: Rowman & Littlefield, 2016.
Ransom, Amy J. "Black Zombie: Race and Voodoo in Haitian-Québécois Literature." Unpublished paper delivered at the International Conference on the Fantastic in the Arts. Orlando, FL; March 17–21, 2010.
_____. "Ce Zombi égaré est-il un Haïtien ou un Québécois? Le vaudou chez les écrivains haïtiano-québécois." *Canadian Literature/Littérature Canadienne* 203 (Winter 2009): 64–83.
_____. "The First Last Man: Cousin de Grainville's *Le Dernier Homme*." *Science Fiction Studies* 41.2 (July 2014): 314–40.
_____. "Yellow Perils: M. P. Shiel, Race, and the Far East Menace." In *Dis-Orienting Planets: Racial Representations of Asia in Science Fiction.* Ed. Isiah Lavender III. Jackson University Press of Mississippi. 2017. 77-88.
Raymond, Emilie. *From My Cold Dead Hands: Charlton Heston and American Politics.* Lexington: University of Kentucky Press, 2006.
Rhodes, Gary D. *White Zombie: Anatomy of a Horror Film.* Jefferson, NC: McFarland, 2001.
Roas, David. Presentación. *Brumal: revista de investigación sobre el fantástico.* 2. 1 (2014). Special issue on Richard Matheson. 7–11.
Rolland, Denis. *Nivelle: L'inconnu du Chemin des Dames.* Paris: Auzas, 2012.
Rossinow, Doug. *The Reagan Era: A History of the 1980s.* New York: Columbia University Press, 2015.
Rovin, Jeff. *The Films of Charlton Heston.* Seacaucus: Citadel, 1977.
Ruiz, Luc. "Ce qui doit être lu d'une histoire de vampires: *I Am Legend* de Richard Matheson." *Dramaxes: De la fiction policière, fantastique et d'aventures.* Fontenay aux Roses, ENS, 1995. 39–53. Rpt. Chenille, Dollé, Mellier 33–45.
Sarovic, Marija. *Metamorfoze vampira : komparativna analiza motivskog kompleksa vampira u delima R. Metisona, B. Pekica, B. Vijana i S. Lukjanjenka.* Ph.D. Dissertation. Belgrade: Institut za knjizevnost i umetnost, 2008.
Schaefer, Sandy. "'I Am Legend 2' with Will Smith Is Officially Moving Forward.'" Screenrant.com 2012. Accessed June 11, 2013. http://screenrant.com/i-am-legend-2-will-smith-sandy-155576/
Schuller, Dorothea. "'Something Black and of the Night': Vampirism, Monstrosity, and Negotiations of Race in Richard Matheson's *I Am Legend*." *Inklings: Jahrbuch für Literatur und Ästhetik* 27 (2009): 78–94.
Shapiro, Jerome F. *Atomic Bomb Cinema: The Apocalyptic Imagination on Film.* New York: Routledge, 2002.
Sharp, Roberta. "Richard Matheson." *Dictionary of Literary Biography.* Vol. 44. *American Screenwriters II.* Detroit: Gale, 1986. 237–44.
Shelley, Mary W. *Frankenstein; or, The Modern Prometheus.* 1818. London: Oxford University Press, 1969.
_____. *The Last Man.* 1826 ed. New York: Dover, 2010.

Shiel, M. P. *The Purple Cloud*. 1901. Omaha: University of Nebraska Press, 2000.
Silver, Alain, and James Ursini. *Roger Corman: Metaphysics on a Shoestring*. Los Angeles: Silman-James, 2006.
Skal, David. "'A-Bombs, B-Pictures and C-Cups.'" *It Came from the 1950s! Popular Culture, Popular Anxieties*. Ed. Darryl Jones, Elizabeth McCarthy, and Bernice M. Murphy. New York: Palgrave Macmillan, 2011. 17–32.
Sobchack, Vivian. *The Limits of Infinity: The American Science-Fiction Film, 1950–1975*. Cranbury, NJ: A.S. Barnes, 1980.
Sontag, Susan. "The Imagination of Disaster." 1966. *Hibakusha Cinema: Hiroshima, Nagasaki and the Nuclear Image in Japanese Film*. Ed. Mick Broderick. New York: Routledge, 1996. 38–53.
Southern, Eileen. "Black Musicians and Early Ethiopian Minstrelsy." Bean, Hatch and McNamara 43–63.
Spitz, Vivian. *Doctors from Hell: The Horrific Account of Nazi Experiments on Humans*. Boulder, CO: Sentient, 2005.
Stam, Robert. "Beyond Fidelity: The Dialogics of Adaptation." *Film Adaptation*. Ed. James Naremore. New Brunswick: Rutgers University Press, 2000. 54–76.
_____. "Introduction: The Theory and Practice of Adaptation." Stam and Raengo, *Companion* 1–52.
Stam, Robert, and Alessandra Raengo, eds. *A Companion to Literature and Film*. Malden: Blackwell, 2004.
_____. *Literature and Film: A Guide to the Theory and Practice of Film Adaptation*. Malden: Blackwell, 2005.
Stanyard, Stewart T. Interview with Richard Matheson. *Dimensions Behind the Twilight Zone: A Backstage Tribute to Television's Groundbreaking Series*. Toronto: ECW Press, 2007. 162–68.
Stephanou, Aspasia. "'The Last of the Old Race': *I Am Legend* and Bio-Vampire-Politics." Mathews and Haedecke 17–29.
Stephens, Gregory. *On Racial Frontiers: The "New Culture" of Frederick Douglass, Ralph Ellison, and Bob Marley*. Cambridge: Cambridge University Press, 1999.
Stewart, George. *Earth Abides*. New York: Random House, 1949.
Stoker, Bram. *Dracula*. 1897. Ed. Roger Luckhurst. New York: Oxford University Press, 2011.
Stueck, William. *Rethinking the Korean War: A New Diplomatic and Strategic History*. Princeton: Princeton University Press, 2002.
Sturrock, John. "Introduction." *Structuralism and Since*. Oxford: Oxford University Press, 1979.
Subramanian, Janani. "Alienating Identification: Black Identity in *Brother from Another Planet* and *I Am Legend*." *Science Fiction Film and Television* 3.1 (Spring 2010): 37–55.
Svensson, Charlotte. *"All Men Are Mad in One Way or Another": Gender, Individuality and Transgression in Four Selected Vampire Narratives*. Ph.D. Dissertation. Syddanske Universitat. Odense, Denmark, 2002.
Tal, Kalí. *Worlds of Hurt: Reading the Literatures of Trauma*. Cambridge: Cambridge University Press, 1996.
Telotte, J.P. *Science Fiction Film*. Cambridge: Cambridge University Press, 2001.
Terramorsi, Bernard. "Richard Matheson: L'équilibre de la Terreur." *Europe* 707 (1988): 89–96.
Thornton, Richard C. *Odd Man Out: Truman, Stalin, Mao and the Origins of the Korean War*. Washington, D.C.: Brassey's, 2000.

Touré. *Who's Afraid of Post-Blackness? What It Means to Be Black Now.* New York: Free Press, 2011.

Trujillo, Nick. "Hegemonic Masculinity on the Mound: Media Representations of Nolan Ryan and American Sports Culture." *Reading Sport: Critical Essays on Power and Representation.* Ed. Susan Birrell and Mary G. McDonald. Boston: Northeastern University Press, 2000. 14–39.

Tunc, Tanfer Emin. "(Re)Presenting the Past: *Bid Time Return* as Historiographic Metafiction." Mathews and Haedicke 197–210.

Tyler, Parker. *Screening the Sexes: Homosexuality in the Movies.* 1973. New York: DaCapo, 1993.

Venkataswamy, Rama. *The Digitization of Cinematic Visual Effects: Hollywood's Coming of Age.* Lanham, MD: Lexington, 2013.

Vickroy, Laurie. *Trauma and Survival in Contemporary Fiction.* Charlottesville: University of Virginia Press, 2002.

Wagar, W. Warren. *Terminal Visions: The Literature of Last Things.* Bloomington: Indiana University Press, 1982.

Walker, William T. *McCarthyism and the Red Scare: A Reference Guide.* Santa Barbara: ABC-CLIO, 2011.

Waller, Gregory A. *The Living and the Undead: Slaying Vampires, Exterminating Zombies.* Urbana: University of Illinois Press, [1986] 2010.

Weaver, Tom. "Richard Matheson." *Science Fiction Stars and Horror Heroes: Interviews with Actors, Directors, Producers and Writers of the 1940s through 1960s.* Jefferson, NC: McFarland, 1991. 289–320.

Weinstock, Jeffrey. E-mail to the author. August 1, 2014.

_____. *The Vampire Film: Undead Cinema.* London: Wallflower, 2012.

Wenk, Christian. *Abjection, Madness, and Xenophobia in Gothic Fiction.* Ph.D. Dissertation. Salzburg University, 2008.

_____. "Xenophobic Monsters: Richard Matheson's *I Am Legend*." *Abjection, Madness and Xenophobia in Gothic Fiction.* Berlin: Wissenshcaftlicher Verlag, 2008. 186–241.

Whalen, Patrick. *Night Thirst.* New York: Pocket, 1991.

Wheatley, Dennis. *Devil Rides Out.* 1935. London: Hutchinson, 1963.

Whitehead, Colson. *Zone One.* New York: Random House, 2011.

Whitehead, Mark. *Roger Corman.* Harpenden, UK: Pocket Essentials, 2003.

Wilchins, Riki. *Queer Theory, Gender Theory: An Instant Primer.* Los Angeles: Alyson Books, 2004.

Wilson, Sloan. *The Man in the Gray Flannel Suit.* New York: Simon & Schuster, 1955.

Winter, Douglas E. *Faces of Fear: Encounters with the Creators of Modern Horror.* New York: Berkley Books, 1985.

Witcover, Jules. *The Year the Dream Died.* New York: Warner, 1998.

Womack, Ytasha L. *Post Black: How a New Generation Is Redefining African American Identity.* Chicago: Lawrence Hill Books, 2010.

Worland, Rick. "Sign-Posts University Press Ahead: *The Twilight Zone. The Outer Limits.* and TV Political Fantasy 1959–1965." *Science Fiction Studies* 23.1 (March 1996): 103–22.

Wyatt, David. *When America Turned: Reckoning with 1968.* Amherst: University of Massachusetts Press, 2014.

Žižek, Slavoj. *Living in the End Times.* London: Verso, 2011.

Index

Abominable Dr. Phibes 61, 194n6
Abrams, Fredrick 33, 202
Abrams, J.J. 182
Abu Ghraib 148
Abu-Lughod, Janet L. 124, 165, 167
Acevedo, Kirk 185
Adam (biblical character) 98, 141–43, 181
adaptation theory 4, 5–6, 63, 69–70, 104–105, 153–54
Addams Family 90
After Earth 153, 161
Agamben, Giorgio 72, 195n11
Agyeman, Freema 183
AIDS 24, 88, 94, 196n6
Air Force (U.S.) 98
Aja, Alexandre 169
Alabama 124, 141, 179
Alfred Hitchcock Hour 19
Alfred Hitchcock Presents 100
Ali 163
Alien 151, 182
alien invasion 2, 25,
Al-Qaeda 11, 148, 151
American International Pictures (AIP) 19, 59–60, 64, 92, 105, 135, 142
American Psychiatric Association (APA) 39–40, 192n14
Anderson, James 135
Anglo-Saxon origins 50, 56, 121
anti-Semitism 52, 53–54; *see also* Holocaust; Nazi genocide
Antioch 146, 169, 175, 178–79
Apocalypse Now 132
Arcel, Nikolaj 182
Army (U.S.) 18,
Arnett, Robert 17, 151, 191n2
Arnold, David 27
Arts Group 99
Aryan 34, 179
Asia 93, 104, 108, 132, 134, 183, 186, 193n17
Asian origins 107, 112, 130–31, 134, 160, 175–76, 188
Astic, Guy 64, 203

atomic bomb 1, 20, 25, 26–27, 34, 53, 55, 66, 68, 70, 135, 137, 144, 187, 210; *see also* nuclear weapons
Atomic Bomb Casualty Commission 55
Attack of the Crab Monsters 27, 135, 195n 9
Attack of the Giant Leeches 27
Auerbach, Nina 20
Auschwitz 128
auteur theory 6
Avalon, Frankie 135
Avengers 182
Aykroyd, Dan 19

baby boomers 16, 103
Bacon, Simon 40
Bad Boys 152
Baker, Houston A. 163
Baker, Ryan 58, 96, 97, 104, 105, 121, 124–25, 134, 171
Bakhtin, Mikhail 5
Bakke, Gretchen 158, 161, 167–69, 171, 173, 180, 182, 189
Baldick, Chris 186
Barnes, Steven 161
Bataan 34
Batman (superhero) 9
Batman (television series) 61, 198
Battle for the Planet of the Apes 127
Bay of Pigs 59
Beaumont, Charles 2, 13, 18, 59, 64
Bean, Annemarie 123
Beat Generation 84, 90
Beatles 116
beatniks 90, 135
Beethoven, Ludwig van 21
Belafonte, Harry 136–37, 140–41
Bellamy, Madge 9
Ben-Hur (1959) 99, 115, 117, 196n7
Ben-Hur (2016) 196n2
Beneath the Planet of the Apes 99, 111
Benshoff, Harry 9, 60–62, 77, 81–82, 84, 91, 194n3, 194n5, 194n6
Berger, Christian K. 58, 151, 191n2

214

Index

Berlin Wall 149
Bernstein, Leonard 21
Bethel 160
Bettoia, Franca 75
Bible 115, 135, 193*n*25, 196*n*5
biblical epic films 13, 99, 114–16, 119, 121, 124, 155, 196*n*2
biblical references: in *I Am Legend* (film) 160; in *I Am Legend* (novel) 54; in *I Am Omega* 178; in nuclear apocalypse films 144, 193*n*25; in *Omega Man* 102, 115–16, 119, 121
Bishop, Kyle 151, 167
Biskind, Peter 11
black identity 52, 120–21, 129–30, 147, 153, 160, 162–65, 167, 173, 180
Black Panthers 104
Black Power Movement 13, 97, 104, 109, 121–23, 126–129, 133, 162
blackface (make-up) 123–24, 164
blackness *see* black identity
Blade 167, 169, 182
Blade Runner 151
Blaisdell, Anne 64
Blake, Linnie 191*n*2
Blatty, William Peter 99
Blaxploitation 98, 107, 129, 196*n*4
Bloch, Robert 59
Blomkamp, Neil 8, 199
Bloom, Harold 49, 191*n*2
Boal, Iaian 109
Bogle, Donald 129, 141
Boker, Pamela 193*n*20
Bomback, Mark 185
Book of Eli 182
Booker, M. Keith 26, 59, 96
Bosnia 150
Boucher, Anthony 59
Boulle, Pierre 185
Boully, Fabien 193*n*21
Box (film) 19
Boyle, Danny 137, 151
Boys in Company C 133
Bracken, Bertram 195*n*10
Bradbury, Ray 2, 16, 18
Bradley, Matthew R. 16, 19, 20, 58, 64, 65, 151, 191*n*2, 195*n*2
Braga, Alice 155, 159, 172
Brahms, Johannes 21
Bride of Frankenstein 74
Briefel, Aviva 13, 148
Broderick, Mick 55
Bronx Zoo 156
Brooklyn Bridge 137, 159
Brooks, Christopher 3, 11, 17, 37, 97, 123
Brother from Another Planet 157
Brotherhood of the Wolf 175
Brown v Board of Education 51, 53, 103, 123, 125, 141, 172
Bryant, Tiffany 193*n*24
Bucket of Blood 90
Buckskin 18–19

Bugliosi, Vincent 109
Burn, Witch, Burn see Night of the Eagle
Burton, Tim 61, 185
Bush, George Herbert Walker 149–50
Bush, George W. 11, 150, 172
Butch Cassidy and the Sundance Kid 111
Butler, Judith 8

Cajun identity 81
Camus, Albert 27
Canavan, Anne 170
Carbone, Antony 142
Carlin, Bob 123
Carney, Raymond 17
Carroll, Diahann 129
Carroll, Noël 2
Carver, George Washington 138
Casali, Arianna 3, 11, 64, 77, 187
Case, John 109
Cash, Rosalind 100, 102, 107, 117, 126, 130, 159
Castellana, Cristina 49, 56
Census, U. S. Bureau of the 181
Chabrol, Claude 191*n*1
Chafe, William H. 1, 52–54
Chenille, Vincent 3, 11, 16, 33, 42, 191*n*1
Chicago 53, 104, 108, 122, 134
Chideya, Farai 120, 181
Childs, Erica Chito 130
Chong, Sylvia Shin Huey 108, 132–34, 150
Christian Scientists 18
Christianity 29, 33, 65, 124, 160, 175, 178; *see also* Judeo-Christian tradition
Christie, Deborah 58
Churchill, Marguerite 9
Civil Defense 67, 70, 137
Civil Rights 97, 104, 123, 148–49, 151, 160; Act 53, 99, 103; movement 4, 50, 53, 95, 97–99, 103, 125, 127, 141, 149, 151, 188
Clark, Mark 194*n*2
Clarke, Arthur C. 2, 29
Clarke, Lydia Marie 99
Clasen, Matias 16–17
Clayton, Anthony 33
Clayton, Jamie 183
Clemm, Virginia 62
Clinton, Hilary 197*n*7
Clinton, William Jefferson 150
Coffy 107
Cohan, Lauren 183
Cohan, Steven 3, 25, 43–44, 46, 52, 59, 99, 113–15
Cold War 1, 4, 11–13, 16, 20–21, 24–26, 29, 34, 42–43, 57, 59, 67, 70, 72, 76, 82–83, 96, 106, 114, 129, 132, 135, 137, 144, 149, 151, 180, 187–88, 191*n*7
Coleman, Chad L. 183
Collier's (magazine) 42
Comedy of Terrors 62
Comer, Joshua 40
Coming Home 133
communes 109, 149

Compton (California) 196*n*4
computer generated imagery (CGI) 137, 155–56, 158–59, 195*n*2, 197*n*1
Connell, R.W. 112–13
Constantine 152
Coppola, Francis Ford 132
Corman, Roger 2, 19, 27, 60, 62, 64, 70, 85, 90, 135, 142, 193*n*25, 195*n*9, 196*n*5, 196*n*11
Corrington, John 13, 97, 98, 99, 106, 109, 125, 126–28
Corrington, Joyce Hooper 13, 97, 98, 99, 106, 109, 125, 126–28, 153, 188
Cosby, Bill 129
Cosby Show 162
Country Joe and the Fish 106
Craven, Wes 169
Cregar, Laird 62
critical race theory (CRT) 9–10, 119–20
Cudlitz, Michael 183
Cumings, Bruce 42–43

D-Day 1
Dacascos, Mark 2, 14, 145, 147, 174–78, 189
Danieli, Emma 68, 89
Dark City 99
Dark Tower 182
darkseekers 151, 154–55, 158–59, 165, 167–69, 171–73, 189
Dartmouth College 136
Darwinism 175, 179
Davis, Wade 195–96*n*3
Dawidziak, Mark 20, 26, 62, 63, 92, 96
Dawn of the Planet of the Apes 185
Day the World Ended 2, 27, 70, 135
Deer Hunter 133
Defoe, Daniel 186
DeGraw, Sharon 155, 161–62, 165, 167–68, 173, 180–81
Dehn, Paul 127
Delli Colli, Franco 65
del Toro, Guillermo 152, 182
Democratic Party 61, 98, 104, 129, 150
Dendle, Peter 151, 195*n*12
Denmark 16
Depression, Great 17
De Sade 64
Desai, Tina 183
Descent 169
Desert Shield *see* Gulf War
Detroit 108, 122, 126
Devil Rides Out (film) 64
Devil Rides Out (novel) 64
Diaz, Cameron 167
Die! Die! My Darling see Fanatic
disaster films 13, 25, 148, 151
Disney, Walt 76
Disney Studios 61
Do the Right Thing 150
Dr. Phibes Rises Again 61
Dollhouse (television series) 182
Dollé, Marie 33

domino effect 42, 132
Douglas, Lord Alfred 194*n*4
Douglas, Kirk 59, 99
Douglas Aircraft 18
Douglass, Frederick 166
Dracula (1931 film) 29
Dracula (1974 film) 19
Dracula (novel) 5, 19, 63, 159, 193*n*15, 193*n*19
Dracula's Daughter 9
Dragonwyck 60–61
Duel (film) 2, 47
"Duel" (short story) 18
Dumbrell, John 97, 107, 108
Dushku, Eliza 182
Dyer, Richard 4, 6–7, 8, 10, 50, 112–13, 114, 120
Dziemanowicz, Stefan 48

Edward Scissorhands 61
Eisenhower, Dwight D. 61, 194*n*6
Elba, Idris 182
Ellison, Ralph 138, 166
Elysium 8
Energy Crisis 148
England 64, 93,
Enlightenment values 33, 164, 187
U.S.S. *Enterprise* 195*n*9
epidemic 2, 14–15, 21–24, 26–28, 30–31, 33, 40–41, 47, 55, 60, 65, 68–69, 72–75, 83, 88, 93–94, 96, 101, 107–108, 110–11, 113, 115, 137, 151, 154–55, 158, 177, 180–81
Esquire 113
Ethridge, Benjamin Cane 16
EUR (Esposizione Universale Roma) 77
Europe 1, 12, 27, 34, 53, 56, 68, 77, 88, 93, 107, 116, 120, 140, 153, 177, 179, 181, 187
Eve (Bible character) 141–42
Everyman 2, 4, 17, 47, 62, 67, 155, 195*n*9
Exodus: Gods and Kings 196*n*2

Fain, Kimberley 129, 141, 152, 153, 161, 162, 182
"Fall of the House of Usher" 62, 85
Family Affair 90
Fanatic 64
Fantomas 196*n*12
fatwa 170
Ferrer, Mel 140
Finney, Jack 18
Fisch, Audrey 186
Five 27, 70, 134, 135–36, 137, 138, 140, 144, 193*n*18, 193*n*25, 196*n*5
Fly 60
Fonseca, Anthony J. 3, 11, 16, 17, 22, 35, 48, 49, 51, 59, 62, 79, 100, 191*n*3, 191*n*2, 193*n*21
Foster, Gwendolyn Audrey 49–50, 57, 79
Foster, Jodie 8
Foucault, Michel 195*n*11
Foxy Brown 107
France 16, 34, 186, 194*n*4
Franco, James 185

Index 217

Freeman, Morgan 162
French 3, 16, 27, 33, 42, 73, 81, 140, 175, 185, 191*n*1, 192*n*11, 193*n*16, 195*n*3, 196*n*12; Resistance in WWII 27
Fresh Prince (rapper) 152; *see also* Smith, Will
Fresh Prince of Bel-Air 152, 162
Friday the 13th (1980 film) 13
Friedrich, Caspar David 146
Fringe (television series) 182
Full Metal Jacket 132
fundamentalism 109, 171
Furst, Griff 2, 145, 147, 174, 176

Galaxy Science Fiction 18
Gardena (California) 19, 196*n*4
Gates, Jaym 45
Gault, William Campbell 18
Gauntlet Press 18, 19
Gégauff, Paul 191*n*1
Genesis (biblical) 98
German shepherd 146, 154, 175–76
Germany 33–38, 50, 53–54, 77, 82, 124, 136, 187
Giles, James R. 27
Gilliam, Seth 183
Gilliard, Lawrence, Jr. 183
Gilligan's Island 195*n*9
GIs 17, 60, 88, 171
Gladchuk, John Joseph 7
Glasgow, Adryan 20, 58, 192*n*10, 193*n*23
Glasnost 149
Goldsman, Akiva 151, 153, 182
Goméz Martín, Mario 191*n*1
Gothic (genre) 16, 18, 20, 29, 32, 56, 61, 70, 108, 110, 146, 158–59, 169
Gould, Stephen Jay 172
Grainville, Jean-Baptiste Cousin de 137
Grant, Cary 59, 99, 113
Great Mouse Detective 61
Great Society platform 103, 148
Greene, Eric 127, 160, 185
Greensboro sit-ins 53
Griffin, Sean 62, 91
Gulf War, First Persian 150
Gurira, Danai 183

Hackman, Gene 19
Haedicke, Janet V. 3, 16
Hagood, Amanda 59
Haitian folklore (zombie) 58, 101, 125, 195–96*n*3
Hall, Donald E. 8
ham radio *see* short wave radio
Hammer Films 64, 92–93
Hancock 153, 161, 168
Hand, Richard J. 186
Hantke, Steffen 3, 11, 57, 78, 100, 148, 151, 153, 155–56, 172, 180, 196*n*10, 196*n*6
Hardt, Michael 195*n*11
Haring, Kristen 67

Harrison, Craig 142, 196*n*13
Harvey, Paul 160
Hatch, James V. 123
Hautecloque, Isabelle 16
Have Gun—Will Travel 19
Hawaii 147, 175, 189
Hawaii Five-O 175
Hawkins, Corey 183
Hayden, Tom 128
Heffernan, Kevin 60, 194*n*5, 194*n*6
Hefner, Hugh 118
Heimdall 182
Heineman, Kenneth J. 104, 122, 128
Heinlein, Robert A. 2
Hendershot, Cyndy 79
Henry, Patrick 27
hero, concept of 4–5, 8–9, 11, 13–14, 17, 20, 29–33, 37–38, 56, 63, 70–71, 78, 93, 97, 105, 111, 115–19, 127, 143–44, 147, 155, 157, 160–71, 182–84, 185–88, 191*n*3, 192*n*11
Herrera, Alfonso 183
Herzberg, Bob 111, 206
Herzog, Werner 159
Heston, Charlton 2, 7, 8, 12–13, 57, 59, 95, 96–101, 105, 107–109, 111–21, 124, 130, 132–33, 138, 141, 146, 154–57, 159–62, 165, 167, 175, 177, 185, 188, 193*n*25, 195*n*1, 196*n*2; *The Actor's Life* 99, 109; *In the Arena* 98–99, 111, 130
hibakusha 55–56
Hills Have Eyes (1977) 169
Hills Have Eyes (2006) 169
Hillyer, Lambert 9
Hispanic identity 140, 173
Hitchcock, Alfred 19, 100, 114
Hitchcock, Susan Tyler 186
Hitler, Adolf 1, 34, 50, 76, 124
Hoge, Charles 22, 192*n*9, 194*n*27
Holden, Gloria 9
Hollywood 2, 43, 48, 59, 60–61, 64, 76–77, 78, 84, 99, 105, 108, 111, 120–21, 132, 149, 152, 153, 161–64, 167, 176, 178, 180–82, 188–89, 195*n*12, 197*n*1
Holocaust (Shoah) 1, 14, 31, 33–34, 38, 52, 55–56, 72–73
Holt, Erika 45
"Homega Man" 196*n*2
Homeland Security, Department of 170
homosexuality 9, 59–60, 82, 88–92, 194*n*3, 194*n*6
horror (genre) 2–4, 8–9, 11–13, 16–21, 24–26, 28, 35, 38, 43, 48, 56, 58–61, 64–65, 67, 70, 74, 76, 79, 82, 84, 85, 86, 104, 105, 108, 110–11, 135, 144, 148, 151, 158, 159, 167, 172, 174–75, 180, 186, 189, 191*n*2, 191*n*5, 194*n*1, 195*n*9, 195–96*n*3, 197*n*1
House Committee on Un-American Activities (HUAC) 34, 76–77
House of Usher 2, 62
House of Wax 60
House on Haunted Hill 60

Hudson, Janice Hagwood 16
Hudson, Rock 113, 196*n*6
Humphrey, Hubert H. 99
Hunchback of Notre Dame 77
Hunger Games 152
Hunt, Lester H. 2
hydrogen bomb 1, 26

I Am Legend (film) 2–4, 84, 97, 135, 137, 145, 146–74, 180; criticism of 10–14
I Am Legend (novel) 2, 5–6, 15–57, 70, 72, 127–28, 132, 134, 142, 184, 187–89; adaptation to film 58–59, 63–64, 70, 92–94, 96, 98; criticism of 3, 10–14, 76, 82–83, 87
I Am Omega 2, 5, 14, 84, 145, 146–47, 174–80, 181, 189
I, Robot 151, 153
I Spy 129
Illinois 98, 121
In the Flesh 196*n*9
Incredible Shrinking Man (film) 2, 49, 57, 64, 80
Incredible Shrinking Man (novel) see *Shrinking Man*
Independence Day 161
Indian Arts & Crafts Board 194*n*6
Indochina 129; *see also* Vietnam War
Ingold, Charles 3, 11
Internal Revenue Service 116
interracial relationships 82, 97, 103, 117–18, 129–30, 134, 139, 141, 144, 150, 161–62, 179, 183, 188, 196*n*8
Iron Chef America 174
Iron Man (film) 182
Islam 163; Nation of 122; and terrorism 151, 171
It Came from Outer Space 2
Italy 58, 64–65, 77, 105

Jackson, Michael 61
Jackson, Peter 197*n*1
Jackson, Samuel L. 182
Jackson, Shirley 18
James, Lennie 183
Jancovich, Mark 59, 79, 97, 99, 111, 114, 119
Janicker, Rebecca 87
Japan 1, 34, 53, 55, 182, 187
Jaws 3-D 19
jazz 67, 84, 90, 118, 123, 165, 195*n*11
Jellenik, Glenn 153
Jeremiah Johnson 112
Jim Crow laws 53, 123–24, 161, 170
Johnson, Haynes 150
Johnson, Lyndon B. 99, 103–104, 108, 124, 133, 148
Johnson, Russell 195*n*9
Jones-Moreland, Betsy 142
Judeo-Christian tradition 33, 52, 112, 114–15, 119–20, 159, 182, 187
Julia (television series) 129

Kamen, Henry 110

kamikaze pilots 34
Karloff, Boris (William Henry Pratt) 61
Kennedy, John F. 103, 104, 108
Kennedy, Randall 130, 137, 162
Kennedy, Robert F. 104, 133
Kent State University 104
Khader, Jamil 12, 82–84, 112, 193*n*15, 193*n*19, 194*n*27, 196*n*10
Kilpatrick, Lincoln 101–102, 122
Kim, Hun Joon 43
Kimmel, Michael S. 150
King, Martin Luther, Jr. 104, 141
King, Stephen 13, 16, 17, 182
King and I 114
King Kong (2005 film) 197*n*1
"King-Vampire" 22, 84
Kinsey Report 83, 88
Kirk, Capt. James T. 9
Kirkman, Robert 158, 183
Korean War 12, 14, 38, 42–43, 57, 132, 187
Kosovo 150
Krulik, Ted 20, 47, 97
Ku Klux Klan 101, 123–24, 126, 133
Kubrick, Stanley 132
Kurtzman, Alex 182
Kuwait 150

LaCapra, Dominick 38
Lampin, Charles 135
Lampley, Jonathan Malcolm 58, 64
Lancaster, Burt 99, 114
Laneuville, Eric 102
Lang, Fritz 64
Langer, Lawraence 38
"Last Man" (film) 195*n*10
Last Man (literary figure) 2, 6, 10, 12, 15, 19, 23–24, 26–28, 41, 4447, 49, 57, 59, 63, 66–67, 69, 70, 75, 78, 91, 94, 96, 98, 102, 107, 111, 120, 134, 136–37, 143–45, 147, 151, 153, 158, 160, 175, 181, 186, 191*n*7, 192*n*8
Last Man (novel) 23, 27, 156
Last Man on Earth 2, 5, 6, 7, 12, 58–79, 82–92, 94–95, 96105, 137, 142, 156, 174, 187, 200, 209
Last Woman on Earth 6, 70, 135, 142, 193*n*18
Latinos 107, 130–31, 178, 183,
Laughton, Charles 77
Laura 60
Lauro, Sarah Juliet 58
Lavender, Isiah, III 9–10
Lawrence, Bruno 143
Lawrence, Francis 2, 11, 16, 97, 134, 145, 148, 152, 156, 169
Lawrence, Martin 162
Lee, Earl 135
Lee, Spike 150, 163
Leiber, Fritz 64
Leicester, William F. 64, 92–93
Leie, Roger 21
Lennix, Harry 182
Leskosky, Richard J. 26, 191*n*7

Life (magazine) 42, 77
Lincoln, Andrew 183
Lindow, John 182
Lippert, Robert L. 64
Lithgow, John 166
Little Big Man 112
Little Shop of Horrors 90
Lloyd, Ryan 176
Look (magazine) 77
Loose Cannons 19
Lord of the Rings trilogy (films) 197n1
Los Angeles 18, 19, 83, 100–101, 105, 117, 122, 150, 156, 175–77
Lott, Eric 123–24, 164
Lovecraft, H.P. 18, 26
Loyola University 127
Luddism 101, 109, 128
Lugosi, Bela 9, 60, 61
Lunde, Giuliana 27
lynching 124, 139, 161, 168, 178

MacArthur, Douglas 42
MacDougall, Ranald 136, 143
Magazine of Fantasy and Science Fiction 18
Malcolm X 163
Man in the Gray Flannel Suit 59, 99, 113, 142, 194n1
Man Who Knew Too Much 114
Manhattan 137
Mann, Michael 163
Manson, Charles 97, 101, 109
Mao Tse Tung (Maoism) 1, 43, 108, 128
Maōri 142–43, 196n13
March on Washington 53, 98, 141
Marines (U.S.) 43, 178
Marley, Bob 165–66, 211
Marshall, Neill 169
Marshall Plan 88
Martin-Green, Sonequa 183
Marzorati, Harold J. 136
masculinity 4, 5, 8, 11–13, 17, 43- 49, 51, 56, 58–60, 79, 82–83, 89, 94–95, 97–99, 111–14, 116, 118–19, 122, 136, 142, 146–47, 150, 160–63, 181, 187–88, 193n21, 196n6
Mask of Fu Manchu 61
Maslany, Tatiana 182
Masterson, Alanna 183
Mata Hari 90, 93, 174
Matheson, Ali 18
Matheson, Chris 18, 194n26
Matheson, Richard 2-4. 10–14; 16–19; 25–26, 29, 33–35, 42, 48, 56–57, 58–59, 62, 64, 90, 92, 94; *Abu and the 7 Marvels* 19; *Beardless Warriors* 12, 33–38, 50, 56, 79; *Bid Time Return* 2, 18; *Earthbound* 45; *Generations* 19, 81; *The Gun Fight* 19; *Hell House* 18; 32; *Journal of the Gun Years* 19; *Memoirs of Wild Bill Hickock* 19; *Night Creatures* 92–94; *Now You See It* 19; *The Path* 19; short stories 18–19, 193n22, 193n24, 194n26; *Someone Is Bleeding* 18; *Twilight Zone* episodes 2, 13, 18–19; 40; 48; 59; 64; 193n22; 194n26; *see also* "Duel"; *I Am Legend* (novel); *Shrinking Man*; *Somewhere in Time*
Matheson, Richard Christian 18, 19, 194n26
Matheson, Ruth Ann (Woodson) 18, 194n26
Mathews, Cheyenne 3, 16, 48, 49
Matrix (films) 182
Mature, Victor 114
Mayersberg, Paul 194n5
McCabe and Mrs. Miller 111
McCarthy, Joseph 1, 76–77, 83; *see also* McCarthyism
McCarthyism 34, 43, 151
McClelland, Bruce 29–32, 36
McCoy, Dr. Bones 195n9
McFarlane, Brian 5
McGavin, Darren 19
McGee, Marty 2, 210
McGilligan, Pat 16–17, 29, 49, 192n12
McNair, Leslie 34
McNamara, Brooks 123
McRoy, Jay 186
Meed, Geoff 174, 176
Meikle, Denis 61, 62, 64, 194n2
memory 22, 39–43, 85, 107, 133, 167
Men in Black 153
Mengele, Josef 128
Merril, Judith 20
Mexican 178
Meyer, Stephenie 23
Michigan 98, 121
Middle Ages 50, 110, 192n9
Middle East 148, 178
Mihok, Dash 152, 168
Milland, Ray 70, 135
Miller, Sam J. 13, 148
miscegenation 131, 162, 179, 193n19
Mitchell, Charles P. 58, 62, 63, 65
Mitchum, Robert 59, 114
mockbuster 175
Modleski, Tania 114
Monster Club 61
Montalbano, Margaret 5
Montgomery Bus Boycotts 53
Moral Majority 149
Moreland, Sean 58, 209
Morey, Anne 23, 59, 209
Morrell, David 133, 209
Morrison, Toni 10, 41, 209
Moses 114–15, 130
Motion Picture Association of America (MPAA) 92
Mozart, Wolfgang Amadeus 21, 41
Munsters 67, 90
Murnau, F.W. 159
Murphy, Cillian 151
Murphy, Eddie 153, 166
Murphy, Geoff 142
My Lai 104
Myers, Mike 166
Mystery (PBS television series) 61

myth (*I Am Legend* as) 3, 12, 14, 106, 171, 181, 185–88

Nama, Adilifu 13, 97, 121–22, 125, 130, 131, 134, 141, 153, 161
National Commission on the Causes and Prevention of Violence 133
National Council on the Arts 99
National Guard 104, 134
National Rifle Association (NRA) 98, 120
Native Americans 175, 178
Nazism 33, 77, 136; anti-semitism and genocide 34, 38, 50, 53–54, 72, 128, 171–72, 187; experimentation 31, 50, 55, 211; Occupation of France 27
Negri, Antonio 195*n*11
Neilson, Keith 29, 47
New Jersey 18
New York City 13, 53, 99, 136–37, 140, 148, 155–57, 160, 164, 167, 172
New Zealand 135, 142–44, 196*n*13
Night and Fog 73
Night Gallery 18
Night of the Eagle 64
Night of the Living Dead 58, 73, 108, 120, 167, 174
Night Stalker 19
9/11/2001 *see* September 11, 2001
Nivelle, Robert 33, 192*n*11
Nixon, Richard M. 99, 104, 108
Noah (film) 195*n*11
Nobel Prize for Literature 27
Nolan, William F. 18
Northwestern University 99
Norwegian origins 18, 50
Northwestern University 99
Nosferatu (1922) 159
Nosferatu (1979) 159
nuclear energy/weapons 1, 12, 16, 20, 24, 25–27, 34, 55–56, 70, 72, 77, 135–38, 142–43, 180, 187, 195*n*9
Nuit et brouillard see Night and Fog

Oakes, David A. 24, 29, 194*n*26
Obama, Barack 160, 197*n*7
Oboler, Arch 27, 70, 135
O'Connell, Jack 16, 22, 25, 48, 192*n*12, 195*n*13
Omega Man 2, 5, 6, 12–14, 52, 53, 84, 95, 96–134, 146, 149, 151, 153, 154, 155, 159, 161, 174, 175, 177, 185, 188, 195*n*12, 195*n*2, 196*n*9, 196*n*10
Orphan Black 182
Orzi, Roberto 182
Other(ness) 4, 9, 27, 30, 34, 41, 50–51, 55–56, 62, 78, 81–84, 91, 108, 112, 134, 144, 155, 158, 170–71, 176, 187, 193*n*24
Outer Limits 18
Overbrook Productions 151

Pacific Rim (film) 182
Pagnoni Berns, Fernando Gabriel 59, 193*n*21

Palance, Jack 19
Panama 28, 32, 40–41, 76, 83, 150
Panavision 105
Panic in the Year Zero! 70, 135, 144
Pascoe, Peggy 141
Patriot Act 148, 151
Patterson, James T. 34, 52–53, 97, 103–104, 108, 123–26, 141, 150
Patterson, Kathy Davis 13, 51–53, 76, 97, 172, 193*n*19, 196*n*4
Patton 133
Pearl Harbor 1, 13, 34, 150, 151, 188
Pearson, Wendy Gay 8
Peck, Gregory 59, 113
Penikett, Tahmoh 182
Perry, Tyler 162
Peyser, John 192*n*13
Pfeil, Fred 180
Pharr, Mary 22, 55, 84, 97
Philadelphia 152
Phillips, Kendall R. 169
Phipps, William 135
Pit and the Pendulum 2, 62
Plague (novel) 27
plague *see* epidemic
Planet of the Apes (1968 film) 99, 111, 133, 160, 185
Planet of the Apes (2001 film) 185
Planet of the Apes (novel) 185
Platoon 132
Playboy 18, 100
Poe, Edgar Allan 2, 18, 19, 60, 62, 64, 85, 89
Poitier, Sidney 138, 153
Polanski, Roman 109
post-black 163
post-9/11 era 4, 57, 145, 147, 148, 151, 162, 170, 176, 188
post-traumatic stress disorder (PTSD) 35, 38–43, 192–93*n*14
post-white 14, 173, 180–85
post–World War II era 1, 3–4, 12, 14, 16, 24, 44, 46, 52, 54, 60, 72, 79, 96, 137, 146, 171, 188, 194*n*19, 193*n*23, 194*n*1
Powell, Colin 160
Premature Anti-Nazi Sympathizers 76
Presnell, Don 2
Price, Victoria 60–61, 76
Price, Vincent 2, 7, 12, 57, 58–67, 71, 72, 74, 76, 78–79, 82–83, 85–89, 91–94, 97–99, 100–101, 103105, 108, 110–12, 116, 146, 154, 157, 163, 174, 175, 177, 187, 194*n*2, 194*n*3, 194*n*4, 194*n*5, 194*n*6, 195*n*9, 195*n*1
Pro-Life movement 149
Prometheus (film) 182
Pulliam, June 3, 11, 16, 17, 22, 35, 48, 49, 51, 59, 62, 79, 100, 191*n*3, 191*n*2, 193*n*21
Purple Cloud 27, 136–37, 192*n*8
Pursuit of Happyness 152, 163

queer theory 4, 8–9, 12, 60–62, 73, 79–92, 94,

Index

112, 116, 162, 183, 194n27, 194n6, 195n9, 196n7
Quiet Earth 135, 142–44
race 4–5, 9–10, 12–14, 82, 95, 97, 136–45, 150, 153, 169–70, 181, 185, 187–88; in *I Am Legend* (film) 146, 154, 157, 160–69, 173, 177, 180–81; in *I Am Legend* (novel) 23–24, 42, 49–56; in *Omega Man* 97, 103, 111, 117–18, 119, 120–36
race riots 13, 95, 97, 104, 108, 121–26, 150, 165
Ragona, Ubaldo 64, 77
Randolph, A. Philip 53
Ransom, Amy J. 125, 193n17, 195–96n3
Rastafarianism 165
Rau, Umberto 74
Raven (1935) 61
Raven (1963) 62
Raymond, Emilie 97, 98–99, 121, 195n1
Reader's Digest 77
Reagan, Ronald 13, 76, 143, 149–50
Rear Window 114
Red Scare 14, 76–77
Reedus, Norman 183
Reeve, Christopher 18
Reeves, Keanu 152
Reeves, Matt 185
Republican Party 98, 104, 172
Reyher, Ferdinand 136
Rhodes, Gary D. 195–96n3
Rice, Condoleezza 160
Riemelt, Max 183
Rise of the Planet of the Apes 185
Roas, David 16
Robin (superhero) 9
Robinson Crusoe 47, 186
Rocketship X-M 25
Rolland, Denis 33
Rome 60, 64, 77, 92
Romero, George A. 58, 73–74, 108, 120, 167, 174
Rooker, Michael 183
Room 222 107
Rossi-Stuart, Giacomo 67, 71, 73,
Rossinow, Doug 149
Routledge, Alison 143
Rovin, Jeff 98, 105, 109, 117
Rubes, Susan Douglas 135
Ruiz, Luc 21
Running Man 151

Sagal, Boris 2, 12, 96, 97–98, 100
Sagal, Katey 100
Salkow, Sidney 2, 64, 187
Sallis, James 16, 22, 25, 48, 192n12, 195n13
Sarovic, Marija 16
Saturday Evening Post 42, 77
Sawtell, Paul 65
Sayles, John 157
Schlesinger, Arthur, Jr. 113
Schoenberg, Arthur 21
Schubert, Franz 21

Schwarzenegger, Arnold 149, 151, 155
science fiction (SF) 1–2, 8, 10, 18–19, 24–26, 60, 81, 108, 111, 144, 153, 180, 182–83, 185, 189, 191n5
Science Fiction Hall of Fame 19
Scott, George C. 133
Scott, Ridley 151, 182
Scream Blacula Scream 196n4
Scream of the Wolf 19, 161
segregation 51–52, 53, 013, 123, 125, 141, 157, 166, 187; *see also* Jim Crow laws
Seltzer, Walter 99
Sense8 183
September 11, 2001 11, 13, 148, 156, 161, 173, 192, 196n1; *see also* post–9/11 era
Serbia 16
Serkis, Andy 185, 197n1
Serling, Rod 2, 13, 18, 48, 183n22
Serratos, Christian 183
Seven Pounds 152, 153
Seymour, Jane 18
Shakespearean theater 99, 121
Shapiro, Jerome F. 26, 66, 70, 79, 135–36, 143–44
Shefter, Bert 65
shell schock 38; *see also* post-traumatic stress disorder
Shelley, Mary W. 23, 27, 137, 156, 186, 192n8
Shiel, M.P. 27, 136, 137, 192n8
Shoah *see* Holocaust
shortwave radio 66–67, 143
Shrek 156, 166–67
Shrinking Man 2, 12, 18, 32, 35, 48, 49–50, 55–57, 60, 79–82
Shyamalan, M. Night 153
Silver, Alain 105, 142
Silvestri, Miguel Angel 183
Simmons, K. Merinda 163
Simpson, Nicole Brown 150
Simpson, O.J. 150
Simpsons (television series) 195n2
Six Degrees of Separation 152, 162
Skal, David 67, 144
Smith, Jaden 153
Smith, Pete 143
Smith, Will 2, 7, 11, 13–14, 57, 134, 145, 146–47, 151–57, 159–68, 170–71, 173–75, 177, 181, 184, 188, 197n7
Smith, Willow 160, 162
Snipes, Wesley 152, 167, 182
Sobchack, Vivian 25, 191n5
Somewhere in Time (film) 2, 18
Somewhere in Time (novel) *see Bid Time Return*
Sommers, Stephen 174
Sontag, Susan 25, 194n5
South Carolina 141
Southern, Eileen 123
Southern California school of writers 17, 25
Soviet Union 1, 16, 20, 76, 132, 149
Soy leyenda 191n1

Index

Soylent Green 99, 111
space race 1, 27
Spain 16
Spanish Inquisition 101
Spitz, Vivian 31
Spock 9
Sputnik 1
SS (Nazi Shutzstaffel) 76
Stalin, Josef 43
Stallone, Sylvester 149
Stam, Robert 5, 63, 153–54
Stanyard, Stewart T. 2
"star" theory 4, 6–7, 8, 60; *see also* Dyer, Richard
Star Trek 9, 19, 195n9
Star Wars (strategic defense initiative) 143
Star Wars (film) 111
Stephanou, Aspasia 31, 166, 195n11
Stephens, Gregory 165–66
Stevens, Inger 136, 139
Stoker, Bram 5, 19, 22, 29, 31, 63, 159, 193n15, 193n19
Stout, William 19
Stueck, William 43
Subramanian, Janani 120, 157, 160–65, 167–68, 172–73, 180, 196n4, 197n7
Supreme Court 51, 53, 125
Sutherland, Kiefer 183
Svensson, Charlotte 16
Swanson, Logan (Richard Matheson) 64
Szwarc, Jeannot 18

Tahan, Charlie 155, 172
Tal, Kalí 38
Tales of Terror 62, 85
Tate, Sharon 109
Taylor, Rosemary R. 109
Technicolor 98, 105
Teenage Caveman 70
Telotte, J. P. 191n5
Ten Commandments 99, 114–15
Terminator 13, 36, 151
Terminator 2 13
terror (genre) 25
terrorism 11, 13, 148, 151, 170–71; *see also* War on Terror
Tet Offensive 104
Thatcher, Margaret 13
Them! 2, 25, 26
Theron, Charlize 161, 199
Thing from Another World 25
13 Ghosts of Scooby Doo 61
Thompson, Emma 154, 165
Thor (film) 182
Thornton, Richard C. 43
Thriller 61
Tingler 60
Tomb of Ligeia 62, 85
Tor Books 19
Torv, Anna 182
Totall Recall 151

Touré 163
Towne, Robert 62, 142
Townes, Jeffrey (D.J. Jazzy Jeff) 152
Transformers 36
trauma 12, 15, 20, 38–43, 77, 79, 92, 98, 132, 133, 148, 150–51, 172, 187, 192–93n14, 193n15, 193n19; *see also* post-traumatic stress disorder (PTSD)
trench foot 192n12
Trujillo, Nick 113
Truman, Harry S 34, 43
Trump, Donald 179
Truth and Reconciliation Commission of the Republic of Korea (TRCK) 43
Tunc, Tanfer Emin 40
Tuskegee Institute 138
28 Days Later 137, 151
24 (television series) 183
24: Legacy 183
Twilight Zone 2, 13, 18, 19, 25, 40, 48, 59, 64, 100, 193n22, 194n26
Twilight Zone Magazine 29
Tyler, Parker 12, 59

Underworld 168–69
unidentified flying object (UFO) 72
Universal Soldiers 174
Universal Studios 74, 110, 192n13
urban legend 24
Ursini, James 105, 142
USSR *see* Soviet Union

vampire 2, 9, 12, 14, 15–16, 20–24, 26, 28–41, 47–52, 54–58, 60, 65–75, 78, 83–89, 91–92, 94, 101–102, 105, 107–11, 117, 134, 145, 147, 151, 156, 158–59, 168–70, 173–74, 186, 188, 192n9, 193n19, 194n27, 195n11, 195n12, 196n4
vampire slayer 22, 29–37, 49, 54, 66, 70–74, 118, 124, 134, 147, 158–59, 174
van Damme, Jean-Claude 149
van Helsing 22, 29, 31, 35, 70, 174, 192n10, 193n15
Venkataswamy, Rama 156
Vermont 155, 172–73
Vertigo 114
Vickroy, Laurie 38–41
Viet Cong 134
Vietnam (War) 4, 13, 43, 57, 96–98, 100, 103–104, 107–108, 128, 131–34, 149–50, 163, 171, 188
Virginia Slims 118

Wachowskis 182, 183
Wadleigh, Michael 106
Wagar, W. Warren 10–11
Walking Dead 67, 158, 174, 183
Wall Street 149
Waller, Gregory A. 22, 31, 73, 192n10
Wanted: Dead or Alive 19
War for the Planet of the Apes 185

Index

War of the Worlds 25
War on Terror 147, 150, 169–71, 180, 188
Warner Bros. 98–102, 106, 151–53
Washington *see* March on Washington
Washington, Denzel 152, 163, 182
Washington Square 155–56
Watergate 148
Watts (California) 108, 122, 124, 126
Watts, Michael 109
Weaver, Dennis 47
Weaver, Tom 47, 58, 64
Weinstock, Jeffrey A. 22, 78, 170
Welles, Orson 98
Wenk, Christian 16–18, 22, 54–55, 194n26
werewolf 24, 174–75
West, Adam 61
West Indies 141
West Virginia 137
Western (genre) 18–19, 65, 111, 137
Western civilization 3, 9, 11–12, 14, 15, 33, 38, 49–53, 59–60, 68, 75, 88, 94, 101, 107, 112, 114, 116, 119, 129, 136, 144, 148, 157, 164–65, 170–73, 181–82, 187, 189, 193n17
Whalen, Patrick 23
What Dreams May Come (film) 19
What Dreams May Come (novel) 19, 45, 194
Wheatley, Dennis 64
Whedon, Josh 182
white anxiety 13, 51–52, 56, 97, 121
White Zombie 9, 195–96n3
Whitehead, Colson 170
Whitehead, Mark 142
whiteness 10, 49–50, 52, 120–21, 130, 167, 173, 180–81, 193n23
Wiater, Stanley 18
Wiggins, Jennifer Lee 174
Wilchins, Riki 8
wild work (vampire slaying) 73, 78, 192n10
Wilde, Oscar 61, 194n4
Will Penny 112

Williams, Tyler James 183
Wilson, Sloan 194n1
Winter, Douglas E. 18, 35, 191n2, 192n12
Witcover, Jules 104
Wolvesbayne 174
Womack, Ytasha L. 163
Woodstock 106, 115, 156, 167
World Horror Writers Association 16, 19
The World, the Flesh and the Devil 6, 25, 66, 70, 71, 102, 117, 134–41, 144, 156, 193n18
World Trade Towers 11, 13, 148, 173
World War I 33, 38, 40, 72, 187
World War II 1, 3, 12, 15, 27, 29, 31, 33–35, 38, 50, 52–53, 56–57, 72, 77, 83, 88, 92, 95, 98, 124, 132–33, 150–51, 168, 187–88
Wright, Frank Lloyd 135
Wyatt, David 104, 113, 131–32
Wyatt, Rupert 185

Xavier University 126–27

yellow peril 43, 193n17
Yeun, Stephen 183
Young Warriors 192n13

Zerbe, Anthony 100–102, 109
Žižek, Slavoj 3
zombie (apocalypse) 3, 9, 27, 31, 37–38, 45, 54, 58, 67, 69, 74, 86, 101, 108–10, 120, 125, 144–45, 147, 151–52, 155–56, 158, 165, 167–68, 170, 173–77, 179, 183, 189, 191n6, 195n12, 195–96n3, 196n9
Zombieland 158, 174

www.ingramcontent.com/pod-product-compliance
Lightning Source LLC
Chambersburg PA
CBHW032052300426
44116CB00007B/699